Natural
Magic

Natural Magic

Spells, enchantments and personal growth

Pamela Ball

This edition published in 2020 by Arcturus Publishing Limited
26/27 Bickels Yard, 151–153 Bermondsey Street,
London SE1 3HA

AD000321UK

Printed in the UK

CONTENTS

INTRODUCTION

'We must seek for knowledge where we may expect to find it. He who wants to study the book of Nature must wander with his feet over the leaves. Every part of the world represents a page in this book, and all the pages together form the Book that contains her great revelations.'

So declared Paracelsus some 400 years ago and it remains just as true today. If we are to become practitioners of Natural Magic we must first learn to understand Nature. We must learn of the cyclical character of the seasons, we must learn of the inherent power in that cycle and above all we must learn to handle that power both in ourselves and in our surroundings. Today, and in the future, this means learning to cooperate with the world in which we live, not trying to gain mastery over it. Rather, it is gaining mastery over ourselves and the power that we have. Some of that power is self-evident and comes from within ourselves and some is inexplicable and comes from beyond – the supernatural.

We cannot come to an understanding of what magic – 'the art of influencing the course of events by the occult control of nature or the spirits' – really entails until we take a look at the religions of the world and find out how they learned to deal with the inexplicable and the supernatural. When we do this, we discover that man is – and always has been – trying to deal with a duality which he perceives within his world, that which is within him and that which is beyond. When he gains a degree of control over this duality, he begins to recognize that he is on the way to becoming a magician. The term 'magician' can be taken to mean all practitioners of magic whatever system they have developed in order to impose an element of control on themselves and their surroundings – whether they call themselves shaman or High Priest.

Broadly there developed two systems of practice: Shamanism, nature-based practices which celebrate the wilder physical creative power inherent in the union of polarities; and High Magic, a more philosophical system – or the Western Mysteries – which is perhaps more controlled in its operation and gains its inspiration from alchemy, astrology and the Kabbalah.

Man has, in the past, done his best to influence nature or natural forces and the elements by showing them what he expected them to do, or by inveigling them into gratifying his wishes. He first developed certain set actions – for instance, he would jump up and down to show a plant how to grow bigger. Such actions later developed into rituals that appeared to have the desired effect. Even later, the rituals were seen to be the cause of the effect, to actually make things happen. Feasts and festivals were then added as part of the actions needed in the carrying out of magic.

For instance, in the Jewish religion one of the most popular annual feasts performed in the Second Temple of Jerusalem was the 'Joy of the House of Water Drawing'. Any action undertaken in this rite was designed to do one thing, to draw down the waters – the life-giving rain so needed by the people, whose economy relied on a good harvest. Each part of the rite 'showed' what was supposed to happen in the natural world. The union of the water and the earth was symbolized by sexual freedom or 'light-headedness'.

This union was sought in ancient mythological stories which spoke of the separation of the waters, the Upper Male from the Lower Female. They were constantly yearning to be reunited, and succeeded in doing so through the creation of rain. In many ways, of course, this echoes the rites of sacred marriage enacted by the High Priests and Priestesses within the ziggurats of Babylon, and also celebrates the union of the spiritual and physical realms. This gives rise to an emotional release – a celebration of the fruitfulness of the union and a recognition of Duality.

The Temple, therefore, as the place where this union was celebrated, was seen as the centre of the whole universe. Its foundations bore down upon the Waters of the Abyss (primeval waters beneath the earth) and it was located at the highest possible point on earth, as close to the heavens as possible. The Temple symbolically represented the entire universe, and every single rite or ritual performed in it had an effect on the part of nature which the ritual reflected. At that time, the function of the Temple was of such importance that the very existence of the entire world appeared to depend on it.

There was later a complementary notion that a central personality, such as a patriarch, king, or pious and saintly man had it within his power to influence the weather and thereby ensure the well-being of his people, either directly, by working with the laws of sympathy, or indirectly by ensuring the intervention of God. He could choose which method – sympathetic manipulation or direct appeal – worked best. Such a man was, in truth, a natural magician.

Still later, long after natural ritual had become an integral part of pagan religion, Christian thought required that such rituals were assimilated into a more acceptable framework. The development of new solutions to problems, using both Christian and pagan rituals, was partly a product of the interaction between Christianity and Paganism. The local clergy, by default, became a primary source of this whole assimilation process. The mixing of liturgical, medical and folklore medicine was a sort of conglomeration of ideas as to how nature functioned. The line between these ideas was very unclear – liturgy blended into medical practice or was mixed with apparently magical, and certainly ritualistic, pre-Christian practices. This coming together is evident in a charm ritual for blessing the land, the Aecerbot ritual, which was performed yearly and is still retained centuries later on Plough Monday (usually the first Monday after Epiphany – 6 January).

Originally an Anglo-Saxon fertility ritual, it was gradually Christianized. In this agricultural – or field – remedy for witchcraft, four pieces of turf were taken from the four corners of the land, along with other agricultural products such as fruit, honey, herbs and milk as well as holy water. Certain words (such as 'grow' and 'increase') were said in Latin over these goods. The turfs were then anointed and blessed along with the fruits of the farmer's labour, taken to church and placed carefully under the altar. The priest then said four masses over the altar. The turf was placed back in the ground before sunset, along with four crosses marked with the name of the Apostles. Words and prayers similar to those above were said, including a specially written prayer calling on God, the earth and heavens to help in bringing forth the power of the earth for a successful crop. The ritual was closed by the owner of the field turning around three times while reciting Christian prayers. There followed a similar ritual for blessing the plough using herbs and other sacred items. The strong similarities to the rites calling upon Mother Earth and the Sun God and the Lower Female and the Upper Male in pre-Christian rituals are quite marked.

Every ritual has three dimensions. The mundane material dimension is the actual external rite. Then we have the spiritual dimension, which is not visible, but is assumed to be the more real act. The change actually takes place within the spiritual realms and the physical act is the reflection or image of the spiritual. Finally we have the ultimate fulfilment of the ritual, where the physical and spiritual meet and create a new reality. This interpretation is somewhat different to the one we have seen insofar as the Temple Rituals were concerned, but it is up to us to decide which way we wish to think of our magic. When we emphasize one interpretation over the other, we get confused over what the ritual actually is and what it means. What we actually have to do is to be able to perceive ritual in both ways.

Let us take baptism as an example. The ceremony has the dimensions mentioned above:

Physical: The physical immersion, washing, sprinkling or pouring of water signifies a cleansing and a giving up of old ways, of previous wrong doing.
Spiritual: The change within the physical initiates a process of purification and repentance. The inner spirit is awakened to its task. There is a New Birth when the Holy Spirit becomes an integral part of the individual's life.
Final Fulfilment: Eventually there is the promise of resurrection of the Body, and life Everlasting.
We can see that the Spiritual follows the Physical and then comes the implementation.

If we look at this act in a slightly more magical way, we can put a different interpretation to it, and one that is probably closer to the original Essenic way intended by Jesus when he was baptised by John the Baptist.

The act of baptism then was more one of initiation into a body of knowledge. It signified a cleansing certainly, but then an anointing and consecration into discipleship – a promise to live life on earth in a certain way according to the highest principles. The initiate was entering into a new community where each one was a priest, or holy person. It is this initiation into a body of knowledge that we hope to help you achieve with this book.

We look first of all at the various religions of the world in an effort to understand their attitude to magic. Following that we look at why magic has persistently been vilified over the centuries. Fear of the unknown is one of the most potent causes of aggression there is, or ever has been. It is a natural human reaction to try to discredit and destroy what is misunderstood and found to be unacceptable. Sometimes it is possible for religious conviction to become so entrenched in its own beliefs that there is no capacity for change. When this happens, the cycle of growth and decay – a natural process – occurs and it can be something very simple or basic that causes an upheaval, making room for expansion. Often it is the most cultivated system of belief that is most easily threatened.

Finally, we set out the most widely accepted procedures and protocols for ritual. Every system of belief has a basic way of dealing with the energies and powers that develop as the individual looks to learn how to control himself and his environment. To enable you to work with the maximum freedom, we have left you plenty of scope for your own creativity and your own beliefs. We have deliberately not insisted that one way or another is right or wrong, but have gathered together an eclectic series of tips, techniques and rituals to help you to develop into a truly magical practitioner. Should you find yourself becoming confused – which we trust you will not – it is worth remembering that working through the confusion and refining your processes is part of the learning curve.

May your magic be all you would wish it to be.

1.

MAGIC AND BELIEF THROUGH THE AGES

To understand how magic works within the world we do have to have an understanding of how mankind sees the world in which he lives, and the beliefs he has accrued in the process. In the main, over the centuries, he has developed two perspectives; one is naturalistic (shamanic) which suggests that the man of knowledge has the ability to travel between two worlds and thus gain understanding. The other (The Mysteries) postulates that understanding is gained through careful consideration of a spurious reality and the attainment of perfection. This approach is philosophical.

While it is not possible to make mention of every belief system in the world, we have loosely grouped the main ones in an effort to illustrate our point that there are two principal ways of understanding and using magic.

In exploring the development of belief systems, we usually discover that man is trying to deal with the duality that he perceives – that which is within him and that which is beyond. When man sets out to gain a degree of control over that duality and tries to find out how to make use of the energy available to him within the inexplicable and the supernatural, he is on the way to developing his ability to become a magician or, rather, a practitioner of magic. His belief system – and therefore his practice – will depend upon whether he believes that he has power over the world around him or whether he must call on powers beyond himself in order to have control. It is the way in which he calls upon those powers beyond himself which defines whether he works as a Shaman or as a High Priest.

SHAMANISM

From archaeological and anthropological evidence, we know today that the practice of shamanism has existed for thousands of years, perhaps since the beginning of the human race. It has been around certainly since the Stone Age, and is still practised today. Shamanism attempts to bring in good fortune and drive out misfortune, to manage a duality that can cause distress. Yet, insofar as ritual is concerned, it shows a unique religious form in which the shaman contacts deities spiritually, using singing and dancing in a largely spontaneous way.

It is a practice that combines divination and healing as its main components. Evidence of shamanism has been found in all parts of the world. Particularly in isolated regions, it has survived almost unscathed and as a result the world is now coming to a better appreciation of the beliefs of the aboriginals of the Americas, Asia, Africa and regions of Europe and Australia.

Although there are differences of ritual found among the various peoples, similarities are also apparent. There is what has become known as the 'shamanic state of consciousness' or 'ecstatic trance'. In this, the shaman puts himself in touch with information not available to him in a non-trance state. The ecstatic trance is common to all shamanic cultures – without this change of consciousness the shaman will not be able to perform all the assignments and responsibilities appropriate to his calling. This ability sets him apart from priests and adepts of non-shamanic persuasion, though some of the Christian sects which rely on speaking in tongues show a similar ability. In his altered states of consciousness the shaman remains in control, is capable of perceiving non-worldly realities, and is happy to act as a go-between among the various states of reality.

So that the shaman can access the shamanic state when required, he learns certain practices that help him to do so. He integrates singing and dancing into a standardized ritual, where he contacts his gods by dancing and placates them through singing. Rhythmic activities such as drumming, rattling and chanting; purification activities – isolation in darkness, sweat baths and sexual abstinence – and gaining greater mental control by, for instance, staring at a flame or concentrating on imagery gains him control over his own 'inner' environment. Some societies use psychedelic drugs for this purpose, though most claim drugs are not essential, perhaps even harmful.

The shaman accepts that he has access to three worlds – Earth, Sky and the Underworld. They are connected by a central alignment represented by a World Pillar, World Tree or World Mountain. This same idea resurfaces in the tenets of the Kabbalah with its Tree of Life.

Remaining lucid throughout all of his experiences, the shaman has various abilities that are not apparent in ordinary reality. He can ascend to the heavens, using mythical animals or by shape shifting (actually a type of change of consciousness similar to the ones seen in Celtic practices), and he can descend to the underworld. In both places he can communicate with spirits and souls, and he can also act as intermediary between the gods and his tribe.

Traditionally, shamans are called to their profession in two ways: by heredity or by spontaneous and involuntary election by the Supernatural beings, this often being the way in which women became shamans. In this day and age it is permitted to seek out shamanic training, but traditionalists are aware that these individuals may not be considered as powerful as those who have inherited the ability. This is believed to be because, for many, contact with other worlds is not considered normal within their culture and is therefore a learned response. Many such seekers will, however, undertake a 'vision quest' assisted by an initiated shaman, thus gaining knowledge of the relevant world.

Central to the belief of the shaman is the idea that he or she has a guardian spirit, usually an animal or plant. In a vision quest, most often used by North American Indians, the initiate seeking his totem animal either deliberately goes into a 'trance' state or has a vivid dream in which his guardian spirit manifests. Sometimes he receives advice directly from the Great Spirit. The vision quest provides the average individual, not just the medicine man, with access to spiritual realms for help.

In more primitive societies vision quests are mostly undertaken by males, usually as part of the rites of passage during puberty. Such quests exert a huge influence on the individual on his way to maturity. They provide a focus, sense of purpose, personal strength and power. Initially, since for most tribes power was to be obtained for hunting and fighting, only the male could be a shaman, and measurement of his ability was by the greater number of his guardian spirits, by the intensity of his vision and by his greater power. Some tribes do have minor rites for girls to acquire guardian spirits, and as shamanism spreads it is now much more acceptable for women to be shamans, particularly within the healing traditions.

Most vision quests are solitary undertakings, but some are done on a collective basis, such as the Sun Dance ceremony discussed later. Usually, sweat-bath purification rites precede the vision quest. The individual goes either alone or with his mentor into the wilderness to a sacred place where he may fast, abstain from liquid, pray and 'meditate' for a vision – that is, he deliberately induces a change in consciousness. This vigil can continue for several days and nights. During this time he meets his guardian spirit, who empowers him with magical strength.

When seeking a guardian spirit, the individual most often asks to be given certain qualities or abilities, such as for hunting or healing. Vision quests are also undertaken in times of war, disease, death, and childbirth (to seek instructions for naming the child) – in other words occasions that affect the whole community. Most Native Americans believe that the vision seeker should abstain from sex for a period prior to his quest. In the full shamanic state the shaman has various powers that he does not normally possess. He sees spirits and souls, and communicates with them; he makes magical flights to the heavens where he serves as intermediary between the gods and his people; and he descends to the underworld, the land of the dead.

In imparting powers the guardian spirit may prescribe food taboos, for example in ancient Celtic lore it was forbidden for the hero Cuchullin to eat the flesh of a dog and for the bard Ossian to eat venison; give instructions for adornment (such as shells, feathers, stones and robes) and for the assembly of the personal medicine bundle or talisman bag. The guardian spirit may teach a song or chant, which is used to reconnect the shaman with his guardian at any given time – almost like a self-hypnosis – and also serves as the shaman's alter ego, giving him animal power. This is very similar to the power of the magician in Celtic magic. The guardian spirit usually appears in animal form, though it may later change to human form, and becomes then similar to the spiritualistic concept of a guide.

All the instructions received by the individual must be followed to the letter or it is thought the person will lose the power of the animal. The spirit will usually leave behind a physical token of the vision, such as a feather or claw, or will manifest some symbol that the new shaman may use. Sometimes the shaman cannot handle the magnitude of the energy, or feels it to be wrong or unsuitable, in which case a further attempt will be made later to contact the guardian.

The belief in spirits in the form of animals comes from a strong conviction that animals and humans were once related. So within an altered state of consciousness, such as during ecstatic dancing, the shaman assumes the form and power of his favoured animal and then is able to perform his duties. He sees the animal, talks to it, and uses it to help him achieve his aims. The guardian's task is to escort the shaman through the underworld or to be with him in his ascent to the skies. The animal spirit is never harmful to the shaman, though he may stretch the individual's powers to the limit.

Guardian spirits may also protect an entire tribe or clan with the collective or individual power of the animal, when they are known as totem spirits. Totem guardian spirits are part of the Native North American's culture, especially among the tribes along the Northwest Coast. Different totem animals are sacred to each particular tribe; no member of that tribe is permitted to kill a bear if that is the tribe's totem animal, but the tribe may use the flesh or skin of its totem if it is killed by another tribe.

In Northern Siberia and the Far East, Shamanism was based on a more dualistic conception of the universe, and showed a number of mythological and cult forms. The natural world had its parallels in the spiritual world, each level of which was inhabited by spiritual beings. Again the shaman, a pivotal figure, acted as an intermediary between them. His clothing and paraphernalia were particularly important as part of his ritualized entry into the other worlds. His clothing symbolized animals and birds found in the spirit world which helped him to communicate with the world of the spirit, his tambourine summoned his ancestor spirit upon whom he rode and his head-dress and warder, a symbol of authority, characterized the centre of the Universe.

Other figures of birds, beasts, reptiles, fantastic creatures and anthropomorphic figures of wood, fur and metal called ongons, which are dwelling places for shamans' helper spirits, are used to form a circular structure that symbolizes the Universe and the cycle of birth, death and rebirth. The ongons are an essential tool of Siberian shamans and are most often taken with the shaman when he or she goes to the location of a ritual. Shagai are sheep anklebones, which are used for divination as well as for traditional games. They are roughly cubical in shape, but each side of the bone has a specific name and meaning.

The shamanism of the Siberian peoples preserved many otherwise archaic forms of worldviews, rituals and artefacts. The garuda bird, for instance, is the king of the birds, similar to the thunderbird of Native American legend. There is a spirit called Mongoldai Nagts (Mongol Uncle) that guards the entrance to the lower world so that spirits cannot travel back and forth to the upper world without permission. This has distinct similarities to the Doorkeeper in spiritualist belief who performs the same function on an individual level.

KOREAN BUDDHISM

When Buddhism was introduced to Korea during the Three Kingdoms Period, the country had religions which were shamanistic in their origin. Korean Buddhism was transformed in the process of fusing with shamanism, unusually adopting a ritualistic aspect from those beliefs. This gives a unique identity to Korean Buddhism, which is still apparent today. Korean Bhuddism spread to Japan when in AD 577 Japanese rulers requested a second contingent of Korean Buddhist monks, nuns, sculptors and architects to spread Buddhism and Buddhist culture there.

A fundamental principle of Buddhism is that one can attain salvation by oneself through self-discipline. It is believed also that one can be reborn into the Buddhist paradise by repeating the name of Amitabha – using chant as a sacred vehicle. This is akin to the use of sound and rhythm in shamanism. At least three aspects are similar in the two religions. Buddhists believe in the Mandala, an illustration of the eightfold path, which bears some resemblance to the Diagram of Assembled Deities revered in shamanism. Mantra is the effective use of sound and rhythm, and Mudra increased Buddhism's affinity with shamanism. Mudra is a series of symbolic body postures and hand movements initially used in East Indian classical dancing which became the prototype of Buddhist ritual dancing. Korean Buddhism has its own music, called bumpae, and Buddhist dance developed in various forms to fit diverse Buddhist rites. With this synthesis, singing and dancing have had an inseparable relation with Buddhist rituals. Even today, Korean Buddhist music retains its unique character and artistically refined form. In some senses, such Buddhism does not require belief – indeed there is no one word meaning belief, but simply the practice of it – thus the enactment of the dance becomes the prayer. We see below how the rituals combine both elements.

Shamanic elements are so widespread in Korean Buddhist rituals that sometimes conflicts do surface. For instance, after various attempts to eliminate shamanic elements from temples – in the name of purification of Buddhism in the 1960s – shamanic Buddhist rituals have experienced virtually no change, though many of the buildings where the rituals were practiced have been destroyed.

During the early period, Korean Buddhism had initially simple practice rituals such as homage to Triple Gems, repentance and the hearing of moral codes; only later, in order to satisfy the folk desire for belief, did it develop a belief ritual with its focus on the Buddhist service. It is here that we can see the unification of Buddhism and shamanism, for the participants in the service paid homage not only to the Buddhas and Bodhisattvas but also to gods revered in shamanism such as the mountain god, the Big Dipper god and the Dragon King god. These latter were given the task of protecting Buddhist Dharma (law). Thus we have a pantheon of gods associated with Buddhism which, in fact in its pure form, does not worship any god at all. In terms of the function there are three rituals which deserve our attention, the invitation-and-parting ritual, the purifying ritual and the feeding ritual.

First, in the invitation-and-parting ritual, the Buddhas, Bodhisattvas, deities and the souls of the dead (in the rites for the dead) are invited and then sent away. The ceremonial steps include reception, moving a Buddha drawing to signify removal, prayer, and parting. However, according to Buddhist belief, there is no difference between existence and non-existence, or coming and going, so inviting and then sending away must have been adopted from shamanism sacrificial rites such as invocation of the soul, appeasing, and sending away.

Secondly, included in the purifying ritual designed to define and sanctify the place where a rite is performed – much as we do today by casting a circle – is the ritual of inviting deities to protect the Dharma or laws of Bhuddism. This actually has no basis in Buddhism, which believes that the entire universe (Dharmakaya) is pure enough in which to hold a ceremony. It is only ultimately from the mind, through repenting and removing greed, that paradise can be found. A type of folk ritual, this ceremony is similar to the cleansing ritual in shamanism.

Thirdly, in the feeding ritual called the Youngsan (detailed below), food and chanting are offered to lead the souls of the dead to the Buddhist Paradise, appease them, and also to feed the starved devils. The feeding ritual is a sort of Buddhist memorial service for the dead, which is comparable to the consoling ritual, called Duichun of Kamang, for evil spirits in shamanism. A cleansing ritual is held first to sanctify the souls of the dead who have travelled a long way and then food is offered. Hungry demons and wandering souls are also invited to have food.

THE YOUNGSAN RITUAL

Healing rituals and incantations designed to drive out illness were adopted from shamanism, where a special kind of feeding ritual is held to cure someone of an illness through feeding his ghosts or demons. (In Bhuddism, the doctrine of karma and retribution states that one becomes ill because of one's own deeds or misdeeds, not through the possession of ghosts.) Once again Buddhism has responded to the demands of the people.

Of all the Buddhist rituals, the Youngsan ritual is deemed to have the richest artistic and theatrical quality, and has the greatest influence of all. Held to lead the souls of the dead to paradise, it has interior and exterior procedures and is one of several rituals held on the 49th day after death. The process on an interior level completes for the participants the traditional period of 49 days of mourning. The exterior practice is the main part of the ritual designed to protect the Dharma (laws of Bhuddism). It represents Sakyamuni Buddha's sermon given at Mt Youngchuk. This has three parts:

1. The body of teachings expounded by the Buddha.
2. Knowledge of, or duty to undertake, conduct set forth by the Buddha as a way to enlightenment.
3. One of the basic elements from which all things are made.

In the reception part of the introduction, the Buddhas, bodhisattvas, deities protecting Dharma and the souls of the dead are invoked and led into the temple. The parade follows a guiding bodhisattva – one whose essence is enlightenment – then the souls of the dead who were ushered into the temple are treated with tea (which in the shamanic ritual would be alcohol) and all prepare to attend the ritual. The souls of the dead are then cleansed of karma in the body, the mouth and the mind, before proceeding to the altar. Finally, deities that protect Buddhist teaching are invited to purify the temple where the Buddhist sermon is to be delivered. This service is held in front of the main altar, while the feeding is held at a separate altar. Feeding is a combination of the offering ritual of Buddhism and the traditional ritual of worshipping ancestors.

Following the main part, the rite for the souls of the dead is the concluding part. Here, the dead one's deeds are transferred to the living to benefit them, a kind of inheritance of goodness. First, the invited ones are sent away, with an acknowledgement of their assistance, then the clothes and tools used in the ritual are burnt. This signifies that the dead go to the other world riding on fire, a concept easily recognized from other beliefs such as Hinduism and Norse religions. After the ritual is finished, people who participated eat food signifying the sharing of religious devotion. The procedures within this ritual are therefore largely shamanic, while the philosophical part is Buddhist.

Because Buddhism was largely philosophical, and therefore by our definition theurgical, wherever Buddhism was transmitted it could accommodate local deities. Certainly in Korea this adaptability made its acceptance easier. The rather simple Buddhist ritual had the capacity for the incorporation of the theatrical fun and diversity of expression of shaman ritual. This resulted in a blending of both low and high magic.

By raising the awareness of all the people it allowed for rituals and chanting which could have a profound effect on the world in which the participants lived. The ritual of transforming the mundane to the sacred naturally emphasizes the meditative practice seen in Bhuddism, but rituals associated with belief are seen in the prayer and chanting rituals which call on the divine to assist the physical realm.

This same reliance on chanting and prayer rituals is seen in other shamanic cultures and it is first easily perceived in the Celtic religions. In these religions, there was a tremendous awareness of how the divine impinged on the physical realm and vice versa.

CELTIC RELIGIONS

It is unfortunate that our knowledge of Celtic mythology and religion is hampered by the fact that a great deal of existing material has been tainted. Above all, the Celtic religions were rich in oral tradition and story, only recorded later by Christian monks and others. By and large, though, the belief systems of the Welsh and the Irish show remarkable similarities which are echoed by the Gauls. Their gods and goddesses and the stories about them are similar, their names only varying according to the local dialect – Lugh in Ireland matches Llyr in Wales, for instance. Celtic religion featured many female deities such as mother goddesses and war goddesses. The Mother Goddess of the Celts was often conceived as a warrior, instructing the hero in supernormal secrets of warfare and the arts of transformation. This close cooperation with the divine arose principally from the observance of the Wheel of the Year and its seasons in nature.

According to the tenets of the Celtic magician, there was – and still is – a unity in nature that allowed for a degree of transmutation between species. The Celtic magician, in attempting to transform him or herself, used willpower in a very focussed way and actually tried to assume the form and nature of the person, animal or thing he wished to become – in other words to shape-shift. So far as other people were concerned, when he wished to transform them he would transfer the characteristics of the animal or being by the use of his will-power, resulting in the victim having to adopt the shape of the animal or being. This power could obviously be used for good or evil and has overtones of totemism. The incantations (*obaidh*) used at this time were recited in verse.

Among the more potent and important enchantments of the Celts was that known as 'fith-fath' or 'fath-fith' which was employed to bring about invisibility. Invisibility by the aid of fith fath (pronounced 'fee far') was well known in Ireland. It was said to have been given first to the Tuatha De Danann (the original inhabitants of Ireland) by the god Manannan, whose lordship of the sea gave him power over shifting fogs and the creation of illusion. One of the more recent uses was to fool the Excise men on smuggling expeditions. The enchantment went thus:

A magic cloud I put on thee,
From dog, from cat,
From cow, from horse,
From man, from woman,
From young man, from maiden,
And from little child.
Till I again return.

The witch, fairy, or indeed any woman with supernatural powers, was assumed to have a bunch of cords made up of nine cow fetters. This burrach, cow fetter or spancel was a cord or thin rope made from horsehair with a loop at one end and a knob at the other for fastening it. These fetters probably later evolved into the nine-knotted 'witch's ladder.'

Witch's Ladder Charm

This modern-day charm can be of two types. One is a general-purpose charm for protection and good luck, while the other can be dedicated for a particular intent. Nowadays such an implement incorporates ideas from other cultures as well, such as the feathers or coloured objects.

For a General Purpose Charm

Plaiting and knotting is a specific kind of magic. Plaiting, because it makes three strands into one, represents the three aspects of the Triple Goddess – Maid, Mother, Crone – becoming one.

If possible, this ladder should be made on the night of a Full Moon for maximum effect.

YOU WILL NEED

White candles

Incense of your choice

Consecrated water

White Cord

Red Cord

Black Cord

Nine feathers or coloured objects to incorporate the following meanings:

Red for physical energy,

Blue for knowledge, peace and protection,

Yellow for happiness, prosperity and emotional matters,

Green for self-awareness and matters of health,

Brown for steadiness and respect for others,

Black for mystical insight and wisdom,

Grey or White for spiritual harmony and balance,

Peacock feathers – or those with specific markings –

for protection and clairvoyant abilities.

METHOD

Consecrate your sacred space.

Light your candle and incense.

Using about a metre of each coloured cord, tie the ends together and plait them together and say:

Cord of red,
Cord of black,
Cord of white,
Work enchantment here tonight.

About every four inches, securely knot in the feathers or objects.
You can usually tie a secure knot around the feather or object for this purpose.
Whilst doing this, say suitable words, such as, when using yellow:

With this feather and this string,
Prosperity this charm will bring.

Repeat this until the plait is finished and tie a knot at the end.
Tie both ends of the plait together to form a circle.
Pass the finished ladder above the candle flame then through the incense smoke.
Sprinkle the ladder with the consecrated water and say:

In the names of the God and the Goddess
By Air, Earth, Fire and Water
I do thee bless.
Of objects nine and cord of three
As I will, so shall it be.

Hang the ladder in an unobtrusive place, but where you yourself will see it every day.

For a Specific Purpose Charm

The method for making this charm is the same as that for the general purpose charm. The difference comes in ensuring that your cord, objects and/or feathers are geared to your specific purpose. You will probably find that you need only three objects or feathers (representing body, mind and spirit).

Let the words flow naturally and do not be too surprised if you find yourself inspired.

The old style spell associated with this implement especially ensured that a person who was struck, adjured 'by the nine cow-fetters', would carry through any task imposed upon him. The 'wyrd woman', who travelled around the countryside seeking victims, in much the same way as Hecate is said to have done in Greek mythology, would strike him with her deadly cow-fetters which she used when milking deer. Such a blow made the victim so fey that anyone could beat him in combat.

The charm used was as follows:

To lay thee under spells and crosses under (pain of being struck by) the nine cow-fetters of the wildly roaming, traveller-deluding fairy woman, So that some sorry little wight [stooge] more feeble and misguided than thyself Take thy heart, thine ear and thy life's career from thee.

Wyrd, which of course gives us the word 'weird', was a mysterious force that acted as a kind of Fate or Fury – a destructive force. This force or power could not be destroyed once and for all, only avoided on a temporary basis. Any woman having this power was obviously much feared.

We can see in this the archetypal struggle against female authority and power, particularly when it is used in a malign way; the only way to deal with this problem is by each individual alone. This struggle is epitomized over and over again in the heroes' tales in both Celtic and Anglo-Saxon myth – through these it is but a short step to a belief in the power of evil in women.

THE 'EVIL EYE'

Another superstition that held much sway in Celtic folklore was the superstition known as 'the evil eye'. This is not only seen in Celtic folklore but is particularly strongly feared even today in countries of Celtic origin. Different cultures have different ways of dealing with this nuisance. It seems that the evil eye was more often associated with women and therefore inevitably with the Crone, or wise woman, than with men. Anyone with a squint or eyes of different colour could be accused of possessing the evil eye and of using it to cause destruction or illness. Interestingly, a charmed burrach or cow fetter could be used to protect animals. There were a number of other preventative measures that could be taken, some using plants and trees – such as rowan and juniper – and others using horseshoes and iron stakes.

While the owner of the evil eye did not necessarily need to be a witch, the curse did require the services of a magical person to remove it. In Scotland such arcane knowledge was passed from father to daughter and mother to son. The word 'orth' was used for an ordinary spell but a ceremonial magical spell among the Gaelic Celts was signified by the word 'bricht'. It is perhaps interesting that this word also means 'bright' in dialect – perhaps such a ceremony required a moonlit night.

THE SALMON OF KNOWLEDGE

Various stories abound of receiving knowledge through supernatural means. The Irish, for instance, believed in the 'salmon of knowledge' which had acquired its powers through eating the nuts of the sacred hazelnut tree that fell into the well in which it lived. Druids and magicians alike sought this magical fish in the hope of partaking of its flesh. Indeed, Finn McColl, an Irish hero, is said to have caught and cooked the salmon. On burning his thumb, he sucked it and developed the ability to perceive events before they happened. This story bears a strong resemblance to the Welsh story in which Gwion is burnt by the magical potion he is preparing, much to the displeasure of Ceridwen who intended the potion for her son.

SHAPE SHIFTING

Spells designed to bring about a difference in bodily appearance in order to dissolve enchantments by the fairy folk or frequenters of the lower world are legion in most cultures. In Celtic lore, during the process of disenchantment, having cast a magic circle, the rescuer must keep repeating the name of the enchanted person; this is to remind the latter of who he truly is. Traditionally the enchanted one will go through several metamorphoses or shape shifts. These will be in the following order: Esk, adder, lion and finally a bolt of red hot iron. Then returning to human form, he or she is left completely naked. They must then be covered by a cloak – thus rendered invisible – and dipped in milk and then hot water.

These actions actually follow some very ancient occult laws. The sequence of stages mimics the journey that the human soul is said to make through the lower realms of existence on its way to enlightenment. If we accept the idea of the evolution of the soul, we can see that the stage of heating iron until it is red hot represents the process of transmutation from animal to human. The final purification in milk (which in Irish myth is a healing substance) and water restores the victim to his normal self – he is reborn.

PROTECTIONS

Iron as a tool of purification is often seen in Celtic magic but is also apparent in most other cultures. It was said to be a substance dreaded by the darker powers and many amulets and charms fashioned from the substance were used to avert evil. Iron pins or brooches were stuck in the headgear, a piece of iron was often sown into the clothes of children and horseshoes were often used to protect the homes and byres (cowsheds).

Women in childbirth were also said to be protected with iron, sometimes by a row of nails and at other times by a scythe or pitchfork. This was so that mother and baby were protected from evil spirits, particularly from the night demons who were said to steal babies. Up until quite recently in Scotland in some areas, it was considered highly unwise to leave a baby alone at all, lest it be stolen away by the faeries.

There are, in fact, several customs associated with birth and the surrounding period which have survived without people necessarily appreciating their magical significance. They therefore belong more to folk magic and thaumaturgy than to higher magic. The 'toadstone' protected the newborn from evil spirits and the Virgin Mary Nut, actually the seed of the plant *Entada Scandens*, counteracted birth pains. The shell of a sea urchin known as the 'cock's knee stone' – but also representative of the Virgin – has also always been considered to bring good fortune.

Much disease was often considered to have been brought by demons and evil spirits which could be cast out. Magical stones were often used for this purpose and in both Scotland and Ireland there are many tales of the existence of such stones. It was said that healing stones could impart their qualities into water and this ability can still be seen today when healers use crystals, or elixirs infused from crystals, in their healing

Many plants and herbs were regarded as specifics against bad spirits. Rowan or mountain ash even today is often to be found close to isolated cottages or near standing stones as a form of protection. The berries were thought to be the food of the gods. St. John's Wort was often carried as a charm against witches and fairies – in the Isle of Man it is said that a fairy horse will rise from the earth and carry you about all night if you tread on the plant.

THE MEETING OF PAGAN AND CHRISTIAN

The lucky four-leaf clover represents the equal-armed cross and is thus associated with the sun and good fortune. It also suggests the Goddess form, the quaternity – the fourfold aspects of God rather than the trinity as seen in the trefoil. Clover is thought to give the wearer the ability to see the fairy form, and it perhaps here that we can see the cross-over between the old and the new religions. St Patrick is supposed to have used the trefoil to demonstrate the principle of the Holy Trinity to his followers. He would have used material that was readily available to him rather than the rarer and more magical four-leaved plant, and would thus have signified the move away from intrinsic magical knowledge. The more nature-based religion gradually then gave way to the Christian.

Prior to the arrival of the Christians, Celtic spiral designs were already in use commemorating both the Goddess as Mother Earth in her journey from the underworld and also the path that we must take towards enlightenment. We have already seen the changes that the physical form is reputed to go through on that journey and much Celtic art shows this in the form of fantastic animal illustrations. Simple spiral designs developed into more sophisticated ones and then evolved into intricate knotwork that was more labyrinthine than spiral. Sophisticated spirals exist in the same early works where the knotwork and animal designs are still somewhat rudimentary.

Later, the astonishing degree of ornamentation and detail in The Book of Kells, a set of illuminations that decorate a translation of the four Gospels in Latin, demonstrates the way that monks of the period (around AD800) used such artwork as a working meditation – not to the goddess but for Christian purposes. This labour of love was a true offering to the divine, yet remained within the traditions of the culture. Art forms often have the ability to link different ways of thinking and belief systems.

Celtic religion and Druidism are often inextricably linked in the minds of many people. They are not necessarily one and the same thing, Celtic religion being based much more, as we have seen above, in folklore while Druidism was a totally different set of beliefs with a philosophical background based on an appreciation of natural forces.

DRUIDISM

It has long been thought that the word 'Druid' probably came from the Greek 'drous', which means 'oak', therefore suggesting that the Druids would be the priests of the god or gods identified with the oak tree. However, it may also be derived from the word 'vid' meaning 'to know' which would lead one to believe that the druids were considered to be the wise ones of the community.

There were three principal classes of Druids: bards, prophets and priests, although religious teachers, judges and civil administrators would often also be Druids. They were adept at understanding the movement of the planets, the mysterious powers of plants and animals and the art of natural magic. It is for this last reason that they could be considered the wise ones – that is, having knowledge of Nature herself. They regarded the oak tree and the mistletoe, especially when the latter grew on oak trees, with great awe and usually held their rituals in oak forests. These rituals seem also to have been associated with stone circles and other natural groves. The Druids were often assisted by female prophets or sorcerers who did not always enjoy the same powers and privileges.

While druids are mentioned frequently in ancient scripts, little is truly known of their way of life because their traditions were principally oral, i.e. spoken and yet secret. In their society they were accepted as the teachers of moral philosophy and science; public and private disputes were referred to them for arbitration. Their authority was as much social as religious and they enjoyed many privileges, including in Gaul – though not in Ireland – exemption from military service and the payment of taxes. Many received great honours.

From evidence unearthed in modern times it seems that Celtic Druids may have been the linear descendants of the megalithic builders of the late Neolithic and Bronze Age period in Europe. The druids were also educators, particularly of the nobility, and it is almost certain that Merlin in the story of King Arthur, rather than being just a magician, was also a Druid. Their instruction was very wide-ranging and far-reaching. One component was the learning by heart of a large quantity of verse, which presumably meant that their memories were honed at the same time as they learned the traditions of their calling and their community. When the Druidic tradition died out in approximately the 1st to 3rd centuries AD, largely as a result of ferocious Roman oppression, their store of bardic sacred songs, prayers, rules of divination and magic was lost. Much of the information we have today comes from translations made at a much later date, often as late as the 13th century.

Julius Caesar noted that the Gauls held a tradition that Druids were of British origin. He had made as extensive a study as he could of the latters' doctrine and concluded that the principal point was that the soul did not die, and that after death it passed from one body into another. Some Greek writers are said to have believed that the Druids had borrowed this idea from the philosopher Pythagoras or one of his disciples. Certainly, Druids had a philosophy, but it is more than likely that the belief in the continuation of life arose as much from observation of the cyclical pattern of Nature as from anything else. They do not appear to have feared death, regarding it simply as a transition stage in the immortality of the soul. Indeed, they sometimes seemed to have welcomed death – particularly if it was a courageous one – to the puzzlement of those who struggled to understand them.

The practice of human sacrifice, apparently carried out by the Druids, is now known to have been a survival of pre-Druidic custom and more than probably was regarded as an efficient way of disposing of unpleasant elements in their society. Druids would have presided dispassionately at such ceremonies – as much in the sense of being guardians of the correct balance within the community rather than being wanton murdering high priests. Indeed, the druids seem also to have presided over the traditional religious ceremonies such as the placing of deliberately broken objects in the water of streams and wells as offerings to the Gods.

Accounts are given also of the ritual harvesting of mistletoe. This had to be cut with a golden knife or sickle and gathered without it being contaminated by touching the ground, the plant being caught in a white cloth by attendants waiting below. Two white bulls were then sacrificed, after which the priest divided the branches into many parts and distributed them to the people, who hung them over doorways as protection against thunder, lightning and other evils. The folklore, along with the magical powers of this plant, blossomed over the centuries. It was understood, for instance, that mistletoe took on the character of its host tree in some ways. Mistletoe grown on oak was in very subtle ways different from mistletoe grown on apple trees. A sprig placed in a baby's cradle would protect the child from fairies. An entire herd would be protected from harm if a sprig was given to the first cow calving after New Year.

In both Gaul and Ireland, Druids were not just representatives of a religion but an integral part of the community. Written records seem to prove that Druids had withdrawn from Gaul in the face of the Roman army by the end of the 1st century AD, but there continues to be evidence of their existence in Ireland much later. The similarities between the Irish and Gallic druids is quite pronounced. In Ireland particularly they were most often found in the service of kings, in the role of advisers due to their abilities in the use of magic and the voice as a vehicle.

The voice in magic is truly an instrument or tool and it was through the voice that magical change could be brought about. A change of consciousness could be self-induced in the druidic bard and this would then allow for the spontaneous transmission of wisdom – a kind of channelling – which often took the form of poetry. This poetic tradition was known as Roscanna (vision poetry) and was used in magical incantation. The poetry itself was intended to be ambiguous to the uninitiated and was full of arcane and archaic references. Ultimately they were spells in the true sense of the word, i.e. magical words designed to have a particular effect. Unfortunately, as we move away from the purity of true Druidic poetry, in some later magical traditions it descends into mere doggerel verse.

The Triad is central to Druidic culture and has become a rule in much of their later recorded poetry which gives form to a basic belief that everything has a threefold nature. Knowledge, Nature and Truth lead to Wisdom and the bardic tradition allows this to be taught to the masses. The Druidic moral code is based on the premise that each person, not fate or the will of gods, is responsible for his or her own conduct. It is characterized by a sense of fair play, honour and justice. The myths and tales of the heroes of old gave a strong sense of this to a people who often needed extreme courage just to survive.

Opinions vary as to whether the Celts and Druids were a shamanic civilization or not. They had their own pantheon of gods descended from Danu and were therefore the Tuatha de Dannann, meaning 'Tribe of Danu'. In the Irish language the word 'tuath' means 'people' or 'tribe', but it can also mean 'sinister, perverse, malign, evil'. This implies spell making and witchcraft and the conjuring up of less than benign forces.

As with all belief systems based on a closeness to nature, there were certain times of the year when the people were closer to the Otherworld and they were inevitably aware of the power, majesty and implacability of Nature herself. Fire worship was an integral part of the Celtic Druidic tradition, both as a life giving force and also as a potential destroyer or cleansing agent. The ritual 'need fire' lit at the important festivals expressed the high esteem the Celts held for fire, as a source of inspiration as well as light. (It is interesting that on 2 February at Imbolc, the feast of Brighid – who was also the Celtic goddess of poetry – is based on the maintaining of the eternal flame.) There seems to be scant evidence that the Druid actually travelled between two worlds, as the shaman is said to have done. The Druids did, however, understand the varying levels of consciousness necessary to their calling.

Having said that, Druidism actually demonstrates the management of both low and high magic – thaumaturgy and theurgy – for it is within the differing states of consciousness that a particular type of magic becomes possible. We have seen that a central teaching in Druidism is a personal responsibility for one's own actions. The use of offerings, prayers, sacrifices, ritual, taboos and other physical means in order to communicate with – and influence – divine powers is a carefully thought out act of responsibility; the use of trances, visions, spirit possessions and direct connection with the spirit is far more ecstatic and therefore spontaneous.

The first set of actions by the practitioner attempts to lift the physical realm towards the spiritual, whereas the second accepts the ability of spiritual forces to enter the physical realm and therefore to be 'pulled' downwards. The deliberate nurturing of the powers such as clairvoyance and the calling of elemental powers to help others, the ability to bring unjust war to an end and the knowledge of natural patterns and influences suggests that the Druid's powers were actually a function of his place in the community in which he lived. It was a chosen path of service. In other words he chose to become a Druid and to work through the various initiations of bard, prophet and ovate.

The modern practice of Druidism does seem to straddle all aspects of magical practice but is principally a path to personal development and spiritual integrity. To understand the Druid way of thought in the modern day is to recognize that it is living with a sense of responsibility within the flow of natural forces. By making use of the inspiration given to us by Mother Nature and understanding the ebb and flow of the energies around us, we are able to utilize the power within ourselves and the world around us. We can communicate with the spirits of plants, rocks, the earth itself. Even given the frenetic pace of urban living it is still possible to live our lives successfully; though many of the old ways of worship may have gone by the board, we can still adapt and modify our own rituals to enable us to change our lives for the better.

In days gone by it would take as long as nineteen years to become a fully-fledged Druid. This followed the premise that it is better to travel slowly on any path of spiritual development, but also symbolized the return to a starting point – a full circle – since this was the time between two similar eclipses of the Sun and Moon, suggesting an understanding of both the overt and occult forces within the aspirant's being. The novitiate would come to an understanding of body, mind and spirit and their own place in the universe and would then be ready to pass on the knowledge to others.

MODERN DRUIDIC TRAINING

Nowadays bardic training introduces all the basic concepts of Druidism and shows you how it is a vibrant journey following the cycle of the year which you can practise in the modern world. The aim of the training is to help you express yourself fully in the world. Through it you discover the source of your own creative power and learn how to express it in ways that are appropriate for you. You also learn how to use ritual correctly, how to create a sacred space and to use the directions and the elements. These rituals help to attune you to the world around you and to the rhythms of the earth, the sun and moon and the stars. In this way you gain access to your own inner space, that part of you which connects with life itself.

As with all systems of spiritual advancement, there are some people who prefer to work alone and others who need to work as part of a group. There are advantages to both ways and part of the sense of community, working in groups, is that almost inevitably you will find someone who has had similar experiences to your own. Even if you do work alone, much information can be shared using the world-wide community of the internet and cyberspace.

The process of initiation can be completed much more quickly nowadays than previously; the training for each area of understanding taking more or less a year, although full initiation into the various levels of awareness takes place only when the pupil is ready, whether that initiation happens in private or within a 'grove' or group.

To give an illustration of the way Druid thought works, we shall take you briefly through the beginning of a ritual. In common with all belief systems, the beginning of the Druidic ritual is indicated in an appropriate way. Here, the opening phrase 'We are here to honour the Gods', focusses the minds of the participants on the matter in hand. In a group used to working together the Gaelic phrases might be used, but not if there are beginners because this might cause confusion. Sound might also be used to capture attention; perhaps the sounding of a horn or a roll of drums.

THE CONSECRATION OF SPACE

All you need do to dedicate a space for a new ritual is to walk into it with the proper intent, whether that space is a temple or grove. If the area has been previously used as sacred space, it will be activated by this simple action. When you are in a space that has not been sanctified it is easy to mark it by processing around it, much as is done in creating or casting a circle (see page 136). You could physically mark and then consecrate the edges of your sacred space, depending on the nature of the ritual or magic to be done, though the intention should be to create a more open circle.

Druids do not consider it necessary to mark the four quarters as do most Wiccans or Kabbalists. The sacred grove is already sanctified and protected, so there is little need to call for additional power. It is the space which is important. It is an open, welcoming space rather than a closed one, unless the ritual demands it. Introducing the idea of four cardinal points which presupposes some kind of structure is not necessary. One might assume that the druid belief is so much in touch with the four elements of Earth, Water, Air and Fire that demanding their presence is superfluous. For the Druid, Fire is the motivating force with the other three forming a trinity or triangle of power rather than a square.

There is a another basic difference, too, in that Wiccan or other circles are designed to keep the power and the energy in until it can be directed or managed. Druidic circles will work much more on the spiral shape, which expands to take account of additional energy available. If the energy pattern becomes visible psychically it will manifest as a cone of power or vortex.

Creation of a Group Purpose

Druidic thought recognizes the symbolism of the tree – the triad of the roots that drop down into the earth, the branches that spread out towards the sky and towards others and the trunk, all of which give stability.

One way in which you can help to create a group purpose is to learn to make links with others in the group and to think of yourselves as a group of sacred trees – a grove. Here is how you do it.

METHOD

Think of yourself as a tree (on page 261 you will find a list of 'tree personalities') – in perceiving yourself as a tree you put yourself in touch with your essential energy. From that point of essential energy, you can extend your roots and your branches until they meet and merge with others in the group.

From being an individual among many, you are now able to perceive that you have all become a single grove, an entity which is composed of the energies of all of the participants and yet has a 'being' all of its own. You have developed a group mind, and from here can direct your energies in a single purpose.

Note: Remember that this is only one part of a Druidic ritual.

Within the ritual circle or space it is possible to trace out other shapes which have meaning or are appropriate for a particular ritual. Perhaps the labyrinth could be used to suggest the journey undertaken, an egg shape to delineate all life or the triangle to represent the Three Worlds. These might be walked alone or in procession. We will see a similar tracing of patterns in the sun dances of the Native Americans.

NATIVE AMERICAN TRIBES

Although the Sun Dance was outlawed in 1904, a number of tribes have attempted to revive it in its original form and meaning, not just as a tourist attraction. As interest grows worldwide in natural magic, the true beauty and intrinsic significance of the ritual becomes more and more apparent. The Sun Dance originally safeguarded the coming year by recreating the story of creation in much the same way as the Sabbat rituals do in Celtic belief.

The ceremonies and rituals of Native American tribes show a development all of their own; they also show a similar train of thought to other shamanic societies in the acceptance of animal representation. Tribal belief does vary somewhat, although the basic elements are the same from tribe to tribe. The Sun Dance ceremony of the Plains Indians (a diverse group of many tribes) as creation story is not part of the Shoshoni belief. The Shoshonis hold that the lodge, which is a sacred space formed in honour of the ceremony, is a representation of the cosmos. A Christian interpretation of the Sun Dance ritual was attempted in the nineteenth century, but it could only be interpreted as a ritual to restore health and could not easily be adapted to suit Christian thought.

As a sacred space, the Sun Dance lodge is a symbol of the world – a microcosm within a macrocosm – and is used to heal people in an environment where human interference cannot take place. The lodge is left to decay naturally after the four-day ceremony and must not be destroyed by any human agency. When the lodge is first constructed, the central pole is a cottonwood tree that has been particularly chosen and brought home with special ceremonies. It is the channel between people and God and can be seen as the World Tree or the Tree of Life. The Sun Dance facilitates a change of consciousness where visions and wisdom can be received.

The buffalo is considered to be the chief, and wisest, of all animals, so a buffalo head is attached at the top of the pole to represent all game. The eagle also plays a large part in the Sun Dance and is a most sacred totem. The eagle flies high, being the creature closest to the Sun. Therefore it is the link between man and spirit, being the messenger that delivers prayers to the Wakan-Tanka (god). The eagle's nest, which is fixed just below the buffalo's head, signifies the chief of the birds. Together the buffalo and eagle stand for the two levels of the universe: earth and sky.

ETIQUETTE OF THE CEREMONY

There are various preparatory rituals which take place prior to the ceremony proper and after the last preliminary dance. Those taking part in the ceremony camp close to the lodge in a wide circle with the lodge at its centre.

On the first day of the actual ceremony the (male) dancers prepare by painting their faces and arms red with black spots. On the second day, yellow paint or clay is used. The hair is braided, sometimes with other decorations; the use of feathers usually indicates that the dancer has a guardian spirit. An eagle bone whistle is worn round the neck along with a tribal necklace containing eagle down. This down is also attached to the little finger of each hand, presumably to signify allegiance to the eagle as totem. The men are naked from the waist up. On their legs they wear a richly decorated garment similar to an apron.

On the first day of the ceremony as the evening star rises, about 40 dancers march into the lodge and move to the back. Drummers then enter and sit at the front left (the south east). The ceremonial leader stands by the centre pole and asks Tam Apo – Our Father or Supreme Being – for his blessing. Songs are then sung, each repeated four times and the end of each signalled by the blowing of eagle bone whistles. The dancing is a monotonous kind of shuffle designed to induce a trancelike state. The dancers turn their faces towards the east, in the direction of the rising Sun.

The Shoshoni name for the Sun Dance is 'dry-standing-dance'. Only short breaks are allowed during the three days of its duration and the dancers must fast and drink nothing for this period. As in the vision quest, this suffering is intended to make the supernatural forces show mercy and enable the dancers to heal their people. It is when the Shoshoni are in the trance state towards the end of the Sun Dance that supernatural powers are most likely to be forthcoming.

On the second day, at dawn, single or pairs of dancers begin to dance. At sunrise all the dancers form five lines behind the centre pole. There is a great noise made with drumming and whistling; the dancers greet the sun by stretching their hands towards it. With great attention, morning prayers are listened to before the dancers take care of their own physical needs. This ritual is repeated every day of the ceremony, as is the painting of the dancers which takes place each morning.

Now the healing rites begin. Intense drumming and dancing takes place about 10 o'clock and lasts about an hour, presumably to raise the vibration, before the people to be healed are brought into the lodge. They are treated by the medicine man at the centre pole. The injuries are brushed by the medicine man with an eagle wing to symbolize transference of the power from the World Tree – the centre pole. The healing of the sick and the blessing of the dancers both appear to be the same process, designed to offer support and supernatural power as necessary.

The third day is the hardest and most powerful. Medicine bags, which contain herbs and revered objects, are brought out and sacred pipes are passed around. Healing rites are generally performed when the sun is in the ascendancy. The dancing, drumming and noise-making is more intense than ever and where the dancers feet have worn tracks, the pattern can be clearly seen. The third day is often when more vivid and sacred visions appear to the dancers; those that still have the energy to dance often have more intense visions, but by now many people lie on the ground, completely exhausted from the continuous dancing.

The dancers taking part are blessed on the fourth day at the centre pole, but the healings and blessings stop promptly at midday. Gifts, be they money, furs or blankets are offered to the medicine man who, in the late afternoon, pours some water onto the ground whilst facing east, as an offering to Mother Earth. The resting dancers are then given some of the water, the first liquid to pass their lips since the dance started.

The gifts are then passed out to the women for distribution, though some are placed at the base of the pole as an offering. There is then a great feast with much energetic dancing in the evening or – as often happens – the participants are given time to refresh themselves and the feast may well take place on the following evening.

By looking at all the symbolism and ritual involved with the Sun Dance, we can see natural magic in operation. All parts of nature are linked together and are dependent on one another.

Everything has a right to existence and can lend its energy to a greater whole. The changes of consciousness which occur in the dancers allow access to the power of animals which reveal their physical and spiritual powers to the ordinary man as much as they do to the medicine man and initiated shaman. The Sun Dance shows the continuity that there is in life. It suggests that there is no true end to life, but that there is a cycle of death and rebirth in which everything takes part. The Sun Dance carries the message that humans must give of themselves to help keep the cycles of regeneration going.

EXAMPLES OF NATIVE AMERICAN RITUAL
Many shamanic ceremonies such as sweat lodges, vision quests and the Sun Dance are being adopted by the urbanized Westerner. Many practitioners will find, in common with Native American Indians, that suitable rituals are received in dreams. As you become more immersed in the culture and customs, you too can receive this intuitive information.

We give as suggestions two incenses which may help to recreate an atmosphere that is conducive to working in a shamanic way.

Mexican Magic Incense

2 parts Copal Resin

1 part Frankincense Resin

1 part Rosemary

This incense is particularly suitable for use in Mexican and American folk magic rituals and spells.

Nine Woods Incense

1 part Rowan Wood (or Sandalwood)

1 part Dogwood

1 part Poplar

1 part Juniper

1 part Cedar

1 part Pine

1 part Holly Branches

1 part Elder (or Oak)

Take the sawdust of each of the above, mix together and burn indoors on charcoal when a ritual fire is necessary or desired but not practical. The incense emits the aroma of an open campfire and is particularly good when working shamanically or with the spirit of Nature.

It can be seen that many shamanic belief systems, while being very diverse in the actual expression of those beliefs, all seem to have a basic centrality – represented by a central pole or tree.

In the case of African Voodoo, these beliefs go back some 6,000 years.

AFRICAN VOODOO

There are numerous deities and traditions associated with African Voodoo. Below we give a version of initiation based on the accounts of respected observers. Probably as many as 60 million people worldwide practise Voodoo. Generally it seems that Voodoo flourished wherever the slave trade was particularly widespread.

This initiation demonstrates several aspects of magical or ritual practice in the whips, the dancing and the sacred designs. Many such customs are, and have been, misunderstood, without understanding the cultures on which such practices were based. They were seen as aberrations and evil practices but a little thought will reveal that, in fact, they are in keeping with the tenets of African belief. We describe a basic African ritual, though this will vary from local culture to local culture.

INITIATION

As part of their initiation, the candidates (Hounsis) must make their own whips to signify that they give up their old practices. At this time, they dance and chant to Aizan, the oldest of the Voodoo deities; the whips thereafter are known as aizan. The bush priest (Houngan if male, Mambo if female) dances around the poteau-mitan, the post at the centre of the hounfort (the Voodoo temple), then moves to the doors of the various rooms in the hounfort, where the hounsis will spend their time of initiation, and finally to the sacred trees outside where the ceremony is being conducted. The aizan are offered to other priests present to be kissed, then to the candidates and to other any spectators who acknowledge the aizan. The aizan are then put in the room where the novices will spend their time.

The candidates then go through the routine of rites and dances they have been taught until their teacher is satisfied with the performance. They then must lie down on their backs near the poteau-mitan under the peristyle (the roofed area of the hounfort). This done, the priest pours water into each of their mouths, then makes a cross on the face, chest and palms of each candidate using a powdered sacred substance. After this, the Houngan whips their legs and scolds them. Then with a sacred rattle he taps the candidates on their mouths, cheeks and forehead.

After having been reminded by the Houngan never to forget their responsibilities, the candidates kiss the ground in front of him. He spins them around (signifying the beginning of a new life) and kisses them on the mouth (signifying the beginning of a period of mourning). This part of the ritual is a variation on death and resurrection seen so often in other religions.

With the candidates now symbolically dead, everyone begins to mourn. As the weeping and wailing intensifies, bandages are tied around the eyes of the Hounsis. They are then symbolically buried by being pushed into a secret initiation room called the 'djevo'. There they remain until the final day of the initiation rites.

Sacred designs appropriate to each of the gods ('veve' sometimes spelt 'verver') have already been drawn in flour on the floor of the 'djevo'. The priest covers these with mats so that the Hounsis may rest on them for the next seven days in what is now their sacred space.

Veve/ Verver

They are dressed in simple white tunics and sit on beds of sacred leaves while the houngan cuts a lock of hair from the hounsis' head and from other parts of the body. The hair and nail clippings from the left hand and foot are wrapped in a banana leaf along with some grilled corn, feathers plucked from sacrificed chickens and some sweetened starchy liquid and placed in pots. The Houngan uses the pots to protect the initiates against evil spirits and to ensure the hounsis' devotion. This is a good example of sympathetic magic. During the sacred retreat the initiate is not allowed to move or speak without permission. This is only relaxed three times a day: once in the morning, when the candidate washes himself, and twice when he is rubbed down with sacred oils. As to the normal bodily functions, some authorities say he may leave his 'djevo' in the darkness of early morning, others say he may not leave at all.

The only meat the Hounsis may eat is chicken and then only the least savoury parts such as the head, feet and intestines. He is only allowed to drink water. This regime is managed and controlled by a woman who is specially chosen for the task. The Hounsis does have a bell or rattle with which to summon help in the event of an emergency.

THE BIRTH OF VOODOO

Voodoo is probably the best example of the assimilation of African belief into other cultures. The structure of Voodoo as we know it today began in Haiti during the colonization of Hispaniola, although its essential wisdom originated in different parts of Africa long before the Europeans started the slave trade. It was actually the enforced intermingling of African slaves from different tribes that gave rise to the development of Voodoo in Haiti. Little attention was paid to the spiritual needs of the slaves so, in their despair, a common thread had to be found by the slaves themselves. They began to invoke not only their own tribal gods, but also to practise rites other than their own. This tribal mixture can be seen in the names of different rites and in the gods who are still worshipped who were originally deities from all parts of Africa. They mixed practices and rituals from numbers of tribes and in the process developed a completely new religion that very quickly gained popularity.

The French (the colonisers of Haiti) realized that this new religion was a danger to their colonial system and so they denied all Africans the right to their own religious practices severely punishing anyone found practising Voodoo with imprisonments, beatings and hangings. The French decreed that all slaves be baptized as Catholics, and so Catholicism became superimposed on the African rites and beliefs (which the slaves still practiced either in secret or hidden as harmless dances and parties). This religious struggle continued for more than three centuries, but none of the punishments could totally obliterate the simple faith of the Africans.

Followers of this new religion of Voodoo – which originates in shamanic practice – actually considered the addition of the Catholic saints to be an enhancement of their faith and set about incorporating Catholic hymns, prayers, statues, candles and holy relics into their rituals. Tribal deities were often given the aspects of Catholic saints; they did not become the Catholic saints, but retained their original characteristics and personalities while adopting the symbolic trappings of Catholicism and the saints who they seemed to resemble most.

The whole structure of Voodoo reflects its history. The cross as a symbol, for instance, was easy to accept because it was already a powerful representation in the tribal religions as the crossroads where the spiritual and material worlds meet. It was adopted as the symbol of the powerful god Legba, who is the guardian of the gates, messenger of the gods and has multiple faces. As the trickster, he is the child who wants things he cannot have. The saint most closely associated with Legba is St Peter who holds the keys to the kingdom of heaven.

Below we show some other gods who have 'migrated' between religions.

DAMBALLA

This god suffered much in his transition from Africa and is a manifestation of the Fon tribal god, Dan. As the rainbow, he is a spiral around the earth and holds it together. He moves the sun, the moon and the stars and creates mountains. In Haiti, however, he is a snake god – the snake plays a role in Voodoo but only as a symbol.

OBATALA

This is the 'orisha' (spirit) of peace, harmony and purity. Some people see him as an androgynous deity which contains both male and female energies representing, respectively, heaven and earth while in some paths of Voodoo, Obatala manifests as a female. In his masculine form he is the father of most orishas and the creator of humankind; as such he is the owner of the world. He represents clarity, justice and wisdom. Everything that is white on Earth belongs to him: the snow, the sky, the bones and the brain. Obatala is invoked for health, peace and harmony.

OSHUN

This is the goddess of love, sexuality, beauty and diplomacy. She is often invoked in matters of wealth and love as she is the owner of the 'sweet waters'. She is the protector of the abdominal area and the teacher of pleasure and happiness. With her sweetness, she overcomes the most difficult tasks – in this she most closely approximates to the goddess Venus. She is a great giver, but when she is angry it is very difficult to calm her down. In this latter respect she shares similarities with the Indian goddess Kali and other such destructive entities.

SHANGO

Once the fourth king of Yoruba, he is immortalized as the thunder god and is said to have hurled thunderbolts. This links him to the Norse god Thor, whose main implement was the hammer. On Shango's altar, bodyguards appear as thunder axes ('oshe') and thunder-rattles ('shere'). Shango is legendary across the African Atlantic world and, as late as the 1970s has given rise to a cult, the shango-Baptists, which incorporates aspects of the Baptist religion. Shango's storms and lightning are said to cause a cleansing kind of terror that brings a balance to issues to do with morality.

Voodoo priests and priestesses are first of all healers, diviners and protectors from evil spirits, thus showing their shamanic background. In many ways they are more dispassionate in their judgements than perhaps the Judeo-Christian religions and much misunderstanding has grown up over their use of poppets and image magic. Ritual killings and deliberate harm have as little to do with Voodoo as Satanism does with Christianity. The idea of the wholesale sticking of pins into dolls is unfortunately a misapprehension based in Hollywood hype. The art of sympathetic magic used in an apparently negative fashion makes good copy.

The three main elements of traditional healing in African-based religions are:

1. Prevention of and protection from difficulties
2. Discovery of the causes of these difficulties
3. The eradication of these difficulties

Part of any healer's work is the management of the process of dying. A healer will know when no more can be done through his own art, will advise the family accordingly and will hold himself available to aid in the transition process.

The ancestors and recently departed family members play a large part in the rest of the work of traditional healers which relates to protecting clients from possible harm. Healers consult the spiritual realm by invoking and conferring with the ancestors. It is recognized that most afflictions are believed to come from external forces, so protection against them involves warding off the negative aspects of witchcraft and maintaining an equilibrium with other people, and with the spirits.

Thus, protection includes paying penance and seeking forgiveness for real or imagined offences. The healer may use herbs and other substances that are ingested, sniffed or smoked in a ceremonial pipe. They will also use their dreams, through which the ancestors give them the ability to diagnose a problem. Many traditional healers drum, dance or follow specific rituals, after which they perform ceremonial acts; they then provide medicines against imbalance or charms and totems to protect.

Like other shamanic cultures, healers dress in special robes, beaded necklaces and head-dresses. The necklaces they wear consist of beads, objects that have spiritual significance and plant or animal parts that are thought to have medicinal uses. These objects also signify the healer's status.

HOODOO

Hoodoo is neither a religion nor a denomination of a religion, although it does blend elements from several African and European religions. It consists of a great deal of African folklore magic along with a considerable amount of American Indian herbal knowledge and a smattering of European folklore (much of which pre-dates Christianity). Modern-day practitioners of hoodoo also often have an extensive knowledge of medieval manipulation of energy, Jewish kabbalism and some Hindu mysticism.

It could perhaps be said that Hoodoo is the thaumaturgical part of Voodoo, its smaller sister. Voodoo is a set of beliefs, a religion, as we have seen, whereas Hoodoo developed and survived because its techniques and magic are known to work. The ability of an individual to change their circumstances and those of others through ritual and spells is seen as personal power. Practitioners do believe in supernatural powers but they are free to believe in any god or gods of their choosing.

The only god in Hoodoo that seems to have survived from the African pantheon is Legba, the teacher god, whom we have met already. It is he who meets the hapless traveller at the crossroads. It is said that if you wish to learn a skill, such as how to play an instrument, you should wait with it at a crossroads on either three or nine specified nights or mornings. On your first visits you will probably see a series of animals. On your last visit, a big black man or a devil will appear. Provided you are not afraid and do not run away, he will request to borrow the item you have. He will then show you the proper way to use it by using it himself. When he returns it to you, you will suddenly have the power to excel with it.

The lack of the need for overt consecration means that the practice of Hoodoo is a mystical art based in natural magic rather than a religion. Some of its practices may be incorporated and used by priests and priestesses, but the art can also be practiced as a separate worldly skill by anyone, without initiation. Again it is a demonstration of a system of belief which has grown up using material which is readily available to the practitioner. Perhaps it is also for this reason that many of the rituals and techniques are based on the magical properties of herbs, roots, minerals, animal parts and the personal possessions and bodily secretions of people.

Foot track magic, for instance, is often used to force someone to do something they may not wish to do. Hoodoo gives magical power to a person's footprint, and when this particular ritual is used various powders and herbs are placed in the path of the victim – sometimes in a buried container or bottle. When the victim walks over the buried bottle or there is contact between the powder and victim's foot, an outcome is set in train that is commanded by the practitioner or person who has asked for the spell. The name of the powder often gives the clue to the purpose – Go Away powder, Good Luck, Do My Bidding and so on. The commands are often quite arbitrary without thought of the consequences. Many spell bottles contain sharp objects that are perceived by the rules of sympathetic magic to deter intruders. Spell bottles were, however, originally created to break the power of an evil magician or witch. The victim would create a container that could turn back the power against the perpetrator.

Initially these 'witch's bottles', as they became known, would be filled with nail clippings, hair or any bodily fluid or excreta known to belong to the original magician. Later they became objects of protection and would be buried near a home or placed within the walls for this purpose. Such bottles were made up until the early 19th century.

When making spell bottles you might like to enhance your work by lighting a candle as you do it. Magical practitioners who work in African-based traditions, and who work with candles, often pay attention to the way a candle burns and can draw conclusions about the progress of a spell or ritual. When the candle gives a clean, even burn, for instance, things will go well with the spell or blessing and one will most likely get what one desires. If a free-standing candle leaves little or no residue, that is best. If it runs and melts unevenly while burning, you have the opportunity to 'read' the residual wax, much as you would tea-leaves. You will ultimately become quite competent at interpreting the signs. If the flame flares and gutters while you are working, you will probably find that the energy you are using needs adjusting in some way.

Spell Bottles

Today, we use bottles filled with herbs and other personal objects in a similar way largely as protective devices as we show below. All such bottles are an amalgamation of energy, created and enhanced to achieve a specific magical end.

To Protect Your Home

YOU WILL NEED

Small glass jar with a tightly fitting lid

Rosemary

Pins

Needles

Red wine

Red candle

METHOD

Fill the jar with the rosemary, pins and needles while pushing your own energy into them. While you are doing this, repeat words that enhance the action, such as:

Needles, pins, herb and wine
Protect now this house of mine.
In this bottle I now trust,
As in the ground it is thrust.

Pour in the red wine and seal the jar with wax from the candle.

Bury the bottle close to the boundaries of your property or, if you do not have a garden, put it in an inconspicuous place as close to your front door as possible. Trace a protective pentagram over the bottle and leave alone knowing you are protected.

If you move home then dig it up and either destroy it (dispose of the contents in running water) or take it to your new home.

On page 276, there is a Witch's Bottle Home Protection incense that could be placed in your bottle along with the other ingredients or burned while you prepare your bottle.

Obviously ways had to be found of breaking malign spells. Finding and destroying the buried bottle thus breaking the spell, setting out salt, ritual bathing, sweeping and floor washing to remove the powders are all antidotes to this magic, and practitioners will often do a roaring trade in these artefacts. The wearing of protective amulets, or nine Devil's Shoe String twigs (a species of viburnum or blackthorn), in the shoes or around the ankles is also deemed to be protection.

CROSSING

'Crossing' is a variation of foot track magic where a cross or mark is placed where it is known the victim is going to walk. The antidote to this magic is black pepper which is said to keep your footprints from making any sort of impression, so that even if anyone does get hold of them, they have achieved nothing. You wear it inside your socks or shoes. (Note: The old superstition that if you walked on a line on the pavement the 'black man will get you' may have its roots in this kind of magic.)

Magicians and sorcerers will also cast spells to improve one's luck or ward off evil spirits. A frightening aspect of some traditional African beliefs is muti murder, the deliberate taking of life. This practice is founded on the belief that there is only a finite amount of good luck in the world, and any gain over and above one's quotient has to be at the expense of another person's life. An even more powerful way to acquire another person's power is to consume medicine made from their body parts. It is believed that muti killers frequently take the body parts while the victim is alive, which is believed to increase the potency of the medicine.

OTHER FORMS OF AFRICAN-BASED RELIGIONS
MACUMBA

This is the Brazilian form of Voodoo. Macumba is an umbrella term that embraces two principal forms of African spirit worship – Candomble and Umbanda. Candomble ceremonies start with invocations to the gods, prayers, offerings and possession of the faithful by the gods. Umbanda incorporates the worship of the Catholic saints along with the beliefs of the Brazilian Indians.

Macumba is often referred to as black magic, but this aspect is really more the system known as Quimbanda. Quimbanda's practitioners simply draw their power from unruly spirits. The work is more mischievous, and therefore their practices are often considered tainted.

One Macumban celebration held on 1 January is where more than a million celebrants wade into the ocean at dusk and a priestess known as 'mao de santo' (mother of the saint, therefore drawing parallels with the Virgin Mary) lights candles and then purifies and ordains other young priestesses. As the sun goes down, celebrants decorate a tiny wooden boat with candles, flowers and figures of the saints. At midnight the boat is set sail from the shore; if the boat sinks Yemanji, a water spirit, has heard their prayers and accepted their offering, promising her support and guidance for another year.

LA SANTERIA

Santeria is the worship of the ancient African gods through spirit possession and magic.

La Santeria, or the Way of the Saints, came about when the Yoruba people were taken to Cuba and forced to worship the saints of the Catholic church. They would do this by equating their own gods with the saints. This religion is famous for its 'magic', which is based on a knowledge of the mysteries or spirits, which are the servants of God and rule over every force of nature and every aspect of human life. The spirits can be counted on to come to the aid of their followers. It is said that they will guide the practitioner to a better life in all ways and will show him how to interact with them to improve not just his or her own life, but also the lives of others. This means that practitioners of la Santeria live their lives in an altered state of awareness.

OBEAH

Unlike its relative Voodoo in Haiti, Obeah, which originates in Jamaica, has always been strictly opposed to Christianity. Obeah can be viewed as 'a Tower of Power', an enormous source of energy that can be communicated with by the Obeah priest in special ways. Obeah pre-dates Christianity and is an occult tradition that includes healing and divination. The Obi Stick used by the Obeah man of Jamaica is thought to be a representation of the Rod of Moses, which he used to part the Red Sea. The Obi-man and his stick were often used as a threat to young children if they were being naughty. Obeah still has the connotations of evil and black magic attributed to it by many of the white missionaries of years gone by.

Obeah includes many elements easily recognizable as shamanism. These arise out of a simple search for knowledge which later develops further into practices seen within Voodoo. Obeah looks for power over the world and environment in which its practitioners live and can be seen as one of those aspects of awareness which feeds perhaps on fear.

Rather than rigidly adhering to some carefully laid down formula, the African-based religions have grown, changed and expanded to take account of the needs of the people they serve, while maintaining the beliefs that are at their core.

WITCHCRAFT

The roots of Witchcraft are just as ancient as the roots of Voodoo. Like Voodoo, the Craft or Witchcraft should never be confused with Satanism, the outright worship of Satan. The true Witch has nothing to do with such worship, even though there are some Satanists who will, wrongfully, call themselves 'Witch'. It is this type of misunderstanding that led to the persecution of witches in the olden days and, in today's climate of knowledge, is an unnecessary burden.

At rock bottom, modern witchcraft owes its roots to shamanism, although in many ways in being brought forward into the modern day by people such as Gerald Gardner and Alexander Sanders, some of that shamanic integrity has been radically changed. In becoming almost an urban religion, it has become very diverse in its practices and beliefs and, on the surface, it is sometimes difficult to perceive the basic core convictions.

Witchcraft develops through the large number of groups that exist with intrinsic bonds to each other. On the whole, these are looser than those that you will find between the various Christian churches. Each group or coven has its own traditions and beliefs, develops its own rituals and can exist – if necessary – in isolation. It is perhaps this latter quality which has given rise to the huge upsurge in the existence of solitary witches but has also resulted in the survival of the Craft despite persecution and danger.

The basic principles of the Craft are as follows:

1. The first principle is that of love and is expressed in the ethic, 'do as you will, so long as you harm none'. This love is not emotional but is seen as an outpouring and sharing of a basic energy or force as communicated in relation to other beings, whether they are human or otherwise. Harm, which is seen as unethical, is unjustified action with no cause; harming others can be done by word, thought, or deed. Doing something that ultimately harms oneself is obviously also not acceptable.

2. The Witch should act within the structure of the Law of Cause and Effect. Every action has its reaction, and every effect has its cause. This is a principle that acts within the human realm. It is believed that all things happen according to this law. From a human perspective – though not from a divine – nothing in the universe can occur outside this law, though we may not always enjoy the relationship between a given effect and its cause.

3. Supplementary to this is the Law of Three, which states that whatever goes forth must return threefold, whether good or ill. Our actions affect others more than people realize, and the resulting reactions are also part of the package. It is a very basic application of the tenet 'As ye sow, so also shall ye reap'. This is why magical spells and rituals must be very carefully considered and full responsibility accepted before action is taken.

4. For this reason, anyone practising witchcraft needs to recognize and harmonize with universal forces in agreement with the Law of Polarity. Everything is dual; everything has two poles; everything has its opposite; for every action there is a reaction; everything can be categorized as either active or reactive in relation to other things.

5. Recognizing this polarity means that, while the Wiccan religion acknowledges the Oneness of the Divinity, members worship and relate to the Divine as the archetypal polarity of God and Goddess, the Male and Female principle, the All-Father and the Great Mother.

Godhead is one unique and transcendent wholeness, beyond any limitations or expressions; thus, it is beyond our human capacity to understand and identify with this principle of Cosmic Oneness, except as It is revealed to us in terms of Its attributes and operation.

These concepts are supposedly as close as humans can get to the One (Godhead) given the constraints of the human limits of understanding and expression. The practice of the Mysteries, however, allows mankind to live within the divine Oneness.

'As above, so below' is another principle that can be accepted. That which exists in the Macrocosm (the Heavens) exists, on a smaller scale and to a lesser degree, in the Microcosm (the physical World). The powers of the universe are present also in the human being, though on the whole they are not properly utilized. The abilities and qualities of 'being' can be activated and used if the proper techniques and initiations are practised. The secrets of the hidden knowledge must be concealed from the unworthy however, because much harm can be done by those who have power without responsibility.

The universe is the physical expression of the divine – there can be nothing in the universe that does not contain the divine – so the powers and attributes of the Godhead exist in the physical, though to a much lesser degree. The Craft is a natural religion, seeing in nature the expression and revelation of Divinity. It is possible for humanity to exert the power of the gods; to be a channel for the Godhead to manifest in a multitude of ways.

Wiccans accept that everything emanates from the 'One Word' – the universe – and is in perpetual motion. All things rise and fall in a tidal movement that reflects the motion inherent in the universe. Therefore the Wiccan practitioner celebrates, harmonizes with and makes use of, the natural flow expressed through the sequence of the seasons and the motion of the solar system. These ritual observances are the eight great festivals of the year, referred to as the Wheel of the Year. Operating the Laws of Polarity, the Wiccan is also conscious of the forces and tides of the Moon. Examples of spells and rituals using these forces are given elsewhere in the book.

There are numerous ways of honouring the moon and one of the simplest is to honour the sanctity of your own life. This you do by paying special attention to Diana, Goddess of the Moon and the Woodlands, for a short time every day and recognizing the life connection between you and every living creature.

You might hang apple slices, nuts and seeds in your garden for her creatures. At the same time, honour Diana by saying:

Diana, Goddess of the woodlands, I make this offering in recognition of your power to care for your creatures.

You may find that you are then drawn to one animal in particular. If this happens, try to keep a representation of that animal close beside you so that you are constantly reminded that you and your body are the medium between much earth energy and other creatures. This is linking with the idea of totem or soul animals, a special spirit to look after you.

Having a representation of Diana and her creatures in your home or sacred space is a reminder that you honour her each time you do something to give assistance to the earth and its creatures. Whenever you think of this, you might repeat these words:

Goddess of the Silver Moon,
Lady of the Forests,
Hear my praises to you
As you protect your creatures,
Protect now me and mine.

Use of symbolic representations of the natural and divine forces of the universe is an effective way of contacting and utilising the forces they denote. There comes a point though when the personalizations of the gods and goddesses, however seductive, become somewhat superfluous and we move on to a consideration of the energies and entities that are behind our gods and goddesses.

To do this, we need to raise our awareness beyond mundane concerns and consider thinking that is more mystical.

SPIRITUAL PROGRESSION

For the majority of people, common sense thinking backed up by practical action is handier and normally of more use than theoretical or mystical thinking. When there are a wide range of circumstances to be handled in everyday life, normally common sense will prevail. However, sometimes, when people are confronted with the unusual or difficult, or are faced by extreme anxiety, they will immediately tend to theorize as a means of achieving understanding. There is a kind of process gone through which says 'If this is so then such and such is also so'. Simplistic thought says, for instance, that if the crops have failed then the gods must be angry. This was believed for many thousands of years, and in some societies even today offerings are made to the gods for a successful harvest.

When talking of traditional African religions, for instance, where understanding is borne out by experience, it can appear that they are obsessed by aspects that might be called religious. This is not necessarily so – more that they are obsessed by things they do not understand or by things considered to be supernatural. When, for instance, an illness does not respond to treatment or the herbal specific that has been given, a deeper reason may be sought and a diviner or witch-doctor called in.

Just as a Western practitioner would now look for psychological reasons for a sickness, so the traditional African doctor will look for other circumstances, such as disturbances in the sick man's life. The West African, for instance, may think of the body as a meeting place of multiple souls – some helpful and others not so – whereas the more conventionally trained doctor will speak of sub-personalities, or the unconscious side of the personality.

Long ago, West African researchers showed that there was a wide distribution of beliefs in what they called 'multiple souls'. They found that many West African belief systems surrounded the individual with a number of spiritual helpers and agencies and the researchers baptised these agencies with fanciful names such as 'spirit double'.

Within the Tale belief system, for instance, there are three categories of spiritual entities especially concerned with the individual. First comes the 'serge', which has the care of the person as a biological unit – over his body, his sickness and health, his life and death. Then comes the 'nuor yin', which is a personification of the wishes expressed by the individual before his arrival on earth – almost the ideal to which he is aspiring. The 'nuor yin' appears specifically concerned with whether or not the individual has the personality traits necessary for him to become an adequate member of the Tale society. Finally in this trio of spiritual agencies we have what one researcher has called the 'yin ancestors'. These are two or three of the individual's ancestors who have been delegated to look after his personal fortunes; Yin ancestors only attach themselves to an individual who has a good 'nuor yin', and the person must already have proved himself to have the basic equipment for fitting into Tale society. It is worth noting that in this way body, mind and spirit are all taken care of in an appropriate manner.

Often in Western society the understanding of the supernatural is left in the hands of the mystic, but this has meant that magical control of nature, formerly an integral part of most societies, has increasingly been lost. Rites and rituals have come down to us in the form of folklore without a full understanding of exactly why the rituals were carried out. The ritual of the new moon in lunar magic illustrates this very well. The principle of sympathy in nature or cosmic sympathy – which we have considered elsewhere – operates here when, for instance, the ritual is recited in the way it was originally spoken.

On the other hand, the shamanic practitioner is skilled in understanding the supernatural and 'driving out devils'. Using special techniques to deal with hidden inner qualities, he is able to achieve healing which might appear to be miraculous. This could be said to be because of his specialization in matters to do with the supernatural. The more he specializes and becomes adept in the use of rituals and other techniques, the more he moves beyond the awareness of the average individual. The more the shaman knows, the more he needs to know and therefore the more he becomes involved in appealing to – and understanding – the supernatural and mystical thought.

There is often a confusion in many peoples' minds between the supernatural, low magic and religion. Low magic is easily distinguishable from religion in that it is said not to involve relationship with a superhuman entity – i.e. one does not appeal to a higher source. However, religion can also be any set of attitudes, beliefs and practices pertaining to supernatural power – demons, forces for good or evil, gods, ghosts or spirits. When this happens, we must bring in the concepts of mystical and magical power and the recognition that such energy differs from everyday energy. It can be unpredictable and not easily controlled except by those who have been trained so to do.

In ancient times, the Jews had an interesting viewpoint concerning the appearance of apparitions, or ghosts, which deserves to be mentioned. While some might consider these viewpoints to be mere superstitions, in fact they have become embedded in a number of spiritual laws that still operate today.

✦ It was supposed that an apparition had the power to become visible and to injure any particular person who might happen to be by himself in the dark.

✦ If two people were together, although they may be in the dark, the apparition had only the power to show itself, but did not have the power to do either of them any harm.

✦ If three persons were assembled together and in the dark the apparition did not posses the power of showing itself to any of them nor 'of doing them least injury'.

They also believed that the light arising from one single candle was sufficient protection for any person against the power of an apparition and would protect them from invisible injury. Candles grouped as a torch or flambeaux would give as much protection as if three people were together.

It can be seen that these beliefs are a very real interpretation of the Rule of Three when negativity is returned threefold. Christ, having come from a Jewish background, may well have been aware of its significance when he said, 'Where two or three are gathered together in my name there am I also'. He would have known that his followers would believe that he was an unseen presence and power with them.

The relationship between religious power and supernatural power is embodied in the knowledge of what control is necessary. It does not particularly matter whether that control is exercised by priests who have studied philosophical thought and reached conclusions in that way, or by shamans who have learned through direct experience and experimentation – both are appropriate according to the systems of belief.

Both priests and shamans recognize that human actions such as war and aggression come from the need to impose control on other human beings. Going one stage beyond that, at a very basic level the support and control of supernatural beings is gained through rituals and their correct management. This helps to impart a certain kind of order in the universe in the hope that certain happenings – natural magic – will occur. The more complex a society becomes, the less likely it is to subscribe to such a simplistic belief, and the more likely it is that, rather than controlling supernatural entities, attempts will be made to control the energies inherent in those entities.

In simple, mainly Pagan, religions with principally oral traditions, there is likely to be more tolerance of other peoples' belief systems and an appreciation that those beliefs will be appropriate to a particular culture. It is only later, when religions become more complex and institutionalized, that they play a part in forming the laws of the society that created them. Intolerance and conflict then arise when ways of interpreting philosophical thought become confused and go against the normal practice of the particular society. At that point it is often necessary to bring about a return to simplicity and return to the correct use of magical powers.

We must here differentiate between witchcraft and what might be called 'wizardry'. In this sense wizardry can be defined as 'the use of magical power for nefarious ends', while witchcraft is the revival of an ancient form of spirituality which existed in Western Europe in pre-Christian times. There is a belief that wizardry arises from the negative emotions of jealousy, anger and spite. This would come under the definition of thaumaturgy – low magic used for negative purposes. Within a scheme of natural magic anyone who decides deliberately to use magical power in such a negative way, perhaps by ill-wishing someone, would have to believe in his or her own right to manage aggression in this way. However, the law of Karma (cause and effect) does dictate that the 'wizard' puts himself in danger by the use of such power. Most systems of belief hold that the misuse of power is dangerous.

Wizardry may also help the individual to manage anxiety, giving him power over those things which distress him. Having a focus for one's anxiety, particularly when actions are not understood, allows the individual to blame supernatural forces for his own mistakes and gives him the excuse to not take responsibility for his actions. As a way of understanding the inexplicable, deviant members of society can then take the blame. This is seen in the widespread acceptance of the principle of 'the evil eye' in most societies.

It is said that 'every society develops certain patterns of behaving designed to guard, by one means or another, against the unexpected, better to control man's relationship to the universe in which he lives.'

MYSTICISM AND MAGIC

Human beings have looked for explanations and spiritual knowledge since time began. Magic was initially a way of explaining the unexplainable, but as time goes on it becomes a way of making use of that which we cannot necessarily explain or control. When the unexplainable happens we devise ritualistic ways of imposing order and seek knowledge either from those who have greater knowledge or from within ourselves. We are motivated by three basic drives: pleasure, knowledge, and survival. The highest expression of these three combined is mysticism – a sense of connectedness with the divine.

There are two ways in which we can verify truths; one from an external source and one from an internal (within ourselves). When we seek knowledge of deeper inner spiritual truths, we can only verify these by that which we experience directly. This intuitive, right brained, inner approach to spiritual knowledge and experience of the divine from within is known as Gnosticism – the doctrine of salvation by knowledge in its purest form. Most magical practitioners who wish to work effectively within any of the magical traditions will come across some or all of the following systems of belief at some point in their search for knowledge. All of these traditions are part of the Western 'Mystery' traditions, requiring initially a philosophical contemplative approach, rather than an active participation.

Many of the systems shown below are the basis on which natural magic is founded and so, for many people in this day and age, their magical workings will contain elements from every system of belief. In terms of theurgy, magic works when there is some understanding of the guiding principles behind it, and for all of these systems there is an awareness of the power of nature, of God and the interconnectedness of all things.

BELIEF SYSTEMS

NEO-ALEXANDRIAN HERMETICISM

The significance of the group of Greek writings that together are called the Corpus Hermeticum is that, in them, it is seen that man has an ability to achieve immortality through knowledge of the divine. The philosophical-religious concept cannot be summarized in a few words, but was thought to be Egyptian in origin.

The writings take their name from the wisdom of their apparent author Hermes Trismegistus (thrice great), known to the Egyptians as far back as 3000BC as Thoth. In that time it was not unusual to ascribe such wisdom to one of the gods though it has now been proved that the actual transcribers were a group of people writing in the 2nd to 3rd centuries AD in Alexandria.

Until the Renaissance the writings were not generally known in the west, but both before – and since – then they have formed the basis of much religious and philosophical understanding, including that of Plato and others.

Christian Kabbalah

The word 'Kabbalah', whether spelt with a K, C or Q, is derived from the Hebrew QBLH, the literal interpretation of which is 'an unwritten or oral tradition', from the Hebrew verb QBL – 'to receive'. A Kabbalist may be described as a student of the hidden meaning of Scriptures, which he interprets by the aid of what is known as the symbolical Kabbalah. It is this symbolism which is studied at great length by sages from all religions. Nowadays, Christian Kabbalah refers mainly to the interpretation of what might be considered to be the occult part of the Kabbalah from a Christian perspective. Much of its esoteric thought dates from the late 12th century and many rituals associated with Kabbalah form the basis for modern magic. We look more fully at the Kabbalah elsewhere in the book.

Teachings of Paracelsus

Paracelsus (1493–1541), whose original name was Theophrastus Bombastus von Hohenheim, was a Swiss physician and alchemist. His egotism and contempt for traditional theories earned him a great deal of enmity, though he was immensely popular among ordinary people, because he used the German language to instruct rather than Latin. The whole purpose of life, according to Paracelsus, is to realize one's inherent Godhood. We can only work with the power of divine wisdom within ourselves when we accept the existence of God within. There is nothing in which we can place any confidence for the purpose of our own salvation, except the power of that divine wisdom.

It was Paracelsus who first recognized that each substance had its own 'fingerprint' or signature that made it totally unique. He travelled extensively and – settling nowhere – might be said to have been something of a hermit, trusting to providence; he acquired knowledge of alchemy, chemistry and metallurgy wherever he went. Paracelsus wrote a number of medical and occult works that contained a weird mixture of sound observation and mystical language. In searching for the cause of pathological changes giving rise to disease, for instance, he named four entities, which he divided into *ens astrorum* (cosmic influences differing with climate and country), *ens veneni* (toxic matter originating in the food), the cause of contagious diseases, *ens naturale et spirituale* (defective physical or mental constitution) and *ens deale* (an affliction sent by Providence).

PHILOSOPHIA OCCULTA

Heinrich Cornelius Agrippa (1486–1535) was one of the most influential writers about magic at the time of the Renaissance. He called magic 'the most perfect and chief Science, that sacred and sublimer kind of philosophy and lastly the most absolute perfection of all most excellent philosophy'. His extensive writings form most of the basis of Western occultism, and still have relevance today. Written in 1509–10, *De Occulta Philosophia* (the magical vision of the cosmos which unifies Nature and religion theurgically) appeared in three volumes. Circulated widely in manuscript form and therefore open to misinterpretation, they were eventually printed in book form in 1533. He also divided philosophy into natural, mathematical and theological teachings. He himself confessed that he was attempting to rescue ancient magic from charlatans and imposters.

ALCHEMY

Alchemy is based on the belief that there are four basic elements – fire, air, earth and water – and three essentials: salt, sulphur and mercury. It is said that ancient Chinese and Egyptian occult literature is the foundation upon which alchemy is based, not least that of the *Corpus Hermeticum*. Great symbolic and metaphysical systems have been built from these seven aspects of alchemy.

Alchemy is an occult art and called by some a pseudoscience – a set of ideas based on theories put forth as scientific when they are not. Prior to the Renaissance there were many who searched for the secret of life and attempted to reduce everything to the four components. As scientific methods came into being, there was a whole system built up to discover how the elements combined and separated to form new substances. In fact, alchemy is the foundation on which in the modern day the study of chemistry is based. Its main goals have been to learn how to transmute, to heal and to transcend the ordinary.

This has given rise to much misunderstanding because these three goals became in many people's eyes the practical tasks of:

1. Turning base metals (like lead or copper) into precious metals (like gold or silver) (transmutation).
2. Creating an elixir or potion or metal that could cure all ills (healing).
3. Discovering an elixir that would lead to immortality (transcendence).

It was believed there was a magical substance that was to transmute metals, to be the universal panacea and to serve as the key to immortality. This was called the 'philosopher's stone'. As time went on, it was realized that the search for the elixir of life had parallels with the search for understanding of the human psyche – the essence of being – and that search still goes on today. Homeopathy and aromatherapy, which both use very subtle energies, in many ways owe their origin to the principles of alchemy.

ROSICRUCIANISM

According to the Rosicrucian legend, the order began with Christian Rosenkreuz who was born in 1378 in Germany. Beginning in 1393, he visited Damascus, Egypt and Morocco where he studied at the feet of several masters of the occult arts. He began the Rosicrucian Order in 1407 when he returned to Germany, initially with three monks from the cloister in which he had been raised, then with eight. Christian Rosenkreuz died in 1484 and was entombed in the *Spiritus Sanctum* (House of the Holy Spirit) he had erected in 1409. Knowledge of his tomb was lost, but it was rediscovered in 1604 when its opening led to a resurgence of interest in the movement.

Rosicrucianism is a traditional and initiatory movement. An individual or small group of individuals who have been properly trained and initiated into the Rosicrucian system will often work together for a common purpose. This is how some Rosicrucian organizations regained popularity at the beginning of the 20th century. Today there are several Rosicrucian Organizations/Orders.

Modern Rosicrucian groups have different beliefs about Christian Rosenkreuz. There are those who believe he actually existed as the early documents assert; others see the name as a pseudonym or magical title designed to preserve the anonymity of certain other historic people. Still others view the story as a parable and occult legend that points to a more profound truth.

BOEHMIAN THEOSOPHY

Jacob Boehme (1575–1624) was neither a scholar nor a man of letters. He could be said to have became wise by virtue of his own experience. A theosophist and mystic, he was born in Altseidenberg, Germany and became a shoemaker. In 1600 he had a mystical experience which led him towards meditation on the Divine. His wisdom therefore grew from personal revelation and employed symbols and myths as illustrations rather than concepts. His influence spread beyond Germany to Holland and England and he is probably one of the greatest of Christian Gnostics.

MARTINISM

Martinism is a system of philosophic thought which is essentially Christ-based in outlook. The traditions are based initially on the works and writings of the Rosicrucian adept Martinez Pasqually, who is said to have received his initiation from Charles Stuart (Bonnie Prince Charlie), who in turn had received it from the Knights Templars. Martinez founded the order of Elus Cohen, of which Louis Claude De Saint Martin (1743–1803) was a member. However, the latter moved away from the technique used by his brothers to achieve their re-integration with the divine – a technique that involved ceremonial magic. He sought a more inward means to achieve the same result. He thus developed what is known in Martinist terminology as 'The Inner Way' of re-integration.

This 'way' perpetuates a sacred system of initiation, in private, with great secrecy and specific ritual through an unbroken line from Saint-Martin himself. Varying other degrees of initiation were added in later years. The goal is for the Martinist to develop and live a

Christian spiritual life and to become an adept in esoteric wisdom and practice. The Martinist believes that he is theurgically (through the Grace of God) empowered by the initiation. In order to accomplish the task of reintegration, the Martinist needs considerable metaphysical knowledge and theurgic magical abilities. Indeed, it is to his use of theurgical powers that Saint-Martin attributed the fact that neither he nor his students ever suffered harassment.

HERMETIC ORDER OF THE GOLDEN DAWN

The Golden Dawn was a magical fraternity founded in London in 1888 by Dr William Wynn Westcott and Samuel Liddell MacGregor Mathers. It was designed by its founders as a system of magic – not a religion, although religious imagery and spiritual concepts play an important role in its work. It was to be a Hermetic Society, drawing on Hermetic teachings, dedicated to the philosophical, spiritual and psychic evolution of humanity. It was to be a school and a repository of knowledge where students learned the principles of occult science and the various elements of Western philosophy and magic.

Although the society itself only lasted in its original form for a few years, tolerance for all religious beliefs was stressed and the symbolism used within the Golden Dawn came from a variety of religious sources including Egyptian, Greek, Gnostic, Judeo-Christian, Masonic and Rosicrucian. Today therefore it is an outstanding learning tool and people from many diverse religious paths would call themselves Golden Dawn magicians. This requires an ongoing study of the Kabbalah, astrology, the psychic arts or siddhis (which we look at later in the book), alchemy and Egyptian magic among other things.

FREEMASONRY

Chronologically, Freemasonry would seem to best take its place before the Hermetic Order of the Golden Dawn. Freemasonry, in the form that would be recognized most widely these days, first seems to have become manifest in London in the early 18th century, though there is strong evidence of its existence prior to that. Its rituals and forms of initiation were rationalised round about that time and, if anything, it was more magical than it is today. While many freemasons would dislike the idea that their organization is part of a magical system, it could be argued that with its ritualistic initiations it is certainly part of the Western 'Mystery' tradition. In its raising of consciousness and study of symbolism it forms part of a growing awareness of man's part in the overall scheme of things – a step towards understanding. The Truth has to be kept secret except for those who have been properly initiated into the Mysteries.

There are some remarkable and diverse theories as to Freemasonry's origins. One is that the initiations performed in Freemasonry mirror the craft of the stonemason (as the rough is polished to perfection). The initiate is not simply a passive recipient of the teachings and benefits, but must interact personally with the principles of Freemasonry. In silence, in his own time and on his own account he must create a sacred space for himself within. Another and similar theory is that Freemasonry is based on the building and destruction of the Temple at Jerusalem and the subsequent resurrection by Solomon of the knowledge which was lost. By the nature of their work, many stonemasons took part in the building of churches and cathedrals and thereby achieved more than a passing familiarity with the idea of God as the Great Architect.

Masons are men who have voluntarily asked to join a 'lodge'. They will have been accepted by their Brothers (as Freemasons are known) because they are good men who believe in God and hold high ethical and moral ideals. They both learn and teach what friendship, morality and truth really involve – they practise on a small scale the reality of fraternity as well as being aware of the greater world picture. Practical programmes are developed for those less fortunate than themselves and many masons apply the old principle of tithing – giving ten percent of their income for charitable purposes.

In essence the Freemasons are a secret society and, as such, they fulfil their need for hidden meaning in their rituals and ceremonies. This links them even today with the magical practices of old. Particularly through the disseminated practices of the Hermetic Order of the Golden Dawn, many of today's Neo Pagan and New Age movements contain a good deal of Masonic lore. The fact that much of this is based on much older magical practice and philosophy is often lost to the participants. Careful study of ancient texts such as those of Agrippa or of the Kabbalah gives a much wider picture.

MAGIC IN RELATION TO PHILOSOPHY

We cannot look at the traditions of the Mystery religions without trying to understand theurgy. Whereas, initially, understanding the Mysteries is a contemplative act, theurgy is an actual activity not just a theory; an operation not a discussion, a technique for dealing with the gods rather than an understanding. Theurgy was considered a part of religion, a religious duty. As such it was considered a form of worship, possibly the best kind of worship and it quite clearly had its own rewards for those who practised it. In previous times, theurgy meant 'the priestly art', suggesting that the theurgist saw himself as a priest, an evoker of God or light, and in a special relationship with God.

The aim of all theurgical operations is described thus – it is to embrace God and be embraced by God:

Having flown upward, the human soul will embrace God vigorously, free of any mortal element, she will be wholly intoxicated by God.

The theurgist aims at unification with the One God, and in many ways this has shades of the rite of the sacred marriage of the ancients. Here, the God was thought to descend to Earth to mate in privacy with the High Priestess at certain times of the year. Through the mystical union with the One God and the release from the bonds of fate, humans actually become equal to the gods, at least for a short time; afterwards they could assume their human condition again. In previous times, theurgists ranked higher than the theologians because they not only thought and talked about the gods; they also knew how to act upon them.

Theurgy is also considered to be a path to salvation, an aspect that connects it with the Mystery religions. It saves the soul and has the effect of washing the body free of its earthly pollution. These beliefs are based on four main principles:

1. Power
2. Cosmic sympathy
3. Sameness
4. The idea of the soul vehicle

Power – First there is power, a force available in the universe to those who know how to work with it and capture it. Magic is also based on this concept – when one learns to use power it becomes available to us to a greater or lesser degree, according to our knowledge.

Cosmic Sympathy – Magic also operates within the principle of 'cosmic sympathy', which is the second principle. Here, the universe is a huge living organism in which nothing happens without influencing some other part. A stone thrown into a pond, for instance, continues to cause ripples beyond the edge of the visible pool – an action taken at one point of existence has an effect far beyond the perceived one (Rudyard Kipling expressed this beautifully in his story of 'The Butterfly who Stamped'). This acknowledges hidden relationships in the universe that cannot easily be explained by the laws of cause and effect, nor those of time and space.

Sameness – The third principle of sameness connects the subject with the object, those who see and understand with those who are seen and understood. This is demonstrated in the art of clairvoyance when the clairvoyant experiences within themselves what another person has already gone through. There is a relationship of empathy. This principle creates a connection between us and the gods through our shared nature. This connection is seen also in the principle of the microcosm and the macrocosm – as above, so below.

Soul Vehicle – The fourth principle is the vehicle of the soul, the carrier of light. Each of us holds within a vital spark. The calling forth of this light allows us to perceive mysteries that would otherwise be hidden. It might be said that in ancient theurgy the medium or priest stood between two realities, in modern theurgy he or she channels the energy between them.

Truly to be magician in this day and age requires us to be just as rigorous in our spiritual disciplines as were the mystics of old.

As we have seen, much development took place in the 16th century, both in philosophical thought and in an appreciation of the magical nature of the world in which people lived. Mystics contemplated the 'meaning of life' and various belief systems accepted the idea of there being one God, or Source, albeit manifesting in many forms. Pagan thought accepted the idea of a Father-God while others of a more philosophical frame of mind searched for other ways of explaining the existence of mankind and his world. A blending of the old and new gives us a principle on which much magical thought is based today.

CREATION – 'IN THE BEGINNING ...'

There are many theories as to how the world in which we live came into existence. The Emanationist position is based on the idea of a series of 'worlds' arranged perpendicularly, with each lower world being dependent on the one above. Each higher state of existence produces the level below it through emanation (literally 'outpouring') and each realm or universe thus becomes the Creator of the one beneath. Creation is not creation out of nothing, but out of the being of the previous plane of existence. The Cosmos, and finite beings, are all seen as having emerged out of Absolute Reality through this outpouring of energy and power.

We can have a sense of this outpouring if we envisage the Sun – Absolute Reality – giving light which, in turn, gives life which then manifests itself in various forms. These forms are mainly created from water before ultimately becoming dust. It is small wonder therefore that the ancients worshipped the Sun as God. Those who understood the idea of emanation could indeed perform magical acts since they realized that each of the levels, or stages, in this 'spectrum' of existence had its own specific characteristics of which they could make use. Magicians could have an effect on the less subtle aspects of their own creation. Priests and magicians alike were able to have some effect on the plane of existence immediately prior to their own – and, with increasing competence, those above.

There was, and indeed still is, some danger in approaching the more subtle realms without sufficient knowledge. Man knew his place in the hierarchy and learned to co-exist with other realms and entities. Everything was, and is even to the present day, a manifestation of the Divine; the more man understood the hierarchy, the closer he moved to the Divine.

KABBALAH

Broadly, this same idea of emanation is central to Western kabbalistic and alchemical belief. Kabbalah combines both philosophical and magical thought and, in fact, does not see them as being very different. Creation in the Kabbalah, therefore, is seen to have taken place through the following process.

Through a series of expansions and contractions the 'Ain Soph Aur' (Limitless Light), also known as the divine mind of God or the

Absolute, establishes the framework of Creation. The first world is subtle and almost undefined and is known as 'Atziluth'. Closest to the original state of non-being, it is the World of Fire, because of the energetic, formless and almost uncontrollable nature of fire. The next is 'Briah', or the World of Archetypes (basic patterns and form). It is symbolized as the World of Air, and is thus something of a transition, before the creation of the next World, 'Yetzirah', or Water. This is the psychic and emotionally charged world that ebbs and flows immediately prior to the world which might be thought of as the container, or World of Earth. The Hebrew word for this is 'Assiah', and represents solid tangible matter.

It is held in Kabbalistic thought that, when God created, he used what are known as the three Mother Letters. These are known as 'Aleph', 'Mem', and 'Shin'; they are also associated with the first three elements. This meant that the final emanation, or manifestation of energy, from these three into the fourth element, Earth, had to be treated separately and was seen as the densest manifestation of all. Therefore, Earth is a product – for want of a better word – from a pattern of unity (oneness), reflection (making two) then division or re-harmonizing on a denser level. Thus, the world of Air would contain aspects of the World of Fire and in turn a mixture of Air and Fire would be contained in Water, while Earth would contain characteristics of all three. A little thought will show that, in many ways, this is something of a scientific truth demonstrated particularly in the science of genetics and our modern day understanding of DNA.

A slightly different perspective was given by Plato and his student Aristotle. They introduced the concept of a *scala natura* – the scale of nature. Their belief was that there was initially an overflowing profusion in the Godhead. The natural world occurs in accordance with the principles of abundance, a 'first principle', which creates successive life-forms in a hierarchical structure. However, the farther the beings are from the source, the less access there is to the very subtle life energy. The lowest in the hierarchical order is matter without structure at the bottom, then rocks, plants, insects, animals, man, and finally spiritual and divine beings. This idea of the 'Great Chain of Being', consisting of an infinite number of links ranging in hierarchical order from the most simple form of existence to the best possible and most perfect, continued right through the Middle Ages until the scientific thought of the 17th and 18th centuries turned the principle around to formulate other models of creation out of which grew modern philosophical thought. We consider some of these thoughts elsewhere when we look at the ways in which ideas about magic have changed over the years.

We can see that the Kabbalistic ideas of creation move from the more subtle emanation to the denser. Alchemical thought shows that we should be able to transmute material from the more dense emanations back to the more subtle through several processes akin to those used by the early sciences – for instance, distilling gold from base metal. In many ways therefore the two concepts of Kabbalah and Alchemy are reflections of one another and, when perceived in the magical context of having an effect on matter, are not dissimilar.

When we look at Kabbalistic ideas, there is another way in which we see this idea of reflection within each 'World' (any self-contained realm or universe of existence). We have seen that each World is a reflection to a denser or more subtle degree than the one before or after it, depending on whether we are moving downwards into denser matter or upwards to the more subtle. Kabbalists are aware that there must be a stepping down or stepping up of the energy within each world, and perceive that this occurs within each World through a series of ten planes or levels of consciousness known as 'Sephiroth', or spheres of being, which combine with energy-matter. Each Sephira or sphere takes on its own unique characteristics and is only a partial, or slightly distorted, reflection of what precedes or follows it.

Successful creation into the denser worlds takes place through the movement of energy through these ten planes. Dematerialization occurs in the same way but in the opposite direction. This 'zigzag' of Creation is called the 'Lightning Flash' and it is this that the practitioner versed in the Kabbalah uses in his magical practice. In effect he moves what he wishes to manifest very quickly through the spheres of existence. The return of energy from dense matter, back through the various stages, the Sephiroth, and Worlds of Creation is known as the 'Path of the Serpent' because of its reverse, or complimentary, zigzag.

Interestingly, even when we move towards the more scientific position of trying to explain magic logically, this idea of a stepping down (or speeding up) of energy levels still holds, and if today magic is more usefully thought of as making things happen, as a model the Kabbalah is a rich source of information.

ALCHEMY

For the alchemist, however, before something can become tangible in matter, energy must take on the characteristics of the eventual manifestation. This happens between the third and fourth spheres of existence, or Sephiroth, if the materialization is to occur properly on the correct physical level. The energy of Life, called variously *Prima Materia* (literally first material) *Chaos* or *Spiritus Mundi* (Spirit of the Earth), is a mixture of two principles – Fire and Air. Both are active in nature, but Fire is the more active of the two, with Air being slightly more passive; matter, in potential, manifests its energy lower down the scale as Water and Earth.

We can think of energy being divided into active and passive power, the active being the energies of life, and the passive the energy of matter. The Elements – Fire, Air, Water and Earth, before they 'become real' in the physical dimension and therefore recognizable by the majority of people, are all energetic states, each with their own unique characteristics, having within themselves ten levels of awareness or consciousness. There are thus forty different ways in which the combination of energy-matter-and consciousness can manifest in our world. Everything contains the four elements to a greater or lesser degree.

There are, though, preferred ways for the elements to interact with each other, to form the Three Principles of alchemy:

These three alchemical principles are Sulphur, Mercury and Salt. The soul – or basic state of anything – equates to alchemical Sulphur, with the living principles of energy (Fire) and intelligence (Air); Alchemical Salt, the physical aspect, is made up chiefly of unconscious forces, the psychic, and instinctual intelligence (Water) and physical matter (Earth); Mercury in the alchemical sense is the general life force, the bridge or communicating force between the previous two and consists mainly of intelligence (Air) and instinctual forces, along with psychic energy (Water).

To understand these ideas better, it is important to remember that these 'elements' are not chemical or scientific compounds but are philosophical ideas or principles that can be made use of in magic. Extending the principle of emanation, we see that the lower realms of the mineral world, for example, have as their predominant energy Earth, some Water, and very little Air or Fire.

'The Golden Chain of Homer', a treatise written or edited by Anton Josef Kirchweger, was first issued at Frankfurt and Leipzig, in German, in four editions (in 1723, 1728, 1738 and 1757). In this the active energy is called Nitre and the passive energy is called Salt. The treatise states:

When God created this Universal fire, He gave it a power to become material, that is to become Vapour, Humidity, water and earth, although that fire in its own Universal Nature, is, and remains centrally the same. Thus you see the Beginning of the 4 Elements, viz
(1) burning fire; Vapour or Humidity mixed with Cold fire constitutes atmospheric air,
(2) air, which still more condensed becomes water,
(3) and water inspissated becomes earth.
Originally it was but one Element, fire.

The great alchemical work is to refine everything; vegetable matter, minerals – indeed any chosen substance – back to its original components until its essence or life force is discovered and the alchemist learns the meaning of life, or rather how life manifests – how undifferentiated energy takes on its various forms.

There are similarities in the way that Eastern and Western systems of belief think of undifferentiated energy. Many of today's magical and New Age systems subscribe to the idea that there is an all-pervading Spirit or Akasha. There is still a duality in this, however, in that one part is active and the other passive and this brings us right back to Nitre and Salt. Nitre is, in that sense, the secret or hidden fire and Salt the crucible in which it burns. The secret fire is that spiritual energy which, in the end, we use in magical workings.

It is that energy, its misuse and misunderstandings about its use, which has led throughout history to the demonization of the ideas and the persecution of the individual and groups of believers whether innocent or not.

2.

PERSECUTION OF THE SUPERNATURAL

Fear of the unknown is one of the most potent causes of aggression there is, or ever has been. It is a natural human reaction to try to discredit and destroy what is misunderstood and found to be unacceptable. Sometimes it is possible for religion to become so entrenched in its own beliefs that there is no capacity for change. When this happens, it can be something very simple or basic which causes an upheaval, making room for expansion. Often it is the most cultivated system of belief that is most easily threatened.

The cultivated Graeco-Roman systems of belief had great difficulty with the simpler ideas of pagan religion. The very word 'pagan' means 'beyond the city', so a system of belief which could allow itself to be hidden, or practised in private away from the supposed sophistication of the cities, was seen as subversive and immediately suspect. This religion, based on the natural cycle of the year, gave its people an element of control over their own lives; therefore it was not conducive to being easily overpowered by incomers who did not understand its origins.

Religions based on philosophy fared no better than the agriculturally based beliefs however, and any system of belief which recognized that understanding brought power which was supernatural (beyond the norm) was to be feared. The fight for control frequently swung from culture to culture, with each one in turn claiming supremacy. With the coming of Christianity as an organized religion, rather than an underground movement, other religions had to appreciate the threat present in their midst.

PAGANISM AND CHRISTIANITY

By AD398 paganism was truly under attack. Temples were destroyed or closed one after another, holy groves were cut down, statues of gods and altars were destroyed. However, the religion itself, which had survived for centuries, could not be that easily uprooted. There still remained many temples, groves, statues of gods, and altars, where pagan rites were held. The advocates of the old religion obviously always found possibilities, particularly in the country and in remote deserted regions, to serve their gods unseen in the existing temples. Sometimes, the battle with the old Roman religion led to bloodshed between fanatic Christians and pagans. State officials often were slow in the active destruction of temples and statues of gods, and therefore the Christians often took matters into their own hands and arranged for the removal of many temples and statues disagreeable to them.

In the town of Sufes in Tunisia, Christians made several efforts to destroy the statue of Hercules who, while not a god, was a personification of the spirit (energy) of the place. They finally succeeded, but the pagans demonstrated their hatred of the destroyers of a very potent pagan symbol. According to St Augustine's report, they killed 60 Christians. Moreover, the pagans requested compensation for the injuries resulting from the destruction of the statue of their protector.

The two Acts proclaimed by Honorius on 20 August AD399 prove that the event in Sufes was not the only destructive act in a newly conquered country. The point of these Acts was that any remaining temples were to be maintained, but the festivals and feasts based on the old pagan calendar would only take place if they were for amusement: it was forbidden to make sacrifices and practice superstitious acts during these meetings. Later, it became the custom to appropriate elements from pagan feasts to organize similar celebrities in the Roman basilicas on the commemorative dates of their martyrs. This was, of course, part of the Roman practice of assimilating the existing religions of conquered countries into their own. By AD407, laws were passed which decreed that the incomes of pagan temples were to be transferred to the benefit of the army. The statues of the native gods were to be destroyed and the temple buildings themselves were to be passed into public use.

In many spheres of life, however, the influence of the old views and customs could still be recognized. Theatrical plays, mime performances, dancing processions, games in the theatres and in circus, statues and pictures in the baths, in public places and in private houses, all presented – as entertainment – the gods and their mythical lives. At the same time they kept alive a number of the old beliefs so, although it went underground just as Christianity had done in the 1st century AD, it still remained alive. Paganism overshadowed the life of common people, both with regard to spiritual experiences and to external celebrations.

Having said this, there was a certain amount of cross persecution carried out. The edicts of the emperors of the time, which had been directed against the emerging Christians in the first century, had requested the renouncement of belief and allegiance to what was, after all, a pagan cult; previously, emperors had been worshipped as gods. The later Christian emperors persecuted and oppressed the pagan cult, but they did allow for certain vestiges of privilege to be permitted by law. Except for the highest court offices, pagans had access to all the state offices; the law also was supposed to protect them against injustice from Christians.

Perhaps the oddest death through persecution of a supposed pagan was that of Hypatia in AD415. She had been taught science, mathematics and philosophy by her father and came to be mistrusted by the authorities for attempting to simplify the understanding of mathematics. She came to a horrible end when the Christians accused her of pagan activities; they flayed her alive – some say with shards of pottery, others say with oyster shells (a pagan symbol for the Goddess).

According to the Augustine papers, it seems that in the times of Theodosius the Great and of Honorius, paganism had almost completely died out and digression from it was a common phenomenon. In his teachings, St Augustine (354–430), the bishop of Hippo Regius, rejected both the traditional polytheism of the Romans and the pagan agricultural religion which presented the highest god as the lord of the gods, people and things. However, in many cities as a rule many of the officials tended towards paganism and they were not friendly towards Christians.

In Africa, the pagan religion was originally rooted in the higher circles of society, in the echelons of eminent citizens and intellectuals. These educated pagans resisted change for various reasons, probably the most important being that as the authority of the Christian bishops grew, their own diminished, leaving them with very little autonomous power.

Manichaeism

Various Gnostic religions developed which, by the 3rd century AD, were not appreciated in the least by the Christians. Founded by the Persian, Mani, in the latter half of the 3rd century, Manichaeism was a Gnostic religion that purported to be the true synthesis of all the religious systems then known. It actually consisted of Zoroastrian Dualism, Babylonian folklore, Buddhist ethics and some small and fairly superficial additions of Christian thought.

It seems that almost as soon as it was founded, Manichaeism upset the authorities. In AD296, Diocletian, the Roman emperor who hated the Christians anyway, commanded the Proconsul of Africa to persecute the Manichaeans and spoke of them as a 'sordid and impure sect recently come from Persia' which he was determined to 'destroy without mercy'. By AD381 Theodosius I, whom we have already met, declared Manichaeans to be without civil rights and incapable of bearing witness. In the following year he condemned them to death under various edicts. Shortly afterwards, in AD405, Honorius renewed the decrees of his predecessors and fined all governors of cities or provinces who were remiss in carrying out his orders. He invalidated all contracts with the Manichaeans, declaring them outlaws and criminals.

Catharism

If the Christian church did not acquit itself well in its treatment of the Manichaeans, it most certainly did not concerning the Cathars. In March 1244, at Montségur in France, 205 Cathars, whose basic belief was Manichaean, chose to be burned alive rather than renounce their creed. It was not only the uneducated who could be persecuted, but also deep thinkers who challenged the status quo.

The Cathars were true mystics and, unlike many witches, by no means simple country folk. The word 'Cathari' means 'pure' in Greek, and the life of the Cathar was dedicated to trying to achieve purity, or as close to it as he could get. The leaders of the sect were fully aware that not everyone could achieve a state of grace in one lifetime and the masses, or 'believers' as they were called, were allowed to live fully ordinary lives, provided they understood that they were in a cycle of reincarnation allowing them to be reborn on earth and eventually reach a perfect state. The Cathars' influence was at one time considerable, for there is evidence of links with Moslem Sufi communities in Spain and the Middle East and with Jewish Kabbalist scholars.

Central to the Cathar creed was the concept of Duality, the opposition of the material world to that of the spirit. For most people, this translated into the fight between good and evil, light and dark – any two polarities – yet for those who chose to take on the concept of the Cathar creed, it was much more than that. To understand this concept more fully we have to go back to one of the roots of Manichaeism – to Zoroastrianism. This taught that the Supreme Being created two forces of reality and unreality. These are seen as essential elements from which our world is created; they are not just polarizations of good and evil. Reality is taken to be objective meaning, and unreality human subjectivity.

The conflict between the two only becomes a negative force in our lives if we get caught up in the conflict and are unable to perceive it for what it is. Man, because he is composed of both objectivity and his own experiences, can, by living a life of purity, undergo a transfiguration – in effect a double death – so that his spirit is set free and is able to rejoin the Light – the Ultimate. Interestingly, this is very similar to Kabbalistic thought, so one wonders if their beliefs had a common source. The rigorously ascetic discipline necessary to achieve this state was available to the 'Parfaits' (or 'perfects'), the master adepts and a somewhat lower grade of adepts.

The outer appearance and practices of the Parfaits were very simple, though only about one in 100 believers reached that high state of being, transfiguration. Renouncing worldly goods, they ate vegetarian foods, wore plain dark blue gowns and kept strict vows of chastity, believing that sexual intercourse prevented their life force reaching the Light. They worshipped in forests and on mountaintops, utilizing the strong earth currents of the region; their initiations were held in a series of limestone caves, chiefly near the Pic de St Barthalemy.

These caves would truly become sacred spaces, hallowed by use and by the energies of the surroundings. What really set the Cathars apart from other gnostic sects was the ritual of the Consolamentum. This ceremony aided the transition of the soul – either through physical death or as an initiation into the community of those who were pure enough in thought, word and deed to become Parfait. This ritual consisted of the Parfait laying his hands upon the head of the supplicant. A strong transmission of energy was said to take place, presumably believed to be akin to the power of the Holy Spirit at the Last Supper, so inspiring those who witnessed it to greater efforts. This energy transmission permitted the spirit to ascend towards the Light – that is, the dying would actually transcend physical death, and those who were being initiated would 'die' to the ordinary world. This spiritual knowledge and the achievement of not fearing physical death in order to evolve during the transition, was enough to give those left at Montséger the courage to walk, singing, to their death on that day in March 1244.

Branded heretics by the Roman Catholic Church, little remains to speak of their bravery today, other than Inquisition records.

KNIGHTS TEMPLAR

In 1118, sometime before this grievous act, Hugues de Payens, a knight of Champagne and eight companions, all in the presence of the Patriarch of Jerusalem, bound themselves by a perpetual vow – to defend the Christian kingdom. The Patriarch accepted their services and assigned them a portion of his palace adjoining the temple of the city; hence their title 'pauvres chevaliers du temple' (Poor Knights of the Temple). The Order was founded along monastic lines following Cistercian rules but also had a strong military component along with the discipline that that entailed.

There were four levels of membership:

1. The knights, who were equipped like the heavy cavalry
2. The sergeants, who formed the light cavalry
3. The farmers, who dealt with the ordinary day to day administration
4. The chaplains, who were men of the cloth to minister to the spiritual needs of the order

The biggest problem that seems to have arisen is the secrecy surrounding the rites of initiation. These initiations always took place in a chapter that perforce had to be held in secret, due to the fact that there were some very serious matters to be discussed. Any indiscretion by any of the members of the Order led to exclusion from it.

This secrecy had several consequences. There was a degree of arrogance in the management of the initiation which led to abuse of both the beliefs and the ceremonies as they were not always carried out in accordance with the original tenets of the Order. Worse still were the accusations which came from outside the Order. The Templars were accused of spitting upon the Cross, of permitting sodomy, of denying Christ and of worshipping idols – all in secrecy. What could not be proved, could be suspected.

The end of the Templars was brought about by two sequential enquiries. First the royal commission carried out by Philip IV of France, also known as Philip the Fair, and secondly the papal commission carried out under Pope Clement V.

The royal commission After a cursory investigation and on the hearsay of a few dubious confessions, Philip acted fast. He arrested all the Templars throughout France on the same day (13 October 1307) and subjected them to extremely severe interrogation. There was, however, not even enough evidence to keep them locked up so, in keeping with the times, confessions were simply beaten and tortured out of them. Many of them were tortured to within inches of their lives but this severe torture was 'deemed necessary' in order to extract the confessions.

Pope Clement V entered an extremely energetic protest and annulled the entire trial, suspending the powers of the bishops who had acted as examiners. By now, having conferred upon himself the title of 'Champion and Defender of the Faith', Philip the Fair deliberately stirred up public opinion at the States General of Tours against the 'heinous crimes' of the Templars. Moreover, he succeeded in having the confessions of the accused confirmed, in the presence of the pope, by 72 Templars who had been specially chosen and coached beforehand. In view of this investigation, the pope, until then sceptical, at last became concerned and opened a new commission, the procedure of which he himself directed. He ensured that the cause of the Order was tried by the papal commission. By restoring the powers of the diocesan commissions, he guaranteed that that individual Knights could be tried adequately.

The papal commission In most of the other countries where they had a following, the Templars were found innocent, but France was different. Here, the examiners, simply resuming their activities, took the facts as established at the previous trial, and, imposing various canonical penances extending even to perpetual imprisonment, confined themselves to bringing the repentant guilty members back into the fold. Only those who persisted in heresy were to be turned over to the non-religious arm, but, because of a rigid interpretation of this provision, those who had withdrawn their former confessions were considered to have relapsed. Some 54 Templars who had recanted after having confessed were condemned as relapsed and publicly burned on 12 May 1310. Subsequently all the other Templars, who had been examined at the trial, with very few exceptions declared themselves guilty.

The pope, by now vacillating and harassed, finally adopted a middle course: he decreed the dissolution – not the condemnation – of the order. This was done, not by penal sentence, but by an Apostolic Decree (the Papal Bull of 22 March 1312). The Order having been suppressed, the pope himself now could decide the fate of its members and the disposal of its possessions. The Templars who were recognized as being guiltless were allowed either to join another military order or to return to the secular state. In the latter case, a pension for life, charged to the possessions of the order, was granted them. The pope reserved his own judgment in the case of the grand Master and his three cohorts.

The exact status of the Order is still debated by historians. From 1654 to 1908 some writers find them guilty, others not. There is a connection with the Cathars in that a treasure which was said to be left in the latter's safe-keeping and later hidden has long been thought to belong to the Templars. The Order was obviously in existence in one form or another until the 1700s, since Bonnie Prince Charlie seems to have received initiation from them. As a secret society its secret must remain just that.

Persecution in these times took many forms. Much arose from political necessity but, backed up by religious fervour, there arose a fanaticism which eventually resulted in the religious persecution of the Inquisition. Not least was the persecution of those who claimed or were thought to be witches.

WITCH-HUNTING AROUND THE WORLD

As far back as the 8th century, St Boniface, English Apostle of Germany, declared that to believe in witches and werewolves was unchristian. In Paderborn in AD785, however, Charlemagne ordered the death penalty for anyone in Saxony who put to death by fire those whom they had judged to be witches. He held that this very act of burning was pagan in origin and therefore not valid. (Saxony had only recently been converted to Christianity.)

The attitude to witchcraft varied somewhat over the years. In the 9th century St Agobard, Bishop of Lyon, discarded the notion that witches could control the weather, while an unknown church official stated in about AD906 that night-flying and metamorphosis (shape changing or shifting) were hallucinations and that 'whoever was ìso stupid and foolishî as to believe such fantastic tales was an infidel'. This statement was accepted as canon law and became known as the *canon Episcopi* or *capitulum Episcopi*.

By defining witchcraft as 'Devil-worship' but then declaring that it was 'nothing more than a foolish delusion', the canon, however, created almost as many problems as it supposedly solved. It then remained the official doctrine of the Church for some time, although by the mid 15th century demonologists and inquisitors were beginning to question its validity. It was, however, still influential in that although flights and other feats of witchcraft were considered physically impossible they were believed to be achievable in spirit. For another 200 years or so, whoever did such things in spirit was deemed to be just as culpable as though they had actually performed the deed.

In 1022 a group of mystics who did not hold to the key Christian beliefs were burned as witches in Orleans. Also around this time, the laws of King Coloman of Hungary refused to acknowledge witches 'since they did not exist'. In 1141 Hugh of St Victor wrote *Didascalicon*, which included a fervent condemnation of studying or using magic:

... Sorcerers are those who, with demonic incantations or amulets or any other execrable types of remedies, by the co-operation of the devils or by evil instinct, perform wicked things.

Also in the 12th century John of Salisbury (secretary at various times to both Theobald, the archbishop of Canterbury and Thomas a Becket), the Bishop of Chartres from 1176 to his death in 1180, dismissed the idea of a witches' sabbat as 'a fabulous dream'.

In the following centuries though, as the persecution was increasing, this strategy of disregarding the existence of witches would have to be revised and reversed. The laws of Charlemagne and Coloman would subsequently have to be forgotten; and to deny the reality of night-flying and metamorphosis was declared heretical; the witches' sabbat would become an objective fact, disbelieved only (according to a doctor of the Sorbonne as late as 1609) by those of unsound mind.

In 1231 Conrad of Marburg was appointed the first Inquisitor of Germany, laying down a blueprint for persecution. He claimed to have discovered many groups of Devil worshippers and stated: 'We would gladly burn a hundred if just one of them is guilty'. This attitude led eventually to the mass hysteria of the witch-hunts proper. In 1258 Pope Alexander IV declared that Inquisitors should not concern themselves within divination but only those which 'manifestly savoured of heresy'.

After two centuries of careful manipulation the doctrine of acknowledgement, yet non-acceptance, of witchcraft was established in its final form by 1490. There are two documents from which much of the European persecution of witches can be dated. The first is the papal bull *Summis Desiderantes Affectibus*, issued by Pope Innocent VIII in December 1484 which condemned the spread of witchcraft in Germany. The second is the *Malleus Maleficarum* (the hammer of evil) written by the Dominican inquisitors Heinrich Krammer and Jacob Sprenger in 1486. There were 40 editions of this publication. From that point on, it became the policy to apply this set of guidelines, of hunting down, finding and eradicating the witches whose organization was now spelled out. It now became clear that:

A belief that there are such things as witches is so essential a part of Catholic faith that obstinately to maintain the opposite opinion savours of heresy.

Countries where witches had been unknown were suddenly found to be swarming with them; it seemed that witches were multiplying at an alarming rate all over Europe. During this spread of knowledge the witches apparently acquired some quite unthinkable powers, succeeded in setting up a complex international network and indulged in very unsavoury social activities. These are shown by some of the accusations levelled against so-called witches. Many of these accusations were of course founded in jealousies and family feuds. We list below some of the more well-known witch trials and persecutions around the world. We'll start with the New World.

AMERICA

In North America perhaps the most well documented case is that of the Salem witches. This case contains all the elements of hysteria which often characterize witch-hunts, both in the girls involved and within the wider community.

The tale started in 1692, when eight pubescent girls between the ages of 11 and 20 began to show signs of apparently being possessed by demons. The girls were all easily influenced; they are believed to have read and heard much about witchcraft and may perhaps have been affected by tales of possession in surrounding areas of Massachusetts. There is also a theory they may have been affected by ergotism, a disease caused by ingesting a hallucinogenic fungus that infects rye and other cereal crops. The fungus has a similar action to lysergic acid or LSD, which induces psychic states. When, in an effort to find out who had led the girls down their dark path, a dog was fed so-called 'witch cake' made from flour and the urine of the girls, the evil influence was apparently temporarily lifted and the girls were able to name their influencers. It is not recorded what happened to the dog.

The girls most afflicted experienced loss of sight, speech, hearing and appetite along with choking sensations and hallucinations. Later, they claimed to have been bitten and scratched supernaturally by others in the community, whom they named as witches. Modern psychiatrists would probably suggest that the young women were clinically hysterical, as the symptoms they produced were fairly typical of hysteria.

The close-knit community had difficulties in coming to terms with what was going on. Two of the girls were related to the Revd Samuel Parris, the local minister, who was naturally alarmed. What had apparently begun as a harmless game of scrying to determine the identity of the youngsters' future husbands had escalated into a full-blown case of demonic possession.

The Revd Deodat Lawson and the Revd John Hale wrote that the movement of the afflicted girls when they were possessed were 'preternatural', which meant that the girls could not possibly fake them. Hale also said:

Their arms, necks, and backs were turned this way and that way, and returned back again, so as it was impossible for them to do of themselves, and beyond the power of any epileptic fits, or natural disease to effect.

It seemed that those who were least to blame were punished most severely. Mary Warren, one of the hysterics, was a servant in the house of Elizabeth and John Proctor. When Proctor also was arrested on suspicion of witchcraft, Mary was too frightened to support the 50 neighbours who signed a public petition to declare his innocence, although neither was she prepared to give evidence against her employer (who had managed to stop Mary's fits by saying that he would beat her if they continued). Because both Proctor and his wife were in prison, Mary was left to care for his five young children. She was denounced by her friends as a witch.

The girls, the magistrates, the clergy, and everybody else in the Province of Massachusetts Bay believed implicitly in witchcraft, so it was natural for them to conclude that the Devil was behind the manifestations and possessions. The biggest problem for the authorities was that, having chosen to believe the girls and everything they were telling them, they threw out all legalities to do with a proper trial and hanged many innocent people. It is apparent that most of these people were the victims of 17th century superstition, though Revd Parris was reluctant to attribute this epidemic of hysteria to witchcraft. He embarked on a campaign of prayer and fasting, which seems to have brought some of the girls to their senses. The hysterical fits were so appalling that it seemed to the community that witchcraft must be the logical, and only, explanation. Yet Revd Parris recognized that the children's fits were communicable and therefore were a form of mass hysteria.

This mass hysteria was also seen when many respectable and good people could not be totally sure whether their spirit double was tormenting the girls. (It was thought the Devil could use the spectre of an innocent person for this purpose.) Some people came to believe what they were told by the clergy and the judges – they therefore confessed and the madness continued.

The longer the Oyer and Terminer special court sat, the more people suffered fits. The bouts of hysteria were becoming more violent. Finally however, the excesses perpetrated in the name of the law could no longer be condoned; false confessions and accusations obtained by binding the neck and heels of suspects until blood trickled from the nose, bullying suspects and denying legal representation, and the acceptance of evidence from children as young as four or five began to disturb ordinary townspeople.

The girl accusers soon overreached themselves when they were called on by the surrounding villages to act as witchfinders. Disquiet spread about methods used and sanity gradually began to return. The members of the Salem jury began to fear that they had been party to various miscarriages of justice. Later they wrote:

We confess that we ourselves were not capable to understand, nor able to understand, the mysterious delusions of the powers of darkness… we justly fear we have been instrumental, with others, though ignorantly and unwittingly, to bring upon ourselves and these people of the Lord, the guilt of innocent blood …

The courts in later years cleared all those accused of witchcraft and in 1711 the relatives of those accused were given a degree of financial compensation. As late as the middle of the 20th century there were still legal repercussions when all prosecutions relating to the case were reversed.

CONTINENTAL EUROPE

In Europe witch-cleansing provided an easy solution to an economic problem. According to contemporary observations and researchers, and allegedly by their own confessions, thousands of people – mainly old women – made secret pacts with the Devil, who had emerged as a great spiritual potentate, the Prince of Darkness. Co-incidentally, many among these thousands were poverty-stricken crones and were therefore seen as a drain on the community in which they lived.

Every night these thousands of people were said to anoint themselves with 'devil's grease' – supposedly made from the fat of murdered babies, but most likely containing hallucinatory herbs – and thus lubricated would slide through keyholes, cracks and up chimneys and mount spindles, broomsticks and in some cases flying goats to fly off to the sabbat. Apparently there were 800 meeting places in Lorraine in north-eastern France alone. The Blocksberg or Brocken in the Harz Mountains in Germany, Blakulla in Sweden and the giant resort of La Hendaye in south-western France, where no fewer than 12,000 witches gathered for the meeting known as the Aquelarre, were well-known international centres where witches gathered. Initially the interrogators in Lorraine thought that sabbats only occurred on Thursdays but they soon gathered additional 'evidence' that sabbats also occurred on Mondays, Wednesdays, Fridays and Sundays.

The belief was that dozens of demons, their paramours and, most importantly of all, the Devil himself appeared at these sabbats. He appeared variously as a huge black bearded man, a foul-smelling goat or even a giant toad, all of which are manifestations of masculinity or rank power. Those present always recognized their master. When worshipping him, they paid homage by dancing around him and making music with whatever was to hand – be that horse skulls, animal carcasses or even human bones. They then signified their allegiance by kissing him – under the tail if he was a goat or on the lips if he was a toad.

Following this they indulged in wild sexual orgies and feasts. All of these acts, of course, had their origin in pagan rituals to do with the worship of the gods and goddesses – though without understanding and in their excesses they had probably lost a great deal of their original meaning. The food for these feasts varied from country to country – in Spain exhumed corpses, in Alsace stewed bat and in England beef and beer. The food was said to be tasteless, but salt was never allowed, lest it frightened away the devil.

When they were not celebrating the Sabbat the witches would, it seems, be suckling their familiars – or totem animals – who apparently appeared in the form of weasels, moles, bats or toads. Alternatively they were arranging the ailments or deaths of their neighbours and their animals (particularly their pigs), causing storms, blight and also impotence in newly married men. The witches were reputedly having sexual intercourse with the devil, who appeared to she-witches as an incubus (a male demon) and he-witches as succubus (female demon). According to 'the Angelic Doctor' St Thomas Aquinas who, after St Augustine might be regarded as the second father of the science of demonology, the Devil could discharge as an incubus only what he had previously absorbed as a succubus. He could, therefore, appear as either without too much difficulty.

The Devil's 'domination' of the secular world was therefore brought about by those who accepted his perceived control. Magical beliefs and pagan practices gave an element of personal power to those people who had little control over the rest of their lives. Through these hidden practices they could discharge some of their anxiety and dislike of their conditions. It was the lack of control of subversive elements in society that caused mass panic among the authorities, who then conveniently focussed on the terrorisation and persecution of those who could not adequately defend themselves.

Throughout Europe most authorities reacted by instigating savage witch-hunts.

Austria In Austria witchcraft persecution and hysteria peaked during the reign of Emperor Rudolf II (1576–1612). A weak man, he was reliant on his advisers and was heavily influenced by the witch haters among them. He became convinced that everyone who had once been considered mad or out of the ordinary was a witch and would have them burned at the stake indiscriminately. It seems that little evidence was needed for a guilty verdict. Merely holding a pot of ointment, touching bones or being accused by a child was deemed satisfactory evidence. Even being the child of an accused was taken as proof of guilt.

A rumour in Salzburg cost a hundred lives; the accused were tortured into confessing and then beheaded, strangled or burned. In the Tyrol those accused of witchcraft who confessed and then retracted their confession would continue to be tortured until they once more admitted their guilt. Any legal safeguards, such as they were, which were supposed to protect the innocent, were ignored due to the nature of the crime. Only children under seven years of age were safe.

Bavaria In common with other countries, the degree of panic in Bavaria varied. In Werdenfels in the Alps, accusation and subsequent trials meant that 49 members of the community were executed. In Schongau about 1598–99, judges set aside any cases brought before them that were not connected with witchcraft. This meant they could concentrate on the witchcraft trials and put to death those convicted.

France In France witchcraft trials began as early as 1275. An inquisition was set up which undertook, among others, the trials of Bishop Peter of Bayeux and his nephew in 1278 who were accused of using sorcery against Philip III; that of Bishop Guichard of Troyes who was charged in 1308 for using magic against several aristocrats; Ailps de Mons and various associates who were accused of using image magic (wax figures) against Louis X in 1314; Count Robert d'Artois who was banished for fashioning a wax figure to use against the King's son in 1331. In 1398 various suspects were beheaded for causing the madness of the French monarch through the use of witchcraft. Specific towns also held their own trials.

The town of Luxeuil had one trial which demonstrated the continued influence of the inquisition; that of Madame de Lisle la Mansenee who was tried as a witch. The whole case was based on hearsay and malicious gossip. Her neighbours alleged that she had caused much of the misfortunes that had occurred in the town. She was hanged and her body burned to ashes.

The Paris witch trial of Jehenne de Brigue was a remarkable one due to the care that the Parliament took to apply the law soberly and correctly which was not normally the case. Unfortunately, the use of torture was sanctioned which defeated well-meaning attempts to observe the spirit of the law.

Germany In Germany, the torture of witches consisted of both freezing cold baths and immersion in scalding water laced with lime, being force feed with salted herring, laceration of the neck using a rope, scorching the skin of the armpits or groin with burning feathers dipped in sulphur, the prayer (ducking) stool, roasting on an iron chair, scourging, the stocks and thumbscrews – in fact, anything that produced extreme physical pain. On the way to the gallows, convicted witches also had their right hand cut off; a woman would have her breast torn off with red-hot pincers. These tortures were at the instigation of Bishop Johann Gottfried von Aschhausen or the 'Witch Bishop' as he was known. He was responsible for sending 300 witches to death in the years 1609–22.

The Bamberg trials were some of the most brutal. At least 600 people were burned as witches in the years 1623–33. Once a person was arrested they had no chance of escaping the death penalty as they were not allowed to have a proper defence. Many prominent people were brought to trial and hanged for witchcraft; their properties were sold to pay for their trials and anything left went to the bishop. This type of trial eventually ceased on the death of the Bishop.

In Würzburg hundreds of lives were taken due mainly to the fact that the Jesuits demanded the death penalty for all those accused and found guilty of witchcraft. It is estimated that some 2,000 accused witches were burned during the period of the witch hysteria. In 1589 in one town alone 133 witches were publicly burned in just one day. Records show that in the years 1587 to 1594 two towns were totally razed as a result of hysteria.

Italy The bare facts show that 140 witches were burned at Brescia, 300 were executed in Como and 70 died at Valcanonica. A further 5,000 were suspected of witchcraft.

Norway In Norway witches were usually blamed for shipwrecks, murders and other crimes. There was less evidence of pacts with the devil. The witch must have actually committed an evil deed.

Pyrenees The Basque region in the Pyrenees was supposedly inhabited by witches. This is hardly surprising since, in common with other rural areas, many of the beliefs would have their basis in folklore. It was the belief in pagan gods which came under scrutiny and as many as 600 people were killed in the Pays de Labourd. In the early 17th century it is here that Christianity and pagan religion probably ran side by side. A local priest, Pierre Bocal, was burned alive in 1609 after it was rumoured that he performed rituals of both Christian and non-Christian faiths. After three more priests from the area were burned and other innocents killed, the local population opposed the slaughter and further bloodshed was halted.

Throughout the 16th and most of the 17th century, people believed in the reality of the struggle between good and evil. Ordinary people did not necessarily always accept the details, but they accepted the principle of the theory. They were not able to argue against more educated men of letters and so, unsurprisingly, reacted with fear. For two centuries clergy and men of God preached against witches; lawyers sentenced them.

Books and sermons, which were deliberately designed to be provocative, warned the good Christian of the dangers – as a good Christian, one had no compunction against reporting one's neighbours, thereby allowing the authorities to exploit an atmosphere of suspicion. Inquisitors and judges were supplied with manuals spreading the latest information and this incited magistrates to greater vigilance and persecution. Judges considered to be too lenient were denounced as enemies of the people. Torture was frequently used to gain, and boost, confessions.

This persecution had almost no effect on the number of witches – indeed, the more persecuted they were the more numerous they became. By the beginning of the 17th century hysteria had gripped scholars and clerics alike and often indiscriminate purges of entire communities were carried out. By 1630 the slaughter was virtually unrestrained. Lawyers, judges, clergy – in fact anyone who was perceived to disagree with the scholars – were denounced as witches and burnt at the stake.

Almost as though the hysteria had burned itself out, belief in the witch-hunters began to decrease and more and more people became sceptical. By the 1680s the obsession had largely disappeared in European Catholic and Protestant countries alike.

BRITISH ISLES
CHANNEL ISLANDS
On the island of Jersey in the years between 1562 and 1736, 66 trials took place. Most notably the records suggest that all of those tried

were sentenced to death. They were often executed by burning instead of by hanging, although in some cases they were hanged and then burned. Perhaps the most horrific execution was that of a pregnant witch who was burned; during the execution she gave birth and the baby was tossed into the flames too.

Others who were accused but not tried were banished, whipped or had their ears cut off. Reason eventually prevailed at the end of the 17th century, and cases of alleged witchcraft became much more rare.

IRELAND

In Ireland the manic pursuit of witches seems not to have reached the fever pitch it did elsewhere. This was probably partly due to the strong tradition of the Celtic arts and the acceptance of folkloric activities. Another reason could well be geographical remoteness and communication difficulties that would naturally cut down the spread of malicious gossip.

The first notable case was that of a Dame Alice Kyteler in 1324 in Kilkenny. She, her son and many of her servants were charged with heretical practices and occult activities. The trial was instigated by the Bishop of Ossory, who had been trained in France. Petronilla de Milda or Meath, probably one of the Dame's maids, became the first victim recorded as being burnt at the stake. This case is notable because it is the first time that stories of mating with demons and pacts with Satan are mentioned. Dame Kyteler apparently escaped retribution.

The last recorded witch trial to take place in Eire was that at Magee Island in 1711. This trial was different to other witchcraft trials in that it was linked to poltergeist activity, which is now thought to be caused by an excess of psychic energy, particularly in pubescent girls. The household of James Haltridge, the son of a deceased Presbyterian minister, seemed to be the butt of pranks and practical jokes, apparently by an unseen hand. It was not until his mother died soon after feeling a pain in her back that neighbours believed that the perpetrator was Mary Dunbar, a servant girl who was apparently showing signs of demonic possession. Dunbar named eight women who allegedly had the power to send her into hysterics. These women were found guilty by jury, although the judges could not agree, and the sentences handed out ranged from a year in jail to undergoing four appearances in the stocks.

SCOTLAND

The most celebrated Scottish witch was Isobel Gowdie, whose confession provided a detailed insight into the real or imagined activities and delusions of the archetypal witch. In 1662, Gowdie, the renowned 'Queen of Scottish Witches', confessed that she had frequent dealings with what she referred to as 'faeries'. She claimed to have frequently travelled to Faerieland, which she entered through various hills and caverns. According to her account, the entrance to Faerieland was guarded by elf-bulls, whose 'roaring and skoilling' always left her terrified. She stated that the King and Queen of Faerieland, whom she met frequently, were always finely dressed and offered her more meat than she could eat.

While she was in Faerieland, Gowdie, along with other witches and faeries, would amuse themselves by shape shifting (changing into animal form) and destroying the homes of mortals. She was taught to fly by the faeries using, among other things, the charm:

Horse and Hattock, in the Devil's name!

The faeries and the Devil would then make what Gowdie termed 'poisonous elf-arrows', presumably as weapons with which to harm, or enchant, mortals.

Gowdie also stated that she used her broom for a rather novel purpose. Instead of using it to travel to Faerieland or a sabbat, she put the broom next to her husband in their marital bed. She claimed he never noticed the difference, which has to be regarded as more of a comment on the state of their marriage than it is an admission of witchcraft.

One trial that gives us a good deal of information on the changing perception of what had previously been an acceptable use of knowledge is that of Bessie Dunlop, who was tried in 1576 for being a member of a coven. Known as the Witch of Dalry, she was probably more of a wise woman than a witch, since she used herbal cures and remedies and also seems to have been exceptionally clairvoyant.

She was accused of sorcery, witchcraft, incantation and dealing with charms. Many of her experiences, such as seeing her familiar or guardian spirit, would be understood by modern psychics as they develop the 'powers'. She was burnt at the stake, although she was patently a white witch working for the good of the community.

The Aberdeen witchcraft trials of 1596 came about largely as a result of public unease. The main accused were Janet Wishart, Isobel Cockie, Margaret Ogg, Helen Rogie, Isobel Strachan, Isobel Ritchie and Isobel Ogg, each of whom was said to specialize in a particular form of sorcery. Janet Wishart apparently stole body parts from corpses. Isobel Cockie bewitched mills and livestock, while Margaret Ogg poisoned meat and Isobel Ogg raised storms. Helen Rogie brought illness and death on her victims by modelling figures of them in lead or wax. Isobel Strachan was notorious as a fascinator and misleader of young men, while Isobel Ritchie made magical confectionery for expectant mothers.

It would seem that these witches all had one thing in common: the ability to cause 'the sudden sickness' whereby their victims would lay 'one half of the day roasting as if in an oven, with an unquenchable thirst, the other half of the day melting away with an extraordinary cold sweat.' Anything that had gone wrong in the vicinity of this group of women was blamed on them.

Other women were tried at the same time and at the end of the trial no less than 23 women and one man had been found guilty of witchcraft. Their punishment was to be tied to stakes, strangled by the executioner and then burnt to ashes. Some of those tried escaped this fate by committing suicide, but their bodies were then dragged through the streets until they were torn to shreds. Those who had been tried but not had the charges proven were branded on the cheek and banished.

There does seem to be some evidence for the practising of the black art in this area of Scotland. The groups that did meet would seem to have two main things in common. First, the practice of witchcraft was a confidential cult, almost a family concern, where secrets were handed down from generation to generation. Secondly, there was a well organized network, and although each of its members operated individually in their own localities, each was also required to attend general meetings to take part in the ceremonies and to take further instructions in 'working woe' (doing harm).

The North Berwick witches trial in 1590 was one of the most notorious and signalled the beginning of witchcraft hysteria in

Scotland. The case started when a deputy bailiff, David Seaton, became suspicious of the goings on of one of his servants, Geillis Duncan. She, cooperating fully with his enquiries, admitted that she had been present at sabbats and gave a long list of accomplices, including Dr J. Fian (there is some difference of opinion as to whether his name was James or John), Agnes Sampson, Euphemia Maclean and Barbara Napier.

Agnes Sampson refused to admit that she was a witch but after long and painful torture admitted all charges. She claimed that a coven with as many as 200 witches had met the Devil at North Berwick, where he had empowered them to use spells and magic. They were to throw a dead cat into the sea in order to create a storm which was to prevent King James VI's ship from returning from Denmark with his fiancé, Anne.

At first the king was reluctant to have them found guilty of witchcraft as he believed they were not telling the truth, but later Agnes repeated to him the exact words of a private conversation he had had with his wife on his wedding night. Highly disturbed by this, he took it as proof that witchcraft had been performed against him and they were found guilty. At the conclusion of the trial Dr Fian, who had been brutally tortured, Agnes Sampson and Euphemia MacLean were all burned alive. Barbara Napier was released after acceptance of her plea that she be spared because of pregnancy.

ENGLAND

Prior to the accession of James I (of England and VI of Scotland) in 1603, the hunting down of witches in England had been sporadic and nowhere near as structured or fervent as it had been in many parts of continental Europe. In England the first Witchcraft Act was not passed until 1542 and it was then repealed some five years later under Edward VI. This lack of hysteria is most likely due to a combination of factors.

Until the reign of Elizabeth I no one had been executed for being a witch. Henry VIII's Witchcraft Law of 1542 was reinstated by Elizabeth I in 1563. As a matter of interest, astrology and chiromancy, both in use at the time, were not associated with witchcraft, although a number of witches prosecuted probably also were astrologers and chiromancers. The Witchcraft Act of 1563 did not include any penalty or censure specifically against either astrology or chiromancy. Astrology was not witchcraft, for witchcraft meant maleficium, the doing of physical harm to others or their property through the laying on of curses or through bringing about their death. Astrologers and chiromancers were never accused of being guilty of such crimes.

In 16th century England accusations of witchcraft were made from time to time and tales were told but they were usually dismissed as tittle-tattle. The witches of Canewdon, for example, were renowned for their power to halt farm machinery and carts by means of a terrifying stare (the 'evil eye'). At various times, they were also accused of sending plagues of lice and other unpleasant creatures against those who had wronged them. Acceptance by local people of such acts did not, however, unsettle the authorities, clerical or secular.

The Church of England had recently seceded from the Roman Catholic Church and did not wish to be seen to be associated with it. Also, the use of torture to induce confessions was largely deemed wrong in England, particularly after trials for heresy such as that of Anne Askew (1521–46), who had been tortured when she would not reveal who her Protestant associates were. Most importantly, however, in the latter part of that century, there were strong movements towards some kind of religious tolerance following the difficulties between Protestants and Catholics.

When a charge of witchcraft was taken seriously in England, however, the penalty was as severe as elsewhere, as can be seen from the following cases.

According to public records the first person to be executed as a witch in England was Agnes Waterhouse, who was tried at Chelmsford in Essex in July 1566 alongside her daughter, Joan, and a friend, Elizabeth Francis. Francis was the first to be charged with causing illness (to a man named William Auger and a woman named Mary Cocke) by 'ungodly ways'. She and Joan escaped the charge, but Agnes was not so lucky and was also charged with poisoning a woman called Alice Poole. She was found guilty and hanged.

In a trial at St Osyth, Essex, in 1582 14 people were charged with several different counts of witchcraft, including one of the bewitching to death of others. The main perpetrator was a woman by the name of Ursula Kempe. Considered to be the local healer, she was seen as somebody to go to if one was ill. She was especially good at midwifery and as a child nursemaid. Witnesses claimed that she cured of a fever an infant called David Thurlowe by using invocations. However, the parents later refused to employ her as nursemaid to their infant daughter. Unfortunately the baby later fell out of her crib and broke her neck. Local gossip said Kempe caused the accident, although Mrs Thurlowe went to her for help with her arthritis. Kempe helped her but Thurlowe refused to pay, at which point her condition worsened.

Mrs Thurlowe complained and Kempe was placed on trial; she pleaded her case and even accused four others of witchcraft, including Elizabeth Bennet. These four in turn named several others, most of whom were let off on minor charges. Four were acquitted and four were convicted but later reprieved. Only two were hanged for witchcraft: Elizabeth Bennet and Ursula Kempe.

The Warboys witch trial in 1593 involved three alleged witches by the names of John, Alice and Agnes Samuel. It came about because they were alleged to have caused the five daughters of Robert Throckmorton to go mad. They were also accused of the murder of Lady Cromwell.

When the case was brought before justices of the peace, Mrs Samuel confessed to everything. All three of them were found guilty. Agnes refused to claim pregnancy in mitigation though, arguing that 'it shall never be said that I was both a witch and a whore'. All were hanged and their estate was given to Henry Cromwell who used it for an annual sermon against witchcraft.

In Lancashire there were two notable trials; one in 1612, the other in 1633. The first was the case of the Pendle witches, a coven active in Pendle Forest, involving approximately 20 people. The two main characters were Elizabeth Sowthern and Anne Whittle. The local magistrate questioned Elizabeth on whether she was a witch, whereupon she implicated her granddaughter, Alison Device, and Anne Whittle. Elizabeth also confessed that the devil had spoken to her and that she had given him her soul. She stated that, when first approached, she had kept rejecting him until one night he came and sucked her blood, driving her to madness for a period of almost two months. The devil then reappeared when she and her granddaughter Alison went to seek payment from a

Richard Baldwyn for whom her daughter Elizabeth had worked. Baldwyn told them to leave or he would hang and burn one of them, at which point the devil took his revenge.

Alison Device was also charged following her confession over the death of Baldwyn's daughter and was blamed for laming an old peddler. Anne Whittle confessed to, and was charged with, becoming a witch. The families of those imprisoned attempted to hatch an escape plan but were found out; several arrests were made and in all 20 people were tried. Amid the general panic, they all implicated one another and ended up testifying against each other. As a result, 10 people were sentenced to hang, Elizabeth Sowthern, who was 80, died in prison and one woman (Margaret Pearson) was sentenced to the pillory and a year in jail. The rest of the accused were found not guilty.

The second trial, in 1633, again implicated the Device family and involved a young boy by the name of Edmund Robinson. He claimed he had been forced to attend a witches sabbat. Of those whom Robinson claimed had been present, 17 were convicted of witchcraft. The cases were referred to the authorities, however, when it was ascertained that the boy had been compelled by his father to lie. The prisoners who were still alive were released and the boy's father was jailed.

In Salmesbury, Suffolk, in 1613 Grace Sowerbutts brought charges of witchcraft against her grandmother, her aunt and another woman by the name of Jane Southworth. According to Grace they had allegedly taken her to an orgiastic revel where they metamorphosed into black dogs by using an ointment they had made from the bones of a child called Thomas Walshman. She also claimed they had eaten this child's flesh and had invited her to join in but instead she reported them to the authorities, also maintaining that they had had sexual relations. This appears to have been a crude attempt to introduce the idea of a European-style Sabbat.

The jury was not convinced, however, and the charges were dropped. Under pressure, Grace broke down and admitted to being forced to make the accusations by a Catholic priest, one Christopher Southworth. It was claimed that the allegation had arisen out of a family feud when the accused had converted to the Protestant faith.

The Somerset witches were two alleged active covens exposed in 1664. Those involved in these covens were charged and hotly pursued by the local justice of the peace, Robert Hunt, until his concerned superiors intervened, asking him to desist from further enquiries. Other members of the community complained, asserting that there were more covens in the area, but investigations into these were never completed.

The impetus for these trials was almost certainly the new Witchcraft Act introduced by Elizabeth's successor, James I, and passed by Parliament in 1604.

James could be said to have been obsessed with witchcraft. He devoted many years of study to the subject while he was King of Scotland, largely as a result of a trial of alleged witches in North Berwick (see earlier). He is also thought to have observed several other witchcraft trials and in 1597 published a set of three books *Daemonologie*, the object of which was to draw attention to the evils of witchcraft and to encourage the catching of witches. As a consequence, The Act of 1604 broadly used *Daemonologie* as a basis and was much more severe than anything that had gone before.

What had previously been no more than a passing interest for many now, in common with continental countries, became a mania. Records giving actual figures for this time are unclear, but throughout the time of the Long Parliament (1640–53) and the Commonwealth (dissolved in 1660) somewhere in the region of 3,000 people were burned or hanged as witches in Britain. It was into this environment that Matthew Hopkins, self appointed 'Witchfinder General', came.

Comparatively little is known about his early life, except that, born in the early 17th century, he was the son of James Hopkins, a minister of Wenham, Suffolk. His mother was Dutch and there appears to have been a family connection with the Huguenots. He received some education in Holland, had gained some knowledge of maritime law when in Amsterdam and worked in a fairly minor role (akin to a solicitor's clerk today) in the legal profession on his return to England. It was from his travels in Holland and the Low Countries that he first formulated the idea of becoming a witch-hunter.

In 1644 his career as a witch-hunter – a role not formally taken up in England previously – began. In March of that year seven or eight witches had allegedly met in his neighbourhood and offered sacrifices to the Devil. Four of them were hanged for sending the

Devil, in the shape of a bear, to kill Hopkins. Somewhat incensed, he set about discovering 'the devil's work' and shortly afterwards no less than 29 witches were hunted down and executed in one go. Thereupon he abandoned his law career and appointed himself 'Witchfinder General'.

In this capacity he travelled on horseback through Suffolk, Norfolk, Huntingdonshire (now part of Cambridgeshire) and Essex with an assistant, John Stern, and a female searcher.

Hopkins' fees were 20 shillings a town plus expenses, and 20 shillings for each witch convicted – a not inconsiderable sum. Alleged witches had to confess and were then hanged on the strength of that confession. If they refused to confess, they were 'searched'. This searching was all in all a hugely barbaric process but one that Hopkins considered necessary.

He was the first to reduce the practice of witchfinding to what he called a 'science' and to regularize the methods of so-doing. He also added four of his own methods. They were:

1. A suspected witch was stripped naked, shaved and searched for the 'devil's mark', which was deemed a sign of guilt. This devil's mark might be any bodily abnormality such as polyps and scarring and probably often more prevalent among the poor and the old. A third nipple and moles were also assumed to be devil's marks. Indeed, any mark which was insensitive to pain and which did not bleed when pricked was damning enough for the witchfinder. This method, although favoured by Hopkins, was more widely used in Scotland rather than England.

2. This particular method was Hopkins' own invention, according to John Gaule, vicar of Great Staughton, who had it on the authority of a witchfinder and a witness: 'The witch was placed in the middle of a room, sat cross-legged on a stool or table (or in some other equally uncomfortable posture), to which if she submitted not, she is then bound with cords; there she is watched and kept without meat for the space of four and twenty hours (for they say that within that time that her imp will come and suck). A little hole is likewise made in the door, for the imps to come in at; and lest it should come in a less discernible shape, they that watch are taught to be ever anon sweeping the room, and if they see any spiders or flies, to kill them. And if they cannot kill them, then they may be sure they are her imps.'

3. The third method was to make the suspect walk barefoot continually for hours on end until she was totally exhausted and her feet were bloodied and blistered. She was then questioned repeatedly until she was ready to confess to anything so she could avoid further torture. This was known as 'walking the witch'.

4. The following was Hopkins' favourite. The witch was 'swum'. The accused right hand was tied to their left foot and vice versa. The victim was then placed on water (a pond, river or lake) and wrapped in a sheet or blanket. If she sank, she drowned — but as an innocent person; if she floated she was found guilty and burned — the idea being that the sacred element (water) used in baptism refused to receive an accursed witch.

In other words you could not win either way and cruelty became the norm. Such cruelty was felt to be justified because witches were patently not God's children. Fortunately Hopkins' career was relatively short. It was undertaken with the complete support of Parliament who, more often than not, would send along a committee to support him and 'assist' the judges in their decision making. Although this career only lasted three years, Hopkins brought about the execution of hundreds of people.

In 1645 in Bury St Edmunds, Hopkins procured the execution of 18 witches in one day. This figure would undoubtedly have been higher were it not for the fact that the King's troops appeared and forced the adjournment of the trial of the 120 others present. Perhaps the most notable suspect was an elderly clergyman named John Lowes, who was disliked as a Royalist sympathizer. He was subjected to the torture of being 'swum' and the ordeal known as 'walking a witch' until he confessed. Other victims included a woman who was burned for the treasonable murder of her husband by witchcraft.

The second trial involved two widows, Rose Cullender and Amyu Duny, who were both charged with numerous acts of witchcraft, including the bewitching of several children. At the end of the trial both were found guilty and were hanged.

In Yarmouth 16 women, all of whom had confessed to witchcraft, were hanged. One of these women, whose imp (familiar) was in the highly unusual form of a blackbird, allegedly made a wax figure of a child and then buried it. During her trial she revealed the place where it had been buried. When this spot was dug up and no figure was found, the conclusion was reached that the devil had taken it. A child who had been suffering 'grievous torments' up until this point, now made an immediate recovery. The bewitching was thus 'proved', although it is difficult to see the logic behind the argument. It is easy to see how the malevolence generated by Hopkins, who probably relished his financial gain and new status, gave rise to similar malice in others.

Hopkins was also successful in Ipswich where, among many other convictions, was the one where a hitherto very religious woman (whom it was decided had three imps) was convicted of bewitching not only her husband, but also a neighbour who had refused to lend her a needle, to death. For these crimes she was burned.

In Faversham in 1645, Joan Williford, who confessed to witchcraft practices, named at her trial three elderly women – Jane Holt, Joan Argoll and Elisabeth Harris. It was decided that the devil had provided them with money – never more than a shilling at a time and usually sixpence or three pence. For this amount of money, and the promise of an imp, these women had signed away their salvation, lived in abject poverty, been convicted of being witches and finally had been burnt alive. It does not seem to have occurred to their judges to consider what alleged 'bargains with the devil' the women had struck for themselves.

By 1646 Hopkins' witchfinding was becoming increasingly bizarre. In Huntingdon, where he procured the condemnation and killing of many women, one case in particular stands out, that of Elizabeth Churcher. She used two walking sticks which Hopkins decided were two imps named 'Beelzebub' and 'Trillibub'. For this 'crime', Elizabeth Churcher was convicted and burnt as a witch.

His self-appointed task of witch-finding came to an end when he died from tuberculosis in 1646. Although this disease usually affects the lungs, it can also attack the central nervous system. One would have to wonder whether Hopkins' increasingly odd behaviour was as a result of his illness.

Following the Renaissance and the birth of the scientific age, there were few accusations of witchcraft. The last person convicted of witchcraft seems to have been Jane Wenham in 1712.

In 1735 the Witchcraft Act was amended again, as quoted below, this time to include provision only for those who *pretended* to practise witchcraft or use magical powers.

THE FINAL SACRIFICE

The final prosecution under any Witchcraft Act, that of 1735, was against the materialization medium, Helen Duncan, in 1944.

Helen Duncan was born Victoria Helen McCrae MacFarlane on 25 November 1897 into a poor family in the small Scottish town of Callander. Even as a child she spoke of people who had died many years previously and remarked that she could both hear and see them.

When she left school, Helen moved to Dundee to work in the mills. At the outbreak of World War One she volunteered to help the war effort. Rejected due to poor health, she took up nursing, and while nursing, met her future husband, Henry Duncan. They were married on 27th May 1916 and moved to Edinburgh, though due to their poor health, neither was able to find work and they returned to Dundee. They had a growing family to support (out of 12 pregnancies, there were six surviving children) and Helen found work in a bleach factory during the day, supplementing her income by taking cleaning jobs in the evening.

It was Henry who decided to nurture Helen's abilities and they began to use psychometry – the sensing of the vibrations of an object. It soon became obvious that Helen was a natural trance medium (able to channel information from other dimensions and planes of existence). She and Henry decided to form a development circle, which met on Thursday evenings. It was at one of these meetings that Helen's spirit guide at this time, who called himself Dr Williams, appeared and advised: 'Never accept anything at face value, but always question anyone claiming to come from the world of spirit; ask for evidence and proof which can be verified.' This, of course, is a version of the rule that a negative vibration will not stand up to questioning.

It was during this time that Helen became aware of her ability to heal, although it was not unheard of for her to take on the ailments of her clients. This can sometimes occur when a medium or healer is unable to clear the negative vibration of the ailment completely. The small donations she received for this work were often, so it seems, passed on to her local doctor to facilitate treatment for poorer patients.

Her séances were renowned for the appearance of physical phenomena (ectoplasm and materialized spirits) and must have seemed truly astounding. In 1931 Helen gave sittings at the London Spiritualist Alliance, where she came up against psychic investigator Harry Price. It seems Price attended four séances, ultimately accusing her of fraud, alleging that the ectoplasm was produced by regurgitating material from within her body – still a common accusation in Spiritualist circles. Although this was disproved, it still meant that Helen became the target of sceptics.

At a séance in Glasgow in 1933, Helen was disturbed while in a trance and informed that police had been called. She was cautioned and charged with fraud. At her trial (largely a sham, the main prosecution witness was a known associate of Harry Price) she was accused of 'fraudulently materializing the form of the dead'. She was fined, but it did not dim her enthusiasm for mediumship; indeed, she went on to give several test séances for researchers. Accused by some of profiteering from her gift, she was comfortable financially, but could by no means be called rich.

She become more and more well known for her mediumship, or channelling as it is now known, and throughout the 1930s and early 1940s she travelled the length and breadth of Great Britain giving séances in home circles and Spiritualist churches. There are numerous stories of dead loved ones appearing and communicating with living relatives. Such proof of survival undoubtedly brought comfort to many grieving people during such difficult times.

Her guide, who was now a man called Albert, warned those organizing the events to exercise caution over who was allowed to attend. Unfortunately these warnings were largely ignored. One of the places to which she travelled most frequently was the Master Temple in Portsmouth. Situated on the south coast of England, Portsmouth was at that time, and still is, the home port of the British Naval Fleet. Many of Duncan's predictions had been extremely accurate, and it is now widely thought that the authorities were terrified that during one of her events the medium would discover or reveal the date for the D-Day landings, which were then in the final planning stages.

She was holding a séance in Portsmouth on 19 January 1944, when it was raided by the police. They attempted to grab the ectoplasm (which they suspected was a white sheet), but it had disappeared. Helen Duncan and three of her sitters were arrested and charged with vagrancy – it would seem this was the only Act under which they could be charged. At the hearing the court was informed that a Lieutenant Worth of the Royal Navy had attended the séance. He paid 25 shillings (£1.25/$2) for two tickets, one of which he gave to the policeman whose signal started the raid.

Instead of being granted bail, as was usual when on trial for vagrancy, Helen was sent to Holloway prison in London, where she spent four days. Her charge was upgraded to conspiracy – in wartime Britain an offence punishable by hanging. By the time her case had been referred to the Old Bailey – England's central criminal court – the charge had been altered once more. This time she was charged with witchcraft under the Witchcraft Act of 1735. This time Helen Duncan and her co-defendants were accused of 'pretending to exercise or use human conjuration that through the agency of Helen Duncan, spirits of deceased dead persons should appear to be present.' The words of the Act are:

… That if any Person shall, from and after the said Twenty-fourth Day of June, pretend to exercise or use any kind of Witchcraft, Sorcery, Inchantment, or Conjuration, or undertake to tell Fortunes, or pretend, from his or her Skill or Knowledge in any occult or crafty Science, to discover where or in what manner any Goods or Chattels, supposed to have been stolen or lost, may be found, every Person, so offending, being thereof lawfully convicted on Indictment or Information in that part of Great Britain called England, or on Indictment or Libel in that part of Great Britain called Scotland, shall, for every such Offence, suffer Imprisonment by the Space of one whole Year without Bail or Mainprize …

Just in case this didn't work, she was also accused under the Larceny Act of taking money 'by falsely pretending she was in a position to bring about the appearances of the spirits of deceased persons'.

Throughout the trial, which lasted seven days, the prosecution did their utmost to prove that Helen Duncan was a fraud, with many attempts to debunk her abilities. People were enraged at her treatment and a defence fund was set up which was used to bring witnesses, among them respected academics and journalists, from around the world to testify as to her abilities. As a result, the case attracted much publicity in newspapers. It was widely felt that she was being prosecuted to stop classified wartime information from falling into the wrong hands – the authorities behaviour could be likened to paranoia. Many in the law profession were extremely uncomfortable with the case and the Law Societies in England and Scotland issued a statement declaring the case to be a travesty of justice.

The defence decided that the best way to test Helen Duncan was for her to give a demonstration of physical phenomena while in the witness box. This alarmed the authorities because they believed that if she succeeded, the very foundations of the British legal system would be rocked. The offer was therefore rejected and it was suggested that Helen Duncan be called as a witness and cross-examined. Wisely, the defence pointed out that she would be unable to testify in the trance state and would be unable to discuss what happened.

The jury was thus sent out and took only 30 minutes to reach their verdict. Helen and the three others were found guilty of conspiracy to contravene the 1735 Witchcraft Act, but not guilty of all other charges. The trial judge deliberated over the weekend and then sentenced Helen Duncan to nine months in prison. The right of appeal to the House of Lords was denied. The establishment had achieved its objective of silencing someone whom they felt to be a danger.

Helen continued to offer spiritual guidance to others while she was in prison, and was herself the recipient of a great deal of public sympathy. It was even rumoured that Churchill, a member of the Grand Order of Druids, saw her. He had been angry when the case had started, considering it a great waste of time and resources. In a ministerial note to the Home Secretary, he demanded: 'Give me a report of the 1735 Witchcraft Act. What was the cost of a trial to the State in which the Recorder [junior magistrate] was kept busy with all this obsolete tomfoolery to the detriment of the necessary work in the courts?' This did not happen; civil servants had many other pressing duties. The sentence of nine months ensured that Helen Duncan was under surveillance when the D-Day landings took place in June 1944.

Released in September 1944, Helen Duncan vowed not to give any further séances. However, within a few months she was again appearing, although the quality of her séances had deteriorated considerably, so much so that the Spiritualist National Union even withdrew her diploma for a short time.

In 1951, the 1735 Witchcraft Act was finally repealed. Whether or not this was due entirely to the Helen Duncan case and Churchill's interest in it is open to speculation, although without doubt the whole debacle was certainly a contributing factor. The Witchcraft Act was replaced by the Fraudulent Mediums Act. Under this Act, it is still illegal to purport to use clairvoyant or telepathic powers or to purport to act as a spiritualistic medium, especially if money is taken as a reward or payment. In 1954 Spiritualism was recognized as a religion by an Act of Parliament. It was hoped by many that these twin moves would put an end to the harassment of true mediums and allow the prosecution of frauds. Unfortunately, this was not to be the case.

In 1956, police raided a séance in Nottingham. They seized the medium, strip searched her and took many photographs using flashlights. They claimed to be looking for paraphernalia, but found none. In their ignorance, the police had done the worst thing possible. They had touched the medium and violated her personal space. They had effectively 'shocked' her out of her trance. This meant that the ectoplasm returned to the medium's body too quickly and caused colossal damage. A doctor was summoned and found two large second-degree burns across the medium's stomach; the medium was taken to her home and then rushed to hospital. Within five weeks, she was dead. That medium was Helen Duncan.

Popular acceptance of the powers that are developed by those who recognize dimensions beyond the ordinary everyday will always be very mixed. Some people will accept unquestioningly, others will search for alternative causes and others still will remain frightened and disturbed by the manifestation of such powers. They have been called magical; they are, for some, part and parcel of ordinary everyday lives and it is for each individual to decide whether or not they themselves wish to develop those abilities.

No one individual or group *ever* has the right to impose their beliefs on another, nor indeed to persecute *anyone* for their beliefs.

3.

PROCEDURES AND PROTOCOL OF RITUAL

Various cultures have theories about how magic works. Many modern magicians give some very deep hypotheses as to how it works, ranging from philosophical argument to material reasons. Most are searching for a basis for understanding what works well, and what does not. Over many, many years the ceremonial magical ritual in its basic form is known to work. Its form has been handed down in various cultures, with regional variations, over the centuries. The basic form is that the magician works within a cast circle, uses consecrated tools (which we explain later) and the magical names of various entities to evoke or invoke Powers.

The trainee magician finds it hard to admit that their rituals do not always work out, often because there is too much personal or emotional investment or because the ritual has not been properly understood. Sometimes nothing appears to happen, or does not happen at the expected time, sometimes there are unexpected side effects and sometimes it is only with hindsight that we realize that events have occurred which lead to the right resolution. The question then that most people ask is 'does it work? By and large it seems to, at least for some people some of the time. There can, of course, be no judgements about what is good and bad in ritual – what works for one may not work for others.

The way we invoke (bring towards) and evoke (send away) powers and the traditional use and naming of angels, spirits, gods and goddesses, ancestral spirits and so on are useful mental constructs, or rather, creative visualizations. These are a comfort to those who need to be conscious of personalities with whom to work. There are times when difficulty or stress within our personal lives makes it too difficult to gain access to the highest forms of energy without the feeling that we have an intimate relationship with these 'beings' and therefore the need to give them personalities.

Ritual gives an accepted formula for such access but that is not the end of the story. Here we think of the individual approaching a being or beings in whom he stands in awe and therefore requiring intermediaries to make his pleas for him. As soon as he or she moves beyond these 'mediators' the magician has to confront the nature of consciousness itself. He therefore becomes something of a mystic – someone who believes in the existence of realities beyond his own perception or intellectual appreciation and in the transcendence of God. Just as the magician has had to use mediators to gain access to the Supreme Power, so also there is the belief that the Supreme Power must 'step down' its energy from its very high level in order to effect changes on a physical level.

This raising and lowering of consciousness is a first principle of Eastern esoteric philosophy, and is at the root of the Kabbalistic doctrine of emanation – which we discussed earlier – and the Sephiroth, the ten creative forces that intervene between the infinite, unknowable God and our created world. This doctrine has been adopted by many 20th century magicians as a useful complement and tool in whatever traditional model of magic they were weaned on. There is a belief among most magical practitioners that while gods, goddesses etc., may well be simply creations of consciousness or archetypal images they can, and indeed should, be treated as if they were real. Whether one believes that magic is the manipulation of one's own or a Higher being's consciousness, it is useful to address these Higher Beings with respect and to accord them the dignity long-held belief requires.

INDIVIDUAL WORKING

There are certain procedures which most practitioners are prepared to acquire nowadays on an individual level which can also be used in group working. Whether you work in a Kabbalistic manner, are Wiccan/Pagan or are simply interested in enhancing your own magical working, certain techniques will be fundamental to your practice.

This is because the magicians of old recognized that they – in their own way – were intermediaries between the Higher Beings or

Gods and the physical material world. Right from the beginning they needed some way of:

1. Feeling different while working magically
2. Defining those differences
3. Marking a space in which they could work safely without interference from either malign powers or interfering humans

It was often safer to work alone in those days, for there was little understanding by the ordinary person of either what the energies were or even how they worked. If a malign energy did manifest then it could be contained within the designated space; the magician was at his most powerful within that space and yet at the same time he had done all that was necessary to ensure that he was a fit vehicle for whatever he needed to do.

The rituals which were developed then have stood the test of time and can be used today in much the same way. Indeed, as mentioned elsewhere, because the rituals have been performed so often for specific magical purposes, they have developed an energy of their own and become powerful in their own right.

For example, the Lesser Banishing Ritual of the Pentagram can be performed on your own to purify a room for further magical work or meditation and also can be used for protection. It has a much higher vibration than simply casting a circle, however, and in addressing the Archangels appeals to the highest authority for protection and assistance. Rather than appealing to the Elements, we now go to those beings or energies who are in charge of the Elements and make a direct appeal to them. When we use the old names we link into a stream of consciousness that quite literally has a resonance that causes a reaction within the universe. From that reaction there is a shift or response in everything in existence. Not only do we dignify the Archangels, we dignify ourselves.

The Lesser Banishing Ritual of the Pentagram

The first part of this ritual, that of the Kabbalistic cross, is used by the practitioner to open themselves to the powers of the universe and to state that they are present and ready for work. By calling the energy of the universe into the practitioner through the centre of his being, the mind, body, and soul are energized and in aligned with cosmic forces. The practitioner is then able to direct these energies with wisdom and at will. It is suggested that if you can do so, perform at least the first part of the ritual – which deals with the personal self – every day.

METHOD
Stand facing East.
Perform the Kabbalistic Cross as follows.

Touch your forehead with the first two (or index) fingers of your right hand and visualize a sphere of white light at that point.
Chant:

Atah [this translates roughly as Thou Art]

Lower your hand to your solar plexus and visualize a line of light extending down to your feet and chant:

Malkuth [the Kingdom]

Raise your hand and touch your right shoulder visualizing a sphere of light there and chant:

Ve Geburah [and the power]

Extend the hand across the chest tracing a line of light and touch your left shoulder
where another sphere of light forms and chant:

Ve Gedulah [and the glory]

Clasp your hands in the centre of your chest at the crossing point of the horizontal and
vertical lines of light.
Bow your head and chant:

Le Olam, Amen [for ever – amen]

This first part in particular brings about a quiet mind free of 'chatter' from the everyday world. This is useful in meditation and also in spellworking when concentration is needed. In the making of talismans, for instance, this quiet mind is of extreme importance so that the correct energies can be focussed properly into the object. Largely we use English words in our rituals, here we begin to use words which through tradition and long usage have become Words of Power. We acknowledge the archangels in their proper place and create a very positive space in which to work.

The effects of the complete ritual, which is in two parts, are first and foremost on the Astral (more subtle) energies, though it uses the pentagram (5-pointed star traced on the body, see Essential Ritual below) as a sign that the practitioner recognizes his place on Earth as Man. There is, in effect, a stepping down of the energies to make them usable, though you should also understand that the practitioner's own power is raised or enhanced at the same time. The protection that the pentagrams give is to banish any negative energy which may be present on any level whatsoever. In previous times it was thought that the magister or practitioner had mastery over the power he or she was using. Today we would rather think of it in terms of a collaborative effort between spiritual or magical energies and the practitioner. This does not mean there is any less respect.

The Essential Ritual

METHOD

Facing East, using the extended fingers, trace a large pentagram with the point up, starting at your left hip, up to just above your forehead, centred on your body, then down to your right hip, up and to your left shoulder, across to the right shoulder and down to the starting point in front of your left hip.

Visualize this pentagram in blue flaming light.
Thrust your fingers or athame (see Magical Tools section) into the centre.
Chant:

YHVH [Yod-heh-vahv-heh]
(This is the tetragrammaton, a four-letter word of power –
translated into Latin as Jehovah)

Turn to the South.
Visualize the blue flame following your fingers, tracing a blue line from the pentagram in the East to the South.

Repeat the formation of the pentagram while facing South,
This time, chant:

Adonai [another name for God translated as Lord]

Turn to the West, tracing the blue flame from South to West.
Form a pentagram again, but this time chant:

Eheieh [Eh-hay-yeah– another name of God translated as I Am or I Am That I Am]

Turn to the North, again tracing the blue flame from West to North.
Repeat the tracing of the pentagram and chant:

Agla [Ah-gah-lah – a composite of Atah Gibor le olam Amen]

Return again to the East, tracing the blue flame from North to East.
Push your fingers back into the same spot from which you started.
You should now visualize that you are surrounded by four flaming pentagrams
connected by a line of blue fire.

Visualizing each Archangel standing guard at each direction
Extend your arms out to your sides, forming a cross.
Chant:

Before me RAPHAEL [rah-fah-ell]
Behind me GABRIEL [gah-bree-ell]
On my right hand, MICHAEL [mee-khah-ell]
On my left hand, AURIEL [sometimes URIEL aw-ree-ell or ooh-ree-ell]

Before me flames the pentagram, behind me shines the six-rayed star

Repeat the Kabbalistic Cross as you did at the beginning and chant:

Atah
Malkuth
Ve Geburah
Ve Gedulah
Le Olam

As can be seen, Raphael is in the East, Gabriel in the West, Michael in the South and Uriel in the North. Sometimes Michael and Uriel are transposed by some practitioners. These archangels are the four guardians of the cardinal directions and you will find references to these cardinal directions in many of the spells and rituals.

This ritual sometimes seems to be too complicated for most people, so let us try to simplify the process of ritual so you can understand the thinking behind it. As time goes on and you become more proficient, you may wish to return to these individual rituals and familiarize yourself with them.

GROUP WORKING

Rather than working as a solitary practitioner, many people will seek a community of like-minded individuals on the basis that their own individual powers are thus enhanced. We give a method of group working, although it is very easy to adjust this for work on an individual basis. The rituals used for a group represent a cooperative act of worship which widens the scope of the ceremony to encompass larger objectives than just the personal; we can then consider our joint responsibility for the world in which we live and a more universal perspective. At the same time, through working in a group, a more focussed atmosphere can be created – a raising of consciousness so that each participant receives wisdom and energy commensurate with their needs and understanding. True initiation into the mysteries of magic for instance, is a private silent process, but an initiation ceremony accompanied by ritual can be seen as a more formal process for marking unmistakable long-term changes in the consciousness of the practitioner.

The purpose of rituals used in this way is to create an inspiring and expressive atmosphere in which to give life and meaning to the connection between the ordinary and the sublime. Symbolism takes on a meaningful existence and through colour, sound, movement and imagination, becomes a vibrant language of the soul. Rituals help us to do several things:

1. To learn the proper application of a basic structure for personal use and to understand the relevance of ritual.
2. To increase an understanding of the flow of energy which we experience and to develop confidence in the use of symbols.
3. To contribute to the group awareness of members thus helping them make the best use of their individual and group powers.
4. To create spiritual and emotional conditions where initiation on an inner level is accepted and experienced and where we can accept heightened states of awareness as the norm.
5. To use knowledge of ritual and power as a way of achieving personal spiritual health, so that the rituals themselves eventually become unnecessary and are recognized simply as a way of gaining access to the ultimate. They may then be replaced by direct experience.

By using the same rituals for both individual and group work these are seen as complementary and members of the group are able to enhance their experience on both a personal and shared level. We can take the insights gained from group work into the personal sacred space and come into contact with an awareness of a new level of activity and vice versa. A magical ritual is far superior if it succeeds without side effects and therefore can be shocking if there are untoward results. Traditional forms of magical ritual – often first taught in a group situation – tap a basic and, if misunderstood, possibly dangerous force which has to be channelled and directed properly. Group work can form a training arena which is also protected to enable the fledgling magician to learn the craft.

PREPARATION FOR RITUAL
Inevitably there are certain things to remember before the ritual proper begins. While you are preparing for the ritual, when putting on your robes or ritual gowns you might spend time in reflection, silent meditation or prayer. Prior to the beginning of any ritual, and while enrobing, concentrate on the matter in hand, if the ritual has a special intent. Alternatively, simply focus on the Supreme Being, Cosmic Responsibility and/or a successful outcome and ask that the event to follow helps you in your learning.

There is no limit to what can be worn in a ritual. Some groups will suggest white robes with black cords or vice versa for everyone, thus ensuring that everyone starts off on an equal footing. Others may designate certain colours for leaders of the group and other colours for trainees, while yet others will simply suggest that you are comfortable in what you wear. Many people will spend a great deal of time, energy and effort on fashioning suitable robes, and we suggest that you use sigils and symbols appropriate to your own beliefs.

The idea is that when working magically you leave behind the ordinary mundane world, so you will probably prefer to turn off mobile phones, put away keys and name tags and remove money from pockets and so on. It will be a matter of group preference as to whether you wear jewellery or not. In some circles, magical jewellery such as the pentagram, the ankh or rings with magical symbols or significance may be allowed while in others they are not. Many groups will not allow the use of watches, since time is considered irrelevant. It is often better not to use perfume or cologne unless it is based on essential oils which are suitable for the work in hand, or complement any incense being used.

RITUAL BATHING

Many practitioners prefer to take a ritual bath before performing any magical workings. You will probably develop your own routine, but below we show the basic sequences that can work very well.

Bath Salts

Commercial bath salts will do absolutely nothing on an esoteric level – they have too many chemical additives and artificial perfumes, so it is a nice touch to make your own using essential oils, blends such as those shown below and/or herbs. The fact that you have mixed them yourself means that they are infused with your own vibration and therefore will work on a very subtle level. Matching your bath salt perfume to your incense perfume will do wonders for your psyche.

On a slightly more practical level, bath salts with an esoteric theme are an effective and gentle way of introducing someone to the delights of ritual.

YOU WILL NEED
3 parts Epsom salts

2 parts baking soda

1 part rock salt (or borax)

Bowl for mixing

Essential Oils in your chosen perfumes

Handful of herbs (optional)

Natural food colouring

METHOD

Mix the first three ingredients thoroughly in the mixing bowl.
Use your hands as this will enable you to imbue the salts with your own energy.
This is your basic mixture and can be perfumed or coloured in any way
that you please.

Note: It is wise when using essential oils to mix them first if you are using a blend to allow the synergy between the oils to develop.

Add your colouring first and mix to your satisfaction, then follow with your oil or blend a
drop at a time.
Next add the herbs to the mixture and combine thoroughly.
Be generous with the oils since the salts will absorb a surprising amount.
Your nose, however, as with all oils and perfumes is the best judge – there is no right
or wrong amount.

If you wish to call upon one of the water gods, now is a good time to do so since you
should take your time in blending the ingredients.

When you wish to use your salts, add approximately 2 tablespoons to a full bathtub
and mix well.

Ritual Bath

If you are intending to take a ritual bath you should, as you mix in your salts, bless the water and charge it with your intent – be that a particular ritual, a relaxing evening or a successful meeting. In this ritual you will use candles. These can be in the colours of the Elements or the colours most appropriate to your purpose, for example – pink (peace and tranquillity), blue (wisdom), green (self-awareness) and red (passion). For spiritual matters, use purple.

YOU WILL NEED
Bath Salts
Votive candles according to your need
Large white candle
Essential oil to remove negativity, e.g. Rosemary
Large glass of mineral water or juice

METHOD
Anoint the large white candle with the essential oil and ask for positivity, health and happiness as you do so.
Do the same with the votive candles according to your need. You may, if you wish, inscribe a symbol to represent your purpose on each candle.

Run your bath and mix in the bath salts.

Light the candles, the white one first followed by the votives and place the latter safely around the bath. The white candle should be placed wherever you feel is safest. You have now created a sacred space.

Lie back and enjoy your bath and at some point drink your water or juice visualizing your whole system being cleansed inside as well as out.
Before you get out of the bath, thank the water deities for this opportunity to prepare thoroughly for the new energies available to you.
If you are to perform a ritual, then keep your mind focussed on that intent.

On this occasion, for safety's sake, when you have finished your bath, snuff out the candles.

OIL BLENDS

Many practitioners like to anoint themselves before enrobing for a ceremony, or working skyclad (naked), if that is their preference. When using oils in this way, you should always mix them in a good carrier such as almond or grapeseed oil.

The following two oil blends are especially appropriate for wearing at the time of the Sabbats (pagan festivals) because they promote communication with the deities.

Sabbat Oil

3 parts Patchouli

2 parts Musk

1 part Carnation

Sabbat Oil

2 parts Frankincense

1 part Myrrh

1 part Carnation

1 part Allspice

These next two oils can be used to anoint your body when you are to perform rituals at the time of the Full Moon, because they link you particularly with the energy of the Moon.

Full Moon Oil

4 parts Gardenia

2 parts Lotus

1 part Jasmine

Full Moon Oil

3 parts Sandalwood

2 parts Lemon

1 part Rose

Wear these next two oils if you wish to honour the Goddess and the Horned God during their specific rituals. They might also be used when working with the masculine/feminine balance, or at any time when you particularly wish to make a link with the receptivity of the feminine or the assertiveness of the masculine.

Goddess Oil

3 parts Rose

2 parts Gardenia

1 part Lemon

1 part Lotus

1 part Ambergris

Horned God Oil

2 parts Frankincense

2 parts Cinnamon

1 part Bay

1 part Rosemary

1 part Musk

The idea with ritual bathing is that you are in as pure a state as possible when performing rituals. The sacred space is obviously also a pure space and is therefore treated with a degree of reverence.

ENTERING THE SACRED SPACE

Personal preference often dictates the form that next follows. Some groups prefer that people simply acknowledge their own entry into the sacred space surrounding the altar, while others prefer to walk in procession into the sacred circle. In this case, no one should enter the sacred circle before the announced time. The moment of entry can be designated by the sounding of bell, a gong, rapping with a mallet or staff, or a musical or verbal announcement by the leaders.

Many groups follow the custom of entering the circle from the Northwest and circling the altar at least three times. Since many modern day groups are based on the principals of the Hermetic Order of the Golden Dawn it might be accepted that this follows the customs of the Masonic ritual on which that order is largely based. However there is a much older precedent which goes back to the veneration of the *ka'aba* or Holy stone of Mecca, which traditionally has been kissed or caressed during seven circumambulations.

This is a very powerful way of bringing a high degree of energy into a ritual area, so the altar or central point becomes the focal point of power. The circle represents the movement of Divine energy back towards itself as in the orobourus or snake which eats its own tail, representing eternal energy. In the continuous circling is suggested the spiral and the serpent. There are in fact two spirals in existence at this time, that of the participant's energy being drawn towards the divine and a second being drawn down from the spiritual realms to the physical or mundane. On page 218, when explaining spirals, we give a technique of protection which follows this principle. The labyrinths in old cathedrals, such as that at Chartres, are examples of the way that the spiral form has been used in mystical contemplative practices.

Chartres labyrinth

In group working, members often make three circuits of the altar, thus defining the magical circle, though more experienced practitioners will often make seven, designating one to each of the planetary spheres or states of awareness accessible to the practitioner of magic. From a spiritual point of view each planetary sphere holds within it more subtle energies which assist the soul in the journey back to source.

THE RITUAL PROPER

Whatever ritual has been agreed, the structure of it remains the same. Each ritual is required to have at least four parts:

1. An Opening, or general banishing of negativity.
2. An Invocation to the powers to be used.
3. A Meditation in order to focus the energies in the appropriate way.
4. A Closing of the sacred space and/or the release of the powers invoked.

These four parts can be made more complex according to training or belief. Additional steps which many consider necessary are shown in more detail below.

OUTLINING THE STEPS FOR A FORMAL CIRCLE
PROCESSING INTO POSITION

Part of the purpose of processing into position is to help people to concentrate on matters in hand and to leave behind the ordinary mundane world. In this case, tradition dictates that you enter from the north-west corner in single file. Usually those people who have least experience will proceed to the north-east corner, while those with the most ritualistic or esoteric experience will move to the south-east. Making a deliberate motion and peeling off at right angles is for many people a reminder of the idea of rightness and propriety and works within the framework of sacred geometry. Leaders of the group will enter after the members, and proceed to their given positions.

Whether you are working alone or with your own group of chosen people, your first act should always be to state the purpose of the gathering. Your form of words might be something like:

We are gathered here today to create a sacred space to enable us to call upon the gods in their many forms so that we may (state your purpose).

As time goes on, you will find that you develop your own form of words. This will depend on the discipline you choose to follow. For instance, Wiccans may call upon the Goddess, while those working with Egyptian magic may call upon Isis and Osiris.

The following steps indicate the more complex construction of a ritual.

FIRST STATEMENT OF INTENT: TO THE PARTICIPANTS

The purpose of this step is to ensure that everyone knows the intent of the ritual. This means that if anyone has any objections to that intent they may leave before the sacred space is created. Everyone has a right to know the general intent, although there is often no need for you to be aware of specifics unless you are leading the group. If everyone is not of one mind, or has any doubts or fears, then the energy generated cannot be as clear as you might wish. The intent is held to the forefront of the mind throughout the ritual.

Any necessary restrictions – such as that you cannot leave the circle once it is cast until it is closed or that you must not touch the ritualistic tools – should be made quite clear at this stage. The energies used in ritual work are very subtle and can be easily disturbed, particularly by those who do not know what they are doing. Now is also the time to inquire about such things as the use of wine and of incense or camphor, just in case people have respiratory problems or other difficulties.

CENTRING, GROUNDING AND ATTUNEMENT

Centring and grounding are techniques used in most magical systems and are designed firstly to help the concentration of the participants but secondly to withdraw your awareness from the ordinary, everyday world for the duration of the ritual. Thirdly, so that everybody is connected to and aware of the correct energies, both earthwise and spiritually, an act of attunement or atonement (literally 'at one with self') is made. All of these actions facilitate magical work.

In magical work, centring is a means of bringing attention to the ritual and its focus. You begin to turn your attention away from your daily routines using various methods, usually selected as appropriate by the leaders of the group. Starting with the body, everyone is taught how to bring their physical selves into alignment. This may be by learning how to stand in a relaxed manner on the balls and heels of the feet, 'shaking' out the limbs to achieve relaxation or by learning how to feel the energy moving through the body in particular ways. Breathing techniques are a good way of learning how to sense these energies. You are able to raise consciousness working with the chakras or with meditation and so become aware of the subtle energies in the body.

Grounding takes this process a step further and is a way of connecting with the subtle energies of the earth, the sun, the moon and astronomical bodies. One very natural way of grounding is through the guided Tree Meditation shown below. By this method you send 'roots' into the earth and 'branches' into the sky to make contact these energies and unite with them. When you use the image of the tree, you are of course connecting with the idea of Nature – competent magical workers who use these energies as their tools are able to perceive them and feel them in their bodies. The energies are often perceived as the different colours of the rainbow, by what some describe as an audible buzz or as light beams which are actually tangible.

Attunement is the process of connecting with your fellow participants in the circle. This can be done in a number of ways, but especially by holding hands and feeling the energy flow of the circle. Often this can lead to a ritualized dance and this creates a unified circle bringing the energies of the participants into alignment with one another. If your robes are fastened with cords, the cords may be used to form links around, or across, the circle.

Preferably you should finish this part of the ceremony with a few moments of quiet meditation, making mental and psychic links with the others in the group. Indeed for many, as they become more practised, this simple act may be sufficient. Remember too that you are also making your own personal link with your helpers and guides within the spiritual realms.

MEDITATION

An apple may be used as an aid to meditation, since it is seen as a small version of a larger world – a microcosm within a macrocosm. It is the symbol of the Maiden aspect of the Triple Goddess or Persephone, daughter of Demeter the Earth Mother. In the centre of the apple is the five-fold star, which represents the four Elements of Earth, Air, Fire, Water plus the Spirit. This represents the World and ourselves. For the purposes of this meditation technique we shall use the apple and its tree.

Tree Meditation

The apple tree and its fruit represent the magical circle – a group of celebrants; it is also the cycle of birth, death and regeneration. In the seed we may perceive our birth; with the fruit we maintain our lives; as the tree decays we see death. The roots of the tree suggest stability and symbolize our beginnings, the branches epitomize enlightenment and represent many systems of belief. The trunk is the single unifying force that holds everything together.

In this meditation, you shift your perception from contemplating the apple to sensing the energy and finally visualizing yourself becoming the tree. This gives you an empathy with nature.

YOU WILL NEED
Apple

METHOD
Cut the apple in half horizontally.

Begin by contemplating the seed of the apple.
Packed within that tiny seed is the potential of the large tree it will become.
Sense that potential, see it as power, as movement, as energy waiting to become.
Now visualize the tree as it begins to grow.

Shift your perception to the energy of the tree, feel it growing as it draws on the power around it to become stronger, to grow and unfold.
Feel as the energy begins to send roots down into the earth, reaching, seeking, growing out and away from the original point of power (its seed).

Feel the energy also reaching upwards, upwards towards the light, seeking warmth and sustenance, unfurling, uncurling, becoming stronger by the second.
Now as the energy of your middle section, your trunk, begins to lengthen and to grow, become aware of the power that is present.

Your roots are reaching further and further into the earth, stabilizing your whole structure, allowing you to stand firm and yet having knowledge of the earth.
Your branches are beginning to unfold – every experience adding to the strength

of the tree – yet flexible in the wind as it blows, bending and twisting to gain
the best advantage.
The trunk is becoming firmer and firmer and more at peace with its place in the world.

Now, in passing, note the nurturing that goes on through the roots, the stability of the
known world, the energy which runs throughout, this time reaching up into the leaves.
Hear the rustle of the leaves as they communicate.
Sense the light and the power that is still to be gained, and begin to reach out beyond
your own framework towards that light.
Feel yourself growing larger, expanding, and able to take in more and more from the
light above but still firmly grounded in the earth below.

Feel the energy from above now meeting the energy from below. Both are changed,
both enhanced, so allow the combined energy to grow till it can go no further.
At this point begin to allow the excess energy to flow down into the roots and out into
the land around.
Let the energy flow until you feel balanced, poised between Land and Sky, Heaven
and Earth, spiritual and physical.
Now truly you stand between two worlds.

PURIFYING, SMUDGING, ASPERGING AND ANOINTING

When working in groups, the preparation of the ritual area is extremely important. You will probably choose not to do all of these at every ritual, but a full, formal ritual particularly if there are large numbers of people present, will include all of them.

Purifying means that you will purify the space in which you build your circle, if you have not already done so in the earlier preparation of the sacred space by, for example, sweeping it with a consecrated broom. Keep your words simple and concentrate on the matter in hand. You might say:

As this place is swept free of contamination within the physical realm so may it be cleansed of negative influence for what we do tonight.

You may also wish to use a simple brushing technique to clear your own aura (subtle energies). To do this, bring your hands up in an arc above your head. Then, keeping them about four to six inches away from your body, bring your hands down in a sweeping movement.

Some may wish to shake their hands at the end of this movement with the idea of shaking away the negative; others may simply drop them. Repeat this action as many times as you think necessary.

Smudging means sanctifying with the elements of fire and air, most often with incense in the form of a sage brush or stick incense, though it can be done with a lit firebrand if wished. (One of the modern garden flares works very well for this purpose in a large open space.) Again, choose simple words appropriate for the method used.

Asperging means blessing the ritual area and the participants with the elements of water and earth. This is most often done by adding salt (which represents earth) to water and sprinkling both the space and the people with this mixture. You might say something straightforward, such as:

Blessings be upon this place and the people who work therein.

Anointing means to consecrate the bodies of the participants by applying blessed oil, water, earth or perhaps the ash from a smudge or incense stick to the forehead, repeating a particular form of words such as:

I consecrate this body in the service of all that is good in preparation for the work to be done.

You may also wish to anoint your ritual tools if you use them.

INVOCATION OF THE GUARDIAN(S) OF THE THRESHOLD OR OPENING THE GATES

In magical working, opening a circle is, in many ways, also an opening of the gates between the ordinary mundane world and the world of spirit, but sometimes it is easier to think of opening the gates and invoking the guardians as two separate activities. There are times within ordinary everyday life for instance when, as an individual, you may wish to place a circle of protection or power around yourself but do not need to call upon the Guardians for help.

Let us assume that you have had a difficult day at work, but still need to remain alert and focussed into the evening. This might be a good time to create a circle or ring of protection around yourself so that you do not get irritated by the people around you, but also have enough energy to carry out your chosen activities. Your circle of protection acts as a buffer between you and your world.

When you are working in a group, the circle may have already been created for you but, once you are in position, joining in a ceremony designed to call upon those beings and entities who guard the threshold between this dimension and others gives the opportunity to ask for assistance only from those who can be of specific assistance in this particular working. You may like to think of it as seeking permission to enter an area of special significance within the magical or spiritual realms.

These Guardians of the Threshold are there to protect you as much as they protect the gates between the dimensions – it would be unwise to let someone loose who did not know what the rules of conduct are. By asking for the Gates to be opened you are indicating your willingness to be aware of your responsibilities, of your calling. Invoking the Guardians means that you are calling on gods such as Ganesh, who guarded his mother's bedchamber, Janus, who looks both ways, Forcelus who protects the door and Limentinus who protects the threshold. You might also call on the goddess Juno whose sacred geese warned of danger. You will find that you have a certain empathy with some gods rather than others.

Making sure that you obtain the cooperation of such power is a sort of double insurance that you are taking care and being fully aware when entering into magical consciousness. You are opening a doorway through which not just the Gods, but also those spirits and elemental energies with which you need to work, can enter into your sacred space. Rather than a polite request, you may prefer to use a command, so your invocation might be along these lines:

We call upon the guardians of the threshold who stand at the doorway between this world and the next to guard and protect us and to hear our request to Open the Door.

If you wish to be a little more theatrical, you may rap on the floor three times with your staff. Theatricality is in many ways an intrinsic part of magic and allows you to use your own creativity in a very individual way.

Invoking the Guardians

This is a ritual which is also somewhat theatrical but gives a great boost to the energy within the circle when performed properly. It can be done both on an individual basis for private ritual or in a group.

YOU WILL NEED

Incense in burner (Air)

Lit candle (Fire)

Chalice containing water (Water)

Salt in small bowl (Earth)

METHOD

If you use an altar, you will already have prepared it for a ritual.

Otherwise have a safe surface within your sacred space.

Before saying each invocation verse, face in the appropriate direction.

Start with East for the first verse, South for the second, West for the third and finally North for the final verse.

First, address the Guardians of the East as follows:

Awaken, all you along the watchtower, you protectors of the east.
I ask for your protective arms to shield me in this ritual.
Come forth on autumn's final falling gasps that, all at once, catch the strong winter breezes that now blast away the harvest season.
Stir my spirit with life's own spirit.
Let it be, O Guardians.

Then pick up the incense burner which symbolizes the element of air.

Say (speaking as the spirit of Air):

I am all things. I am universal.
I breathe in everything.
I shimmer through secret glade and triumphant forests.
I am the storm and the shelter. Without me you would perish.
I am your keeper. Is this not praiseworthy?

Return the incense burner to the altar.

Address the Guardians of the South as follows:

Awaken, all you along the watchtower, you protectors of the south.
I ask for your protective arms to shield me in this ritual.
Crackle forth from the fireside and shining lamps of the homely heartlands where food
and shelter is being prepared to defend against the oncoming ice storm.
Rouse my soul within the flames of spiritual awareness.
Let it be, O Guardians.

Pick up the candle which symbolizes the element of fire.

Say (speaking as the spirit of fire):

I dwell in the sparks of dying fires. I am the light on the Golden Pathway.
I arise from the crack of thunder and from the power of man's two hands.
I can make you glow. I enlighten you. I can extinguish you.
Without me you would perish. I am your keeper. Is this not praiseworthy?

Place the candle on the altar.

Awaken, all you along the watchtower, you protectors of the west.
I ask for your protective arms to shield me in this ritual.
Come forth from the crisp morning where the pearly dewdrops fall and sink
into frosty fields.
Envelope me with diamonds and saturate my most deepest core,
that I may find Paradise.

Pick up the chalice that symbolizes the element of water.

Say (speaking as the spirit of water):

I surface from the moist hidden and sacred Earth.
I slowly lap the smooth shores of her body or else rage against her,
breaching the pure lagoon.
I come from the sky like tears in the rain. I soothe you. I can drown you.
Without me you would perish. I am your keeper. Is this not praiseworthy?

Put the chalice on the altar.

Awaken, all you along the watchtower, you protectors of the north.
I ask for your protective arms to shield me in this ritual.
Come forth from glowing breast of our Blessed Mother Earth
Provide me with the nourishment so that my dreams may breathe, may sing,
and grow strong.
Let it be, O Guardians.

Pick up the salt that symbolizes the element of Earth.
Say (speaking as the spirit of Earth):

I am your Mother. From me comes all that you need to exist, to live and develop.
I keep you safe from the howling wind. I am your harbour in the morning storm.
You are my heaven as I am Atlas.
Without me you would perish. I am your keeper. Is this not praiseworthy?

Place the salt on the altar.

Now stand quietly recognizing your own spirit, that you are now
complete. Give thanks for the gifts of spirit and say

I give thanks to all,
Praiseworthy it is.

Continue with whatever is the appropriate ritual for the occasion.

135

CREATING THE CIRCLE

When you create or cast a circle, you form a temple of energy within the ritual arena. You will have begun the consecration by walking the circumference of the circle, if you have already processed into position. You may feel that the process of attunement is sufficient to create a simple circle. It will depend upon the beliefs of the participants whether you the wish use a particular tool such as your sword or staff to help you create your circle. (In a more formal framework, you may wish to trace the circle on the ground or to delineate it with stones or flowers.)

If you like, think of this circle as a protective barrier which encloses you, your colleagues and your magical world as you carry out your ritual duties. Equally, it forms a barrier which allows you to build up a focus of contained magical energy which cannot be penetrated from the ordinary mundane world unless an invitation is issued, nor can the energy escape unless it is directed by a competent practitioner. It is thus a small world of itself for the duration of the ritual or procedure. For this reason, creative visualization is a tool which can be used by all participants to create a dome of the appropriate colour and texture, a space surrounded by flame or by a moat of water, or – particularly in working out of doors – a dome of vegetation. If you are leading the group, you might make suggestions as to the basic form appropriate for the task to be performed, but should always allow participants freedom to be spontaneous.

Ideally, once the circle is cast, no one should leave until the ritual is finished. Should it be necessary, then there are usually appropriate procedures or conventions that you must observe. Permission is asked of the leader or high priest/priestess who will then cut a doorway in the barrier to allow someone to pass through. Always remember that manipulating the circle in this way is not a good idea, since it takes energy away from the purpose in hand and weakens the protection. Try if you can to spend a few moments rebuilding the energy to its previous level before continuing. The following ritual demonstrates very well the construction of a simple circle, thus giving the participants a sense of occasion.

Basic Ritual Using the Created Circle for Honouring the Goddess

Whether you subscribe to the idea of the feminine principle, the moon as Goddess or the Goddess in the sense of Mother Nature, this ritual will serve all of these purposes.

To mark your circle you might use consecrated stones, ribbon or any other material suitable. You could, for instance, mark each quarter with a branch of sacred wood, in which case the candles could be placed on these. Suitable surfaces for your altar when working outside might be a rock or a tree stump.

YOU WILL NEED

Circle marker

Altar or sacred surface

Preferred image of the Goddess

Applicable incense

Incense burner

Willow wand (if used)

Five white candles

METHOD

Mark your circle on the ground or floor. Make sure it is large enough to include all participants.

Set up your altar at the centre of your circle.

Place the image of the Goddess in the middle of the altar with the incense and incense burner in front.

If using the willow wand, place it behind the image.

Light the incense.

Place the candles on the altar, four to be placed North, South, East and West. The final one should be placed in the centre of the altar at the front and lit.

Now say:

3. PROCEDURES AND PROTOCOL OF RITUAL

The power of the Goddess extends throughout the world,
Through magic and beauty, both new and old.
Enchantment and freedom are within her gift,
We gather to honour and praise her.

In the north, take a candle from the altar, light it from the central candle then place it at that quarter.
Facing outwards, say

The Goddess is splendid,
The cycle of regeneration is hers to command.

In the east, take a candle from the altar, light it from the central candle then place it at that quarter.
Facing outwards, say:

The Goddess is a Lady of Ecstacy,
The winds do her bidding.

In the south take a candle from the altar, light it from the central candle and place it at that quarter.
Facing outwards, say:

Our Goddess is ardent.
Through her, the sun brings new life.

In the west take a candle from the altar, light it from the central candle and place it at that quarter.
Facing outwards, say:

Our Goddess owns the depth of the sea,
And to her belongs all mystery.

Then take the wand – or use your extended forefinger – and starting at the north, trace an entire circle in the air clockwise finishing up at the north point, saying:

Seal this circle, so all therein
Are held apart from the world mundane.
Let us glorify the Goddess whom we adore.

Now acknowledge the North for a moment and say the following:

As above, so below.
As the universe, so the soul.
As within, so without.

Great and gracious one,
At this time we dedicate to you
Our bodies,
Our minds,
And our spirits.
So be it.

Stand for a few moments in silence and usually you will find that a subject for consideration at this time will come to the minds of the participants.
If you wish, now is a good time to serve some light refreshments.
When you have completed the purpose of the meeting, start at the north and snuff out the candles while moving clockwise around the circle.
While you are doing this, say:

Our rite now is ended
Graceful and benevolent Goddess,
Accompany us as we leave this place.
The circle is withdrawn.

Do not forget to leave the area tidy. If you performed your ritual outside, and if you wish, also thank the nature spirits.

CALLING THE QUARTERS AND THE CENTRE

As can be seen in the above rituals, the elemental powers of the four directions or quarters are usually needed when we perform magic, particularly when we wish to achieve an important work You will probably find that your own group has its own traditions in this. As we see elsewhere, the four worlds manifested in a certain order; Fire, Air, Water and finally Earth, and magical procedures should strictly follow this for perfect manifestation. However, over the years in different traditions, diverse methods have been put forward, so if working alone you must find which suits you best, and if working in a group you will follow given practice. We call the quarters clockwise, starting with the East.

The East represents the Elemental Air, helps give to give us clarity of vision and purpose and represents intellectual power. You would appeal to this element principally in any working to do with the mind – when studying for exams perhaps or when you need inspiration for new projects.

The South is the realm of Fire, the most potent of all of the Elements. It signifies the purifying element in nature, that which consumes all others; through it, mastery of the other three is achieved. It is dynamic force, purification and passion, and is perceived as the Inner Guardian of the Temple. You will use this element in your workings when you need creativity, cleansing or protection from malevolent energy.

The West stands for all those watery things like our psychic and emotional nature so, of course, it represents the element of Water, though it should be remembered that within that representation lies both depth and movement. The qualities are often seen as passive, and feminine, but would be appealed to particularly when removing hexes and curses or when revitalizing is important.

The North gives us the solidity of Earth which in turn allows us to manifest the results of our work. It nourishes and grounds us, giving a solid basis from which to create. While it is a complex element containing within it aspects of all the previous ones, it also shows simplicity to enable us to gain access to greater energy which comes from the Ultimate. You would use this Element to create tangibility and stability as well as for issues to do with fertility and productiveness.

Lastly, the Centre is called. This is the realm of Aether or Spirit and is both the synthesis of all four of the other elements and their progenitor. In calling on Spirit you are calling upon all that is, was and shall be and therefore an energy of high vibration. For this reason it is usually best that the centre is called by a high priest or priestess or at least by someone who has been properly initiated and trained. Spirit manifests in so many different ways that often only someone versed in the process will recognize what is happening.

There are many ways to call quarters and, as with other ritual steps, you might try to ensure that one which is particularly appropriate to the intended ritual is chosen. We have suggested that the Centre is called by the leader, but other functions may be performed by any of the other participants. It is usually best if the words come spontaneously, since learning how to speak intuitively is an integral part of magical training. Over a period, everyone should be able to take their turns at all four quarters in order to experience the different energies and be able to be balanced in the work undertaken. You might finish this step by acknowledging that you stand between the physical and spiritual worlds, where true magic belongs. Whatever happens there has an effect on everything.

INVITATION TO THE ANCESTORS AND ALLIES

This step is not always carried out. It will depend on the leaders of the ritual, whether they deem it necessary and whether it is treated as a separate step or combined with calling the invocation of the deities.

The ancestors of the tradition, of the place and of the participants involved are invited to join the circle. Ancestors are asked that they come only if they mean no harm, and will assist in the ritual work. Allies are invited to lend their energies and are there to aid in particular causes, so you might call on the spirits of the forest in an anti-pollution ritual for instance. You might say:

Hail and Welcome, you Ancestors and Allies. Come in friendship, and join us in our task. Lend us your power here today we pray as we fulfil our charge of cleansing the Earth.

BANISHING EVIL

This step has a two-fold purpose and today might be better named 'banishing negativity'. It was practised in ancient ritual forms to ensure that the sacred space was truly sacred and without evil. It is used to get rid of any unwanted psychic forces with which we may have become contaminated in our day-to-day life. Evil is dismissed by a simple form of words, such as:

Evil, depart now this sacred space.

You may also like to follow a very ancient aspect of this action and throw an offering or libation outside the circle to keep the evil forces away. You might also choose to use noise – rattles, drums, horns and voice – to help negativity on its way. This is also a time to recognize within ourselves the reality of negativity and to let such negativity go. If you wish to work with a personalization of evil at this time it is easy to do so and banish that.

INVOCATION OF THE DEITIES

In this, the most important step, the Gods – or your concept of Ultimate Power – are invited into the ritual space. Always call on the Gods with a tone of respect. Act as though you are welcoming an honoured guest into your home You can do this in many ways, using prayer, music, dance or other gestures. If you use the concept of Ultimate Power, you perhaps should remember that you may still call on the Gods as intermediaries between you and that power. You can then use your favourite God or Goddess. A form of words might be:

Power of the Gods, I call upon you now, in the name of [favourite deity] to honour this ritual.
In turn we honour you and offer our allegiance.

You may, if you wish, appeal directly to your own Gods or Goddesses, for example:

Freya, Goddess of love of the Norse people, we come to you now and ask you to bless this rite.

Do make sure that your Gods are appropriate for your own system of belief, or to the magical task at hand. As the energies build up and the deities draw closer, you should become aware of a change of energy and you can hold yourself ready for some kind of meaningful interchange, whether that is an increase in your awareness of other realms, new information or a sense of presence of your deities. All are equally valid.

THE CAVEAT

In this step, we make it plain that we are aware that we are human – we ask forgiveness for any offence we might cause and for any mistakes we inadvertently make in the ritual. In many ways this is a type of insurance and is akin to prostration in the Judeo-Christian tradition, a sort of *mea culpa* ('it is my fault'). It will depend on your mindset whether you consider that you are taking responsibility for your actions or are passing the buck. You might say:

> *O Holy Ones, we come before thee in humility admitting our faults and asking thy indulgence in all that we do.*

SECOND STATEMENT OF INTENT: TO THE SPIRITS AND DEITIES

You should now re-state the purpose of your ritual as the Gods and spirits have graced us with their presence. Do not make this statement too ornate, but do be focussed in your intent. The statement can be repeated by all those present, or, if spoken by the leader, the other participants must channel their energy through him or her or through the words themselves. Carefully chosen words can considerably enhance the ritual.

WELCOMING THE DEITIES: LIBATIONS AND OFFERINGS

Offerings are made at this stage, partially to acknowledge the presence of the Gods but also to recognize their generosity. Such offerings may include foodstuffs, wine or other beverages. At this time creativity – the offering of any artefact, song, prayer or poem – is also a suitable gift for the Gods and may be performed at this time if you feel it is appropriate and that it would be pleasing to the invited Gods. Offerings are made at the centre of the circle and may be poured upon the earth or burned in a fire.

MAGIC RITUAL OR WORKINGS

This is the most important part of the whole process. It is completely unfixed in that it will change with the season, sabbat, or intent behind the ritual or indeed the needs of the participants. Having already raised the vibration of the sacred space, it must be raised even further by whatever means are appropriate for the group. Some will choose meditation, others will use singing, chanting, music and so on. When the energy is at a sufficient level, as judged by the more experienced members of the circle, it is time to discharge it through the performance of the chosen rite. At this time transformation (change) can take place and often is felt as a distinct change in vibration. When the ceremony is over, it is important to allow any excess energy to return to the earth. This can be done by allowing the energy to stream back into the earth through the soles of your feet or by placing your hands upon the ground.

BLESSING AND CONSUMPTION OF CAKES AND WINE

This involves the blessing of a beverage and cakes. The use of the chalice honours the feminine principle and the Earth Mother and, if you choose to use an athame, you can re-enact the spiritual marriage, the union of the Upper and Lower Waters. You signify this by elevating the chalice and symbolically either inserting an athame into the chalice when consecrating the beverage or visualizing a shaft of light or energy striking the chalice from above. This symbolizes a basic polarity, but the recognition that polarity dissolves into Unity. It also symbolizes mystical union and the fruits of mystical union that are shared with community.

The consumption of the cakes is an avowal of community. The blessed beverage and food are shared, clockwise, around the circle, either from hand to hand or being passed back to the leader each time. You may include appropriate words such as:

Let us share our bounty.

It is nice in group situations for the cakes and beverage to be provided by a different person each time so no-one feels put upon. Consumption of the blessed foodstuffs is an act of worship and was commemorated in the Last Supper. Such an act reminds us of our membership of a cosmic Unity (community); that though we are all individuals we are also part of a Greater Whole.

DEVOCATION OF THE DEITIES

In this step we thank and send the Deities away. You must never command them but always remember that they are there by choice. Hence we address them accordingly. You might say:

Remain if it pleases you, go in peace. Hail and Farewell Ye Gods.

Perhaps the easiest way to think of this, and indeed the next few steps, is to envisage those from other dimensions and levels of existence processing out of the sacred space in order of seniority. Thus, those deities who have graced us by their presence leave first. You may address each god or goddess individually if you wish. This idea of hierarchy may help to explain why magicians sometimes succeed at magic and at other times fail.

DISMISSAL OF ALLIES AND ANCESTORS AND OF THE QUARTERS

In this part of the ritual, the allies and ancestors are thanked and bidden a fond farewell. There is, however, a note of caution to be sounded. The idea of something or someone else doing the necessary work for us is a very materialistic approach to magic. The Allies and ancestors are invited to lend their support, not to do the work. They should therefore be acknowledged in this way and then asked to leave. The words used might be:

Friends and ancestors we thank you for your support and assistance.
Go now in peace to your rest.

As the practitioner becomes more proficient, and after experiencing the reality and illusions of other astral worlds, a direct – or more personal – relationship is built up in which the magician sees the powers being directed as aspects of his or her self, and not as an exterior force. This realization belongs to the level of the adept and mystic.

The elemental and directional powers are also thanked and sent back whence they came. Some practitioners choose to do it in reverse order – a sort of unwinding of the circle. Others continue to work clockwise. The ritual overleaf is one that can be adapted to your own use.

Dismissal of the Powers

This technique is used to send the Elements and their powers back from whence they came. Again, it is one of those things that will depend on your original belief or teaching as to how you do it. This particular ritual attributes the cardinal points as follows; South is Air, North is Fire, East is Water and West is Earth but you must take care to follow your own instincts and do what works for you.

Dismissing the powers acknowledges their presence and their help and also asks a blessing. The words 'Blessed be', should you choose to use them, are particularly Wiccan in origin and you, of course, may substitute any appropriate words for yourself.

Note: These words should be said with some passion.

Northern Passion
You lyrical fire dwellers, keepers of white light, lords of the burning dominions,
We thank you for your presence, your guardianship and your power.
We say farewell, leave us in tranquil peace,
Blessed be.

Water of Eastern Mystery
You charged, passionate, watery beings.
You sentinels of river, sea and lakes of feeling.
Rulers of the deep, the hidden chasms, the watery veils,
We thank you for your presence, your guardianship and your worship.
We say farewell, leave us in tranquil peace,
Blessed be.

Lo! Southern Vital,
Greatest of energies, who swirls and dances through air.
Protectors of the upper realms and reaches,
We thank you for your presence, your guardianship and your ecstasy.
We say farewell, leave us in tranquil peace,
Blessed be.

Lo! Western Intensity,
Beings of strength and constancy,
Earth guardians of all cherished stones and metals,
Nobles of the lower reaches and of Persephone's garden,
We thank you for your presence, your guardianship and your permanence.
We say farewell, leave us in tranquil peace,
Blessed be.

Dismissal of the Centre and the Guardian(s) of the Threshold

At this stage you should acknowledge the presence of Aether and Spirit in your circle. Once again it will be according to your basic discipline how this is done. Were you truly dismissing Spirit you would probably be causing complete chaos, so you should remember to dismiss from this ritual only! You might say:

Great and glorious Spirit of All who holds together the fabric of the universe.
We thank thee for your presence here today and ask for your guidance and protection
as we return to our earthly tasks.

The Guardian(s) are also thanked and bidden farewell. If formality was used initially then they should be dismissed in the same way, but a full-blown ritual is not needed. In the case of the ritual suggested you might say, for instance,

All you along the watchtowers: Fire, Earth, Air and Water

Turn in each direction as you do this, then say:

We thank you for your presence,
We bid you farewell.

Note: We have differentiated between the dismissal of the centre and the guardians and the dismissal of the powers, though in some ways these can be considered to be similar.

CLOSING THE CIRCLE

In this step, the celebrant who cast the circle closes it. A simple way of doing this is to use a single slicing action, either with the athame, wand or hand, and visualize the energy being drawn back through the instrument into the spiritual realms. Each participant may reverse the visualization they used to build up the energy initially to help in this process. Though the leader acts on behalf of the group it is an interactive process.

The leader then may touch the earth with their tool or hand while visualizing the energy of the circle returning to the Earth. A good way to make use of any residual energy is to project it to an appropriate target such as one of the world's trouble spots. The leader then says something like:

Our deeds are done, the circle closed. May our work be blessed.

Note: Experienced practitioners, particularly in a teaching group, might hold themselves available to answer questions or help beginners. Members of the group should not go straight from ritual work into the outside world but should be given time to re-orientate themselves. Refreshments, entertainment and social activities are all a good idea to help with this process.

Not everybody chooses to make use of magical tools, but for those who do wish to enhance their magical workings in this way there are various methods of infusing them with power and energy. Throughout this book, we have attempted to keep all processes as open as possible so that practitioners of many persuasions can adapt the words and actions according to their own belief system.

MAGICAL TOOLS AND IMPLEMENTS

As you will have seen we have, in many of the rituals so far, mentioned tools such as the athame, wand, chalice or candles to help in some of our rites. Some disciplines will use many such tools, others only a few. As always, you will be aware of what works for you and will want to learn more about your own tradition's ways. In nature based religions the tools used are relatively easy to obtain, and since as magical practitioners we can use what is available in both the spiritual and physical worlds we also include the 'tools of the mind' – dreaming, meditation, prayer and the siddhis (powers) – in the next section.

Generally, most magical systems in practice use one or all of the objects that we show below.

OBJECTS FOR CONSECRATION

You will find that you tend to use some objects more than others – some fit more comfortably with your personality. We give below a list of the ones that people most like to use.

Altar Objects

The objects that you place on your altar – candle holders, flower vases, crystals and so on – should be dedicated to the purpose in hand by presenting them to your chosen deity.

Athame

By tradition, the athame is a ceremonial knife used especially in the making of spells. It had to be of the best and purest metal possible, and many witches consider that the most powerful athame is one which has been inherited. Its handle is usually black and sometimes carved with occult designs and symbols.

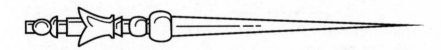

Besom

Another name for a broom, the besom is particularly associated with the 'witch's broom' of old. It is often made specifically for the practitioner, from twigs from the tree of her choice. Like most tools, it is usually kept specifically for the use in the sacred space or circle – this time for cleansing – and is used both symbolically and spiritually as much as physically.

Candles

Candles are such an integral part of the practitioners work that they have become a whole branch of magic all their own. They represent the element of fire, but also light. By varying the colour, they can become an important part of any ritual.

Cauldron

A cauldron of old was usually thought of as a large cast-iron pot. Nowadays they can be made of almost anything and are often of a size that can be stood on the altar. Used as containers for herbs and other magical objects, the cauldron is symbolically associated with the womb.

Chalice

A ceremonial drinking vessel, the chalice is often made from precious metal and is highly decorated. Such decoration may be intricate designs of occult significance or gemstones which have an esoteric meaning.

Pentacle

The pentacle is a shallow dish which is usually inscribed with a pentagram – a five-pointed star. It is used as a 'power point' for consecrating other objects such as water or wine in a chalice, amulets and tools.

Scrying tools

Scrying is the practice of using certain channelling tools – such as crystals, mirrors, coloured water, runes etc – to try to gain an insight into external events around the viewer. Usually, they are made use of by employing the art of concentration and contemplation. The objects used should be consecrated before use.

Staff

The staff directly relates to the wand and has the same attributes and uses. Staves are used very frequently by practitioners today, particularly if they are of the Druidic persuasion. The staff is fashioned from wood taken from sacred trees.

Wand

The wand should be no longer than the forearm and is often made from sacred wood. Since this is a very personal object, it should be chosen carefully and equally carefully attuned to your own energies.

Magical practitioners like to keep their tools entirely separate from ordinary everyday objects. Just as a circle is created to give the practitioner sacred space, so tools are dedicated for the task in hand and are kept for nothing else. If a tool has been used for a mundane purpose then it will be of no use in magical workings; it would ideally have to be replaced or at least cleansed thoroughly and re-dedicated.

Consecration or dedication consists of the preparation, purification and presentation of your objects. You may prepare and purify your tools by soaking them overnight in salt water or by standing them in sunshine or moonlight. This creates the right vibration. You can then use creative visualization (which we explain fully later) to further enhance the connection between you and the object being consecrated.

Here, you hold each object and allow your own energy to pass into the object concerned. Really make an effort to establish a link with it and allow its energy to flow back towards you. When this stage feels complete, allow the energy of Ultimate Power, whatever you consider that to be, also to flow into the object. Perceive yourself as being truly a medium or channel for that Ultimate Power and know that every time you pick up any of your tools that you are performing a sacred task. This obviously means that anything you do must be carefully considered and done only for the greater good. (You may build into your dedication a wish that anything you do that is not within your moral integrity will not succeed.)

There are many ways of consecrating tools, and often the simplest methods are the best. A well thought our prayer may suffice. In the pagan traditions, objects used in rituals are consecrated by presenting them first to the four quarters or points and finally to the Goddess and God. Those practitioners who feel the need to honour the cardinal points will recognize the significance of incense as representing Air in the East, the candle representing Fire in the South, Water signifying its own element in the West with salt or earth symbolizing the Earth in the North.

This next ritual, which is only one method of consecration, can be used to consecrate your magical tools or altar objects and with a little adaptation might also be used to consecrate or dedicate such items as personal jewellery or magical gifts (for example, crystals).

Tool Consecration

YOU WILL NEED
Incense
White candle
Small bowl of water
Small bowl of salt or earth
Your chosen tool

METHOD
Cast your circle.
Ask for a blessing on the articles representing the quarters.
Place the symbols in the appropriate directions.

Pick up the object to be consecrated.
Concentrate on the goals you want to achieve and the actions that you want to carry out then say:

Before you wandering spirits,
I bring this [name tool]
May its benefits be devoted to the work of the Lady and Lord.

Light the incense and waft the object through the incense smoke.
Say:

By force of Air, be purified.
Be devoted to clarity.
May all aspirations be realized for the greater good of all.

Then, having lit the candle, pass the instrument through the flicker of the flame and say the following:

By the power of the dancing light, be purified.
Be devoted to longing.
May all aspirations be realized for the greater good of all.

Sprinkle a few drops of water onto the chosen implement and say:

By the power of Neptune's domain, be purified.
Be devoted to waves of ardour.
May all aspirations be realized for the greater good of all.

Next, take the implement and bring it to the earth or salt and say:

By the power of earth and dust be purified.
Be devoted to resolute intent.
May all aspirations be realized for the greater good of all.

This ritual has two parts; the first honouring the four directions and the second the presentation to the Goddess and the God. Now you must present the implement for consecration by the Goddess and the God.

Presentation to the Goddess and God

Normally when consecrating objects, the chalice is presented to the Goddess first because it is a symbol of femininity, then presented to the God. The athame, by contrast, is presented to the God first because it represents the masculine. The presentation of all other objects is a matter of choice and will depend on your own personal preference. It is often considered preferable to present to the Goddess first. Below are specific invocations used to present the chalice and the athame.

Presentation of the Chalice

Hold your chalice towards the sky in both hands and say:

O beauteous Lady, shower sanctity upon this chalice.
May it be a vessel for activity and achievement, and so appear worthy of your omnipresence.
May it be so constrained that no harm results.
To your service, O Lady, I devote this chalice, that we both shall long in your reverence, serve.

Then say:

O magnificent Lord, sanctify this chalice so that it brings delight and clarity.
Protect the dealings which pour from it that no thing be harmed.
May it be dedicated to thee and thy beauteous Lady, may it serve thee well.
So let it be.

Presentation of the Athame

Hold your athame towards the sky in both hands and say:

O Great Lord, bless this athame.
May it be forever unsullied, bound to your greatness so that no thing be harmed.
O my Lord, bless this athame.
May it be used only for the good and glory of the One,
One heart, one hope, one love.

Then say:

O Beauteous Lady, bless this athame.
May it be untainted in thy service, dedicated to your goodness, harming none.
O my Lady, bless this athame.
May it be used only for the good and glory of the One.
Great Lord and Lady, so let it be.

Now close your circle.

Your most important tools and objects are now ready for use in your magical workings. The two objects above are perhaps the most easily recognizable and well-known magical tools. However, wands are so traditionally tied up with magic that many people will consider the wand to be more important than the athame and chalice.

WANDS

This magical tool is portable and does not require an altar or sacred space for operation. Wands can obviously be purchased, but for those who prefer to work with the energies of nature it is often nice to make your own. For those of you who do wish to use a wand, here is a way of making one of your own using natural materials.

Making a Wand

YOU WILL NEED

Fallen tree branch or a piece of wood that is a comfortable size for you

(Choose one of the sacred woods if you can, or you might use a suitable shard of rock or crystal if that suits you better)

Boline (a white-handled, ritual knife for harvesting herbs woods and cutting them) or any sharp knife

Anointing oil

Coloured cord or ribbons in the colours of the rainbow.

Any decorations which have a magical or special significance for you.

METHOD

Using the knife, scrape off any bark or protuberances from the wood.

Now bearing in mind the purpose for which you require the wand, anoint it with the oil.

Do this as thoroughly as you can from tip to base to draw down the power then from base to tip to make a link with the powers of the Earth Mother and finally from the middle to both ends to make the energies available to you.

If you have time, then it is nice to cover the whole wand with the coloured cords, but it does not matter if you do not.

At least bind the end which you will hold.

Decorate the wand according to your own fancy or intuition. Try to include a crystal tip if you can and glue it securely into place.

When you have completed it to your satisfaction, consecrate it according to the ritual above, after which your wand is now ready for use.

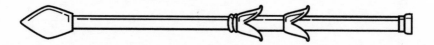

SCRYING TOOLS

Scrying tools are used in the development of clairvoyance – seeing the past, the future and understanding the present. Scrying requires concentration and so you need an object to focus your mind. Before you use any tool for scrying, you may like to prepare your own incense for use while you work. Unfortunately, the scrying incense is not very pleasant smelling, but it does do its job very well. Use it in very small amounts.

Scrying Incense

1 part Mugwort

1 part Wormwood

Crystal Ball

Another of the best known artefacts used by magical practitioners is the crystal ball. Your crystal ball, which will usually be made of clear quartz, can be of any size. Many people feel that it is better if it has been a gift, although nowadays it may be enough to use money which has been given to you to purchase one. Your crystal ball is an intensely personal object, so do choose carefully. Usually you will find yourself drawn to one particular ball, and if you pick it up it will seem to pulsate slightly. When you are not using it, tradition decrees that you should keep it covered with its own velvet cloth, although many people prefer to have it visible either on their altar or in their sacred space.

You will need to practise often in order to feel secure in your use of it. Not everybody finds the crystal ball to be the best divinatory tool for them, so do not worry if occasionally what you 'see' seems to be fantastical or negative. If readings are consistently negative then the best advice is to choose some other form of divination. Do remember that you will develop your own way of working with it.

YOU WILL NEED

Incense or smudge stick

Dark coloured cloth (preferably velvet)

Crystal ball

Votive candle (optional)

METHOD

Clear the crystal ball by holding in the lit incense or smudge stick smoke.

Another way of clearing is to hold the crystal ball in running water for a short while.

Darken the room around you.

Put the crystal ball safely on the dark cloth to minimize reflections.

Place the lit candle so that there is enough illumination for you to see into it clearly
(usually slightly to the left of the crystal ball).

You should experiment with the best position for you.

You may find, for instance, that the candle is best behind you.

Ensure that you are sitting comfortably.

Clear your mind of everyday thoughts and make sure you have made a good
connection with both spiritual and Earth energies.

(You can do this by mentally reaching upwards to spiritual energy and downwards to
the centre of the earth, uniting the two.)

Hold the crystal ball in both hands.

While rotating it gently, think of the purpose you have in mind.

Using you own form of words, call upon your favourite deities or guide for help in
achieving your aim.

Focus initially on a spot slightly in front of or behind your crystal ball.

Gradually you will find your eyes drawn to a particular spot within the ball itself.

Concentrate on that spot and allow your mind to relax so that it can take in new
impressions.

You may experience yourself as 'entering' the crystal or becoming aware of
a different dimension.

Note: Because you are concentrating, your body will probably become somewhat tense. If this should happen, simply breathe out for longer than you are breathing in and allow yourself to relax. As you do this, you will find that your awareness and sense of self changes. You may find yourself becoming apparently larger or smaller. This is not unusual and allows you to transcend the dimensional barriers we all experience in everyday life.

If you find your eyes closing, allow them to do so. If you find yourself moving involuntarily or becoming aware of certain energies, do not become concerned as this also is perfectly natural in changing awareness. This state is known as automatism.

Either out loud or in your own mind, state the question to which you require an answer.
If you have no specific question, then just ask for guidance.
You will now find that impressions come and go and that you can, with some clarity, be aware of the answers you seek.
Let these impressions flow until such times as you instinctively 'know' that there is no more information.

Now begin to become aware once more of your experience of the crystal.
You may find yourself floating inside it, aware of its boundaries.
This experience is totally individual and cannot be quantified.

Gradually become aware of the feeling of the crystal in your hands and the sense of your own body as it returns to normal.
Finally, become aware of the room you are in.
Adjust your breathing and open your eyes.

Sit quietly for a few moments assimilating the experience.
Make sure you have fully returned to everyday consciousness.
If you called on the deities, thank them for the experience then either cover your crystal ball with the velvet cloth or put it back where it is kept.

Simple tools such as the black bowl or cauldron are also very effective for scrying. According to folklore, people used what they had available, and so their tools were often ordinary household objects such as bowls and mirrors.

Scrying Bowl

YOU WILL NEED

Simple bowl whose shape you like, preferably with a dark inner surface
(If it does not have a dark inner surface, paint the inside with non-toxic paint or use a
similar mixture to the one given in Magic Mirror below.)

Note: You may wish to make your own bowl, in which case you can decorate the outside of it with symbols in keeping with your own beliefs. The bowl should be made and/or consecrated during the fourth quarter or waning moon.

YOU WILL NEED

Water or divining liquid
Votive candle

METHOD

First prepare your divining liquid (see below).

Put the scrying bowl safely on a firm surface.
Fill the scrying bowl with the liquid to about an inch from the top.
Place the lit candle so that you can see into the bowl.
You should experiment with the best position for you.

Now use your scrying bowl in the same way as you would do for the crystal ball.

You do not have to use specially prepared liquid for scrying, but it may please you to do so. When you have prepared your own liquid, you have personalized your scrying bowl and therefore the resulting perceptions should be easier to understand.

Divining Liquid

This should be made during the third quarter of the moon to give time for the liquid to infuse sufficiently for use during the fourth quarter.

YOU WILL NEED

Dried herbs e.g. rose petals, jasmine and hyssop

Sea salt

A large clear bottle or jar

Water

Small bowl (not your scrying bowl)

METHOD

In the small bowl, mix the herbs together.

Add one part herb mixture to four parts water.

Stir in 3 teaspoons of sea salt.

Pour mixture into the jar, cover and place in a sunny spot.

Keep an eye on the distillation process. If the amount of liquid diminishes, you can add enough water to sustain the original level.

Leave it as undisturbed as possible so both the moon and sun energy will blend with the herbs and water until needed.

During the time of the fourth quarter, strain the herbs and store the liquid, which will look rather like tea, in a lidded container until you wish to use it.

Magic Mirror

A Magic Mirror can be used in the same way as your crystal ball or scrying bowl. To make a Magic Mirror you should prepare it as the full moon wanes. Ideally you should leave it for one whole cycle of the moon before using it for scrying, turning back negativity or any other magical purpose. Some practitioners will simplify the procedure by merely spraying black enamel paint on the back of a sheet of thick glass. Others may choose to use a double-sided round mirror, with the thought that the magnifying side enhances any working they do. Whatever method you choose, remember to consecrate your mirror before you use it.

YOU WILL NEED

8in x10in photo frame with a removable back and removable glass

Black high-gloss paint (not aerosol spray)

Dried and powdered psychic-enhancing herbs such as hyssop, dragon's blood, orris root, anise seed and any variety of dried moss

Disposable mixing container

Paintbrush

METHOD

Mix the paint and herbs together until you have a thick, tar-like substance.
While mixing, visualize the light of the moon entering the paint and say:

By the Moon's darkest light,
Perception of the night,
Become part of my skills,
And thus banish all ills.

Paint one side of the glass with the paint-herb mixture using long, straight strokes. Cover the surface completely, leaving no gaps.
When dry, re-assemble the frame with the painted side down so that the flat unpainted side shows through the frame.

Leave your mirror outside in moonlight for as long as you can; otherwise keep it covered by a dark cloth.

Your Mirror can also be used to reflect negativity back to where it belongs. If you do use it for this purpose, you should cleanse it and re-consecrate it for the purposes of scrying.

A Mirror Spell of Protection of a Personal Space

YOU WILL NEED

Mirror

9 white candles

A protection incense

A largish round mirror

A representation of the Goddess

METHOD

Light the incense.

Place the candles in a ring around the Goddess image.

Light the candles, beginning with the candle most directly before the Goddess image and say these or similar words:

Light of Luna, Protect me now.

When all are lit, hold the Mirror so that it reflects the light of the candles.

Turn slowly in each direction, ensuring that you throw the light as far as you can in each direction.

Then spin round as many times as you have candles, continuing to project the light and say:

Goddess of love, goddess of light,
Protect this space.

Pinch out the candles and put them away safely until you need to use them again.

In the next technique, sympathetic magic is used to affect the object. You are using the known power of the magnet to draw things towards it in a magical way. Scrying is also being used in a different way by deliberately seeing the objects in the mirror.

To Find Lost Objects

When you have lost an object you need to think like a child initially. For the very young child, when mother goes away, she no longer exists. An older child knows she still exists – she is just beyond his vision. If he tries very hard he can still feel her vibration. So it is with a lost object. If you try very hard you can still feel its vibration and will know where it is. It will draw you to it.

YOU WILL NEED
Mirror
Orange Candle
Black Candle
Small Magnet

METHOD
First create your sacred space and invoke the Guardians if appropriate.
Raise your cone of power by chanting drumming, meditation or visualization.

Then light the black candle (signifying the void, and the negativity of the loss) on the left and the orange candle (for luck and precious objects) on the right.

Pick up the mirror and sit quietly while you visualize the lost objects in the mirror. Now pick up the magnet and stroke it towards you in the space between the two candles and say three times:

By the wavering flame of this black light,
Grant to me of my [name lost object] a sight.
By the power of this orange flame,
Give me luck to find the same.
In this mirror the [nameof lost object] I see
Make the magnet draw them to me.

Say this three times.

Close the circle, but leave the candles burning with the magnet between them until the candles burn right down.

POPPETS AND CORN DOLLIES

Many systems of belief use sympathetic magic as a way of having an effect on their surroundings. Small objects are used to represent the 'real' thing or a larger idea. Small figurines, for instance, were often used to represent the Earth Mother in fertility rites, as has been confirmed by the figurines of apparently pregnant women found in excavations of Neolithic sites. A number of people are wary of using figurines other than as representations of the Goddess since they can be easily harmed or broken. This might well cause harm or injury to others. Therefore, any poppet or dolly should be treated with the utmost respect. Those representing the Goddess can be clothed or decorated according to personal belief or intuition.

POPPETS

A poppet is a small doll or figurine made from wood, paper, material or clay. It is shaped roughly in human form and is used, primarily, for magic spells. The best known examples of poppets are voodoo dolls. Traditionally, while most people do think of the evil aspects of the use of poppets in Voodoo, in fact there are both 'good' and 'bad' voodoo dolls depending on the intent behind their making and what they are supposed to represent. Poppets can be used to represent and help either you or someone else. Only make a poppet of someone else if they have given permission, such as when you wish to help or heal someone. To make one without permission or for the wrong reasons creates the wrong energy vibration.

When you are making a poppet, it is good to have either taken a ritual purification bath or to have meditated both on whether the use of a poppet is appropriate at this time and how best to make use of the poppet. This is to ensure that insofar as is possible, you have removed any subjective feelings and emotions about the subject and are acting only as the creator of the object. You then know that you are acting only as the channel for the energy that is being used.

For ease of explanation, the directions given overleaf are for a cloth poppet.

Making a Poppet

YOU WILL NEED

Paper or card (to act as a template)

Soft material such as felt or cotton

Needle and thread

Straw, paper or cotton wool

Herbs, appropriate to the ritual you are performing, may also be used

METHOD

Draw the outline of a simple human figure on the card or paper, then cut it out.

(It should ideally be at least four inches high.)

Fold the material in two and place the template on it.

Cut around the template.

Sew the figures together, leaving a small area open.

Turn the figure inside out so the stitches are on the inside.

Stuff the figure with the straw, paper, cotton wool or herbs. You can personalize the poppet by adding a lock of hair to the filling.

You can also use buttons for eyes or draw on facial features if you wish.

Finish sewing the material together.

Your poppet is now ready for use. Do not destroy it when you have finished with it – either give it to the person whom it represents or bury it safely in the earth. We give below a way of using a poppet to help someone else.

Healing Image Spell

You can make your poppet as above, this time do try to include within the poppet something that represents the person you are hoping to help. For a short-term solution, you might include hair, nail clippings and such-like; for a solution to a long-term problem you might include a crystal representing the person concerned – perhaps one that matches their astrological sign.

The principle behind using a poppet for healing works on the principle of sympathetic magic. This means that in working with your figurine you are having an effect on the person themselves. For this reason you need to be quite careful as you create the poppet not to represent the problem, but to create an image of the solution.

YOU WILL NEED
Poppet

Blue Candle

Salt Water

METHOD
Create your poppet to represent the person you wish to help already completely healed and whole.

Take the doll into your sacred space.

Light a blue candle (to represent healing).

Sprinkle your poppet with the salt water.

Say something like:

This figure I hold made by my art

Here represents [name person],

By my art made, by my art changed,

Now may he/she be healed,

By art divine.

Pass the poppet quickly through the flame of the candle and visualize the person being cleansed of their problem.

Hold the poppet in both hands, breathe gently on it and visualize first the poppet and then the person being filled with Divine healing energy.
Pay particular attention to the areas in the physical body of your friend which you know are in difficulty.

Then imbue the poppet with the idea of being healed from a mental perspective.
Finally, draw down spiritual energy to infuse the doll and therefore your friend with the spiritual help that they need.
Visualize the person concerned being completely filled with white light, well, happy and filled with energy.

Note: Do remember that healing takes place in the way that the recipient needs it, not necessarily in the way we think it should happen. We are not just asking for alleviation of the symptoms, we are asking for help from a holistic perspective.

Keep the poppet in your sacred space until it is no longer needed.
At this time, enter your sacred space, take the poppet sprinkle it with water and say:

By divine art changed,
By my art made,
Free this poppet from the connection with [name].
Let it now be unmade.

If the poppet contains direct links with the person – such as hair – burn it in an open fire. If it does not, dispose of it in any way you wish.
If you have used a crystal, this should be cleansed by holding it under running water and perhaps then given to the person as a keepsake or for protection.

CORN DOLLIES

The original 'dolly' was actually a straw cage designed to capture the corn spirit. Later it became a representation of the spirit itself, often being intricately woven and braided in accordance with fertility customs and beliefs. It is here that the corn dolly came to represent the Earth Mother. Used in rituals at the time of the harvest, it was kept over the winter to ensure the land's fertility for the next year's crops. The less nimble fingered simply used the symbol of a sheaf of corn dressed as a woman decked with ribbons. Thus, the spirit of the harvest was both saved and honoured at the same time. In the Christian tradition, the symbol of the sheaf of corn became immortalized in the harvest loaf, a tradition which still continues today. It is, of course, no longer dressed as a woman.

'Corn' was a generic word applied to the seeds of the local grass crop. The regional crop was different depending on local conditions, e.g. in England the crop was wheat; in Scotland, oats; in the United States, maize.

The symbol of the Goddess can be decorated simply or elaborately, in any way that is thought to be appropriate, with symbols of fertility and abundance. You may find it interesting to spend a little time deciding which of the corn goddesses you most easily relate to. You may prefer to follow either the Roman, Celtic, Greek or Egyptian traditions, in which case will need to do some research so that you honour your Goddess in her full glory. For example, Demeter as a corn deity was the Greek goddess of fertility, and Ceres was her Roman counterpart. In the rituals for the Sabbats later on, for instance, you may use a corn dolly but will follow more closely the Pagan traditions.

The symbol of the God can also be decorated in a manner befitting his status. Do remember, however, that you must do this in a way that pleases you. It is your creativity that is important.

In this next ritual, we have used the word 'corn' to represent any of the suitable grasses. You will be making two dolls – one to represent the Goddess and one the God.

Making a Corn Dolly

YOU WILL NEED

Two small handfuls of corn stalks

Green and yellow wool or cotton

Trailing greenery (ivy or grape vine are ideal)

Appropriately coloured ribbons for the ritual (e.g. white for St Brigid's day and red
or orange for Lammas)

METHOD

Take one handful of corn stalks.

Just below the top, bind the stalks with the yellow cotton tying securely.

3–5 cm underneath, bind the stalks again; this forms the head of the doll.

Carefully divide the bound bundle into four strands. (The outer two will form the arms,
the middle ones the body.)

Gently bend the stalks which represent the arms and bind carefully with
the yellow cotton.

Bind the two middle pieces together, criss-crossing the cotton to create a body
approximately 10–15 cm long.

Leave the rest of the corn free so that it looks like a skirt.

You have now created a representation of the Goddess.

If you wish, ask for a blessing from one of the fertility goddesses.

You might say:

Demeter, bless now this image of your fruitfulness.

Now make your second corn doll in the same way.

This time, use the green cotton instead of yellow and also bind the two middle
sections to represent legs.

Ask for a blessing from an agricultural god such as Dionysus or Saturn.

You might say:

Dionysus, bless now this image of your fertility.

Decorate both dolls with the ribbons and the male doll with the trailing greenery.
The representation of the male god can be used at the time of Mabon – the Autumn
Equinox or at the time of Saturnalia in December.

Plaiting a Corn Dolly

Corn dollies were also made by intricate plaiting and weaving – an art that was considered in itself magical, akin to knot magic. Here, the heads of corn represented the Goddess and the patterns represented the spirals of life, growth and achievement. Much modern straw is too hard to plait successfully and – should you at some point like to try this ancient art for yourself – you may have to find a specialist supplier.

Simple corn dollies, wheels and other shapes can be made with the standard three-straw plait, though more complex corn dollies involve multiple straws, intricate braids and, sometimes, the creation of a straw core shape around which the outer straw is plaited.

Whereas a corn dolly can be kept in the home, a wish sachet can be used to carry objects with you. You might keep herbs, your stones for geomancy, gems or crystals for example, or a symbolic representation of whatever holds a magical feeling for you – it is your choice.

MAGICAL SACHET

You can keep various things in such a sachet, for it is a repository for your desires. A wish sachet could not be easier to create. If you can find one, a wishbone or perhaps a lucky charm in the shape of a wishbone, is also a good idea. Here is a way of using such a sachet to help your wishes come true.

Making a Magical Sachet

YOU WILL NEED

2 pieces of cloth

Needle and thread

A coloured cord with which to close the bag

Paper or parchment and pen

Any magical items you wish to include

Matches

Fireproof container

METHOD

Sit quietly in your sacred space.

On the paper write out your wishes having thought very carefully about what you really need.

Hold the paper and infuse it with your desires calling on your Higher Power or deity for help in achieving your objectives.

Again think very carefully about how your wish will be fulfilled. For example, if you require money, pinpoint how you want to receive it. If you do the Lottery, ask to come up with the winning numbers.

Read your list out loud. Vocalizing your wishes in this way will give them extra power. Burn the list and remember to save the ashes.

It is now time to make the sachet.

Sew the pieces of cloth together leaving one end open. As you sew, bear in mind your objective in creating the sachet.

Take hold of the wish list ashes and pour them into the sachet. If you like, you can also add an appropriate incense.

Next, take the wishbone and sew it into the sachet so it is secure and will not fall out.
As you do so say:

This is my yearning, this is my will.
Wishes now manifest,
So let it be.

Close the sachet with the cord.

Afterwards, thank your higher power.
Place the sachet in your sacred space.

TRAVELLING TOOLS

A sachet is obviously used to transport articles that are needed and for the magical practitioner it is important that their tools can be easily accessible. Just as most modern-day priests will carry small versions of his consecrated tools with him in case they are needed, so every magical practitioner can do the same. In some ways we are more fortunate, particularly if we work within the nature traditions, as we can often use objects which are readily to hand and dedicate them on the spot.

We have spoken elsewhere about developing a sacred space, and should you choose to work with an athame, wand or chalice you can use representations which are quite clearly associated with the idea behind the magic. You might wish to carry such things with you, however.

Making and Dedicating Travelling Tools

YOU WILL NEED

Material such as linen, velvet or felt to make your travelling roll

Broad elastic or material to hold your tools in place

Needle or small paper knife to represent an athame

Small piece of wooden dowelling or a straight twig to represent a wand

Very small tumbler or oyster shell as a chalice

Coin or dog tag with a pentagram etched on it

Suitable lucky charms or cake decorations as representations of your deities

Birthday cake candles

Four small containers, e.g. phials or empty spice jars

(These will contain your chosen incense or herbs, salt, water and anointing oil)

Matches

Crystals or tumbled stones as cardinal point markers

(Green, yellow, red and blue stones work well.)

METHOD

Make yourself a travelling roll from the material so you can keep your tools together safely. This is similar to the type of carrier in which a carpenter keeps his tools. The elastic will keep them securely in place.

(These tools mean that you can set up an altar anywhere, both out of doors and inside, according to your own beliefs. You might also use the material roll as your altar cloth.) You can also include anything else that you feel is important to your rituals.

Dedicate your objects with an appropriate form of words.

You might say:

O Great Mother,
As I travel over your forests, fields and watery ways,
Bless and empower this pouch with its symbols of your power.

Verdant God,
Have me use them wisely and well,
So that together we manifest your authority.
May it always be with me
So that, wherever I am, so also are both of you.

These travelling tools are now dedicated for use anywhere at any time and under any conditions. Often they can be used unobtrusively without anyone needing to know what you are doing.

In the previous section you will have learnt to think very carefully about the tools you use, and how to look after them, in your magical practice. Obviously you will not need to use all of them all of the time and you should develop for yourself some way of storing them so that they retain their potency. Treat them with respect and they will serve you well.

MAGICAL DREAMING

One 'tool' which is extremely important in the use of magic is the art of dreaming. Obviously this is much more of an internal tool rather than a physical artefact and is only one of a number of such tools we have. Dreams tap into an information database of memory, experience, perception and cultural belief, and help us to form new ideas and concepts. They also present us with ways of making changes which may seem impossible on a conscious level; the mind is free to roam wherever it pleases. Free from inhibition when the limitations that the conscious mind places on the thought processes are removed, it will create scenarios and situations which defy explanation by the logical side of the personality. In looking for explanations we have to become more creative and open in the pursuit of knowledge.

Much of that which we call the unconscious, forms a set of basic physiological and psychological functions. It is our way of surviving – the term 'unconscious' is taken to delineate many dimensions and aspects of Self. It is this Self that is the inner guide that scans our life experience, knowledge of which is retained in a level of memory to which we seldom have access.

As we become more proficient at bringing about changes in our consciousness, we must be willing to open up to our inner guide. Most societies based on shamanic and magical practice use dreams as a form of inner guidance. We too can begin to access the more magical side of ourselves in this way. When we entrust our decision-making to this normally inaccessible part, we have then accepted factors of which we are not consciously aware. When we learn how to ask for direction and assistance through dreams to make decisions which may well be life-changing, we are truly becoming creative.

It is initially difficult to access our inner guide through normal consciousness, but when we are brave enough give ourselves permission to access it through dreams, this can have a profound effect on the way we manage our lives, both physically and spiritually. Such a tool can be effectively used alongside magic and spells both for problem solving and for clarifying feelings with which we are having difficulty. It can also be of assistance in tackling the wider issues which arise within the community in which we live, and also those issues which belong within a more global framework.

However, more importantly, dream management can give us ways of dealing with negative influences, of clearing the ground for action and making preparation for the magical working that we are getting ready to do. Often the ritual or structure of a spell can be perceived in dreams, when we have no idea that such information is available to us. We can be quite literally told what to do – we tap into some hidden wellspring of arcane knowledge. Enhancing our natural abilities and talents for magic is easy when we learn to trust our own inner processes.

ASKING FOR THE DREAMS YOU WANT
This technique is most successful for those who have already learnt how to recall and record their dreams. This technique works because

the lines of communication have already been established between the conscious and unconscious self – the inner and the outer world. Just as initially one might initially send a simple e-mail, so later one learns to send links and attachments giving more and more complex information. For this reason the method also works well for those who have learnt to meditate, or for those who use other kinds of self management tools such as creative visualization or chanting.

It is of most use when there is a strong, passionate, deeply-felt association with the question or request. The technique is a very easy one, particularly if one has learned through work or other experience to remain focussed on issues at hand. You simply remember to use as a memory jogger the word CARDS:

- ✦ **C**larify the Issue
- ✦ **A**sk the question
- ✦ **R**epeat it
- ✦ **D**ream and document it
- ✦ **S**tudy the dream

C means that you spend some time in clarifying exactly what the issue really is. If you are using dreams to help you in working magically you will need to decide whether you are working thaumaturgically or theurgically. If thaumaturgically, then you are trying to manipulate the energies on this plane of existence and perhaps need guidance. If theurgically, then you will be seeking the help of the powers that be. By identifying these basic issues you are then able to make a more effective link with the correct stream of knowledge – to tune into the right channel.

Try to state the issue as positively as you can, because the subconscious tends to latch on to negative statements in preference to positive. So you might say, 'I require guidance as to how to achieve my aims.' Or you could say, 'I require help in achieving my aims.' It also helps to be quite specific in your choice of words.

A suggests that you ask the question with as much relevance as possible. Using an old journalistic technique, ask the questions 'who, what, where, when and why' and sort out in your own mind exactly what the relevant question is. For instance, in our example, you might ask:

✦ Who can best help?

✦ What must I do?

✦ Where do the best opportunities lie for achieving my aims?

✦ When will I be able to use my greater experience?

✦ Why have I created the circumstances I have?

All of these questions are, of course, open questions and are not necessarily time specific. If you ask a question based on confused thinking you may well receive a confusing answer, so always try to get as close to the heart of the matter as you can. Conversely, by asking inappropriate questions you may notch up answers you do not wish to have, and your magical technique based on your dreams may not work.

Repeat the question. By repeating the question over and over again, you are fixing it in your subconscious. Often blocks of three repetitions work very well, which is according to occult law as stated elsewhere in the book, so repeating three sets of three means that you have covered all possible bases – practical, emotional and spiritual.

The art of Dream Command, as it might be called, is that of informing your inner self that you will have a dream which will help you to achieve your objective. As you compose yourself for sleep and use whichever relaxation techniques help you, you must tell yourself that you will have a dream which will give you an answer or the assistance that you need.

One word of warning. It is difficult to say what will actually happen since it will be pertinent to you and what you are doing, rather than being a 'blanket' answer. The dreaming self is quite capricious, so to begin with you may not receive an answer on the night you requested it. You may only receive part of an answer, or nothing for several nights, and then a series of dreams which tell you what you need to know. It is a highly individual process, and no-one can tell you how it should be. With time you will recognize your own pattern, but be prepared to be patient with yourself.

Dream it. When you do dream, document it briefly as soon as you can, noting down the main theme of the dream. With practice you will recognize the difference between a dream which helps you to clear away the everyday problems and one which is more to do with magical guidance. Look carefully at the imagery within the dream which will probably be fairly clear-cut and straightforward.

Study the dream in more detail when you have time enough to do so. Look for details, clues and hidden meanings, and see whether you can apply any or all of them to situations in hand. Sometimes the answer to your request can come from applying your knowledge to a different sector of your life, before tackling the information for which you have asked.

As you become better at communicating with the Inner Self you may find the nature of your questions changing. For instance you may find yourself asking 'How can I make so and so happen?' or 'What if I did...?' This is true magical creativity and is a manifestation of the inner you appearing in your external life. It is an exciting process, and often can lead to dreams of the future, known of old as prophetic dreams.

In days long gone, prophetic dreams such as those experienced by the Delphic oracle, were most likely induced by the natural seepage of carbon monoxide and other noxious gases from fissures in the ground below the temples, though they probably also used incenses such as the sacred laurel, inhaling its smoke before prophesying. The hierophantic (priestly) class among the ancients therefore did not scorn the use of drugs and narcotics altogether, though they kept their secrets so well hidden that much of the knowledge was lost or forgotten. Nowadays, such knowledge is retained by the shamans within many cultures who will often use plants native to their own areas to bring about a change of consciousness.

For anyone who has an interest in the use of dreams in a magical sense, it is often difficult to sort out what can be accepted as 'real' dreaming and which dreams are definitely caused by the use of drugs and herbs.

HERBS FOR SLEEPING AND DREAMING
There are many herbs used today which are helpful in making our dreams more accessible and for obtaining a good night's sleep.

Sometimes, rather than attempting to actually influence our dreams, it is often advisable when working magically simply to let the content of our subconscious come to the fore. For this we may use the group of herbs known as hypnotics or soporifics. Different herbs work for different people so the order here is alphabetical, without any particular preference:

Hops are often used as an infusion or tincture and should not be used when you are depressed. This herb has an effect on the central nervous system, and can be used when tension is making you restless. Gentle slumber is induced from the hop pillow, causing soothing dreams. (See how to make a dream pillow overleaf.)

Jamaican Dogwood can be taken combined with hops, although it is a fish poison and should be used with care. It is used in cases of insomnia or broken sleep patterns.

Passion flower acts without leaving any kind of a hangover effect and makes it easy for those who suffer from insomnia on a regular basis to find restful sleep.

Skullcap has a sedative action par excellence. Working on the central nervous system, it is particularly useful in cases of nervous exhaustion.

Valerian, which is included in many pharmacopoeias as a sedative, is used to manage tension and sleeplessness caused by tension.

Wild lettuce is invaluable where there is restlessness and excitability; it is both sedative and hypnotic – that is, relaxing and sleep inducing. As a gentle remedy, it is particularly useful for children.

Nervines have a beneficial effect on the nervous system. Some which are relaxants are Balm, Black Haw, Bugleweed, Camomile, Damiana, Lady's Slipper, Lavender, Oats, Pasque Flower, Peppermint and Vervain.

Many people prefer to use the herbs in incense and sleep pillows rather than ingest them. If you are having problems sleeping, here are six incense that may help, the last two if your dreams are particularly troubled.

Sleepytime Incense

1 part Poppy Seeds
1 ½ parts Camomile
1 ¼ parts Willow

Rest and Sleep Incense

½ part Catnip

½ part Dill

¼ part Poppy

1 part Lemon Verbena

½ part Motherwort

Few drops of Lemon Verbena Oil

Note: The following two incense can be used when you wish to enhance either aspects or the power of your dreams

Psychic Dream Incense

2 parts Sandalwood

1 part Rose

1 part Camphor

Few drops of Tuberose Oil

Few drops of Jasmine Oil

Prophetic Dream Incense

2 parts Frankincense Resin

1 part Buchu

1 part Mugwort

Burn this incense before you go to bed to stimulate the psychic mind and to ensure that your conscious mind remembers your dreams in the morning.

End Nightmares Incense

1 part Thyme

1 part Willow

1 part Camomile

Nightmares Incense

¼ part Star Anise

¾ part Lemon Verbena

¾ part Thyme

1 part Willow

Few drops of Lemon Verbena Oil

DREAM PILLOWS

Dream pillows may be used for several purposes. You can use them to enhance sleep, in which case any of the following six herbs may be used: Catnip, Hops, Lavender, Thyme, Valerian, Vervain (to prevent nightmares). Should you wish to affect your dreams, you could consult the incense section and use the herbs listed for Psychic Powers, Divination and Prophetic Dreams.

To Make a Dream Pillow

YOU WILL NEED

1 part each of at least five dried herbs from those shown above

Dried orange and lemon peel

½ part Mugwort

1 part Myrrh or Frankincense Resin

2 pieces of lightweight cloth such as muslin

Your personal choice of decoration i.e. ribbon, buttons (optional)

METHOD

Burn a little of the Frankincense or Myrrh Resin to cleanse your working area.

Mix the five dried herbs in whatever proportion feels right.
While doing this, think carefully about the purpose of your dream pillow – e.g. Hops will give a sound sleep, Mugwort induces psychic dreaming and Camomile promotes a feeling of wellbeing.
Crumble the dried peels into small pieces and add the rest of the finely ground resin to this mixture.

Sew together three sides of the material, leaving one side open so you can easily fill the pillow with the herbs.
While you are doing this, make a mental link with Hypnos, the Greek God of sleep or Demeter, Earth Mother.

Decorate the bags with magical symbols, moons or your own personal preferences.
Fill the pillow (not too full) with the herb and resin mixture and sew up the final side.

You may now use your dream pillow whenever you require. Slip it into your pillow case and inhale deeply.

THE VOICE

Another internal tool is the voice. It is possible to use sound to achieve a different state of consciousness, and perhaps a state of ecstacy, and this is the basis of chanting in most languages – to enchant something or someone initially meant 'to surround them in sound'. We have seen already in the section on prayer how the rhythmic use of words enhances magical work.

Most religions have their own traditions for chanting. Hebrew mystics and magicians used the secret names of God – such as Yahweh, Adonai and Elohim. Biblical texts are used for chant in the Jewish religion. In the Christian religion plainchant was influenced by Jewish synagogue music. Various forms developed, the best known being Gregorian. Other forms are Gallican, Mozarabic and Ambrosian; there are also Eastern Christian forms. Followers of Islam chant the 99 names of Allah called 'the Beautiful Names'; Native Americans also observe chanting in preparation for many activities and ceremonies. Mantra today is another widely accepted form of chant, initially used by the Eastern Mysteries.

For those of you who do not consider yourselves to be particularly musical, think of chanting in its original sense of producing a vibration rather than producing a musical note. The vibration should start somewhere near the Point of Power and rise up to be expressed as sound.

One of the simplest chants is the sound of 'Om'. This actually consists of three sounds – A (pronounced Ahhh), U (pronounced ooo) and M (hummed mmm) – and is traditionally the vibration of Creation. It returns us to essential energy, allows clarity and perception and puts us in touch with power and energy. 'Om' often induces a heightened state of consciousness.

Using spontaneously a language that is not the speaker's natural one (speaking in tongues) is known as Glossalalia. Normally a heightened state of consciousness accompanies this and the speaker is not aware of what they are doing.

When you use this technique the aim is to become filled with the power and energy of whatever you are calling upon and to make that energy tangible within the physical realm. When practising, it is often useful to have someone making notes or recording what has happened.

Basic Guidelines for Glossolalia

YOU WILL NEED

A safe or sacred space where you will not be disturbed

A basic (seed) sound, preferably of three syllables.

This gives the correct lilt to your voice.

You might use Om (A U M), Eh vo he, Je ho vah, the name of a deity, or even your own name if you feel it is appropriate.

METHOD

Sit or kneel in a comfortable position.

Choose your seed sound.

Establish an energetic connection with the earth by reaching towards the centre of the earth and visualizing yourself strongly linked to that centre.

If you wish, also establish a connection with the realms of spirit by reaching upwards in the same way.

Begin uttering your seed sound.

Let yourself go and just let the sounds emerge.

(You will probably find that an unexpected emotion emerges and you may laugh or cry. Don't let it bother you, simply allow it to pass and appreciate the feelings.)

When you feel that the practice has run its course (you will find that your consciousness will begin to return to normal and you will become more aware of your surroundings), ground the power by placing your hands on the ground and visualizing the energy streaming through your hands back to the centre of the earth.

Sit quietly and re-centre yourself by finding your own point of power within your body (probably in your solar plexus) and re-ground.

To achieve an altered state of consciousness we need to have some procedure that we can use to switch from external stimuli and distractions and become more conscious of what is going on at an internal level. Meditation is the process by which a person learns to shut off the thinking mind and to begin sensing.

MEDITATION

The ultimate goal of meditation, if there is one, is to be aware of everything around you and within you – to live life mindfully and to do it without making comparisons, appraisals or judgments. You learn to turn off the thinking mind and the physical senses of sight, sound, taste, smell, or touch. You learn to work on an intuitive level and just 'feel' whatever is there, whether that is internally or on an external level. In the process of meditation, you are learning to activate sensitivity of feeling and using it deliberately.

Meditation helps us to preserve objectivity which can become clouded by emotion – a state of being where a person is happy, angry or reacting in some way to a given situation. This does not mean that when we meditate we suppress emotion, simply that we can put it into its correct context and feel things more clearly. Extreme emotion can also cloud thinking and, since one of the aims in meditation is to suspend thinking, the meditator is eventually able to move into an altered state of consciousness where everything just 'is' and he or she is untroubled by the circumstances around them.

The thinking mind is only useful when you are needing to use logical thought – that is, perhaps to develop a strategy or work out a reason for something. Most of the time, the mind is capable of making connections that do not necessarily follow logical thought. It can make leaps of awareness that allow us to use symbolism and other representations in order to understand the surroundings we are in or to make decisions which are right for us. This can give us a deeper and more accurate assessment of our abilities and potential and allow us to live life to the full. Once the mind is set free from having to think in straight lines it can enter the wider world of 'all that is'.

Meditation is a process whereby you are able to suspend thought and to reach your true feelings, by focussing your attention on something constant, like your breathing or a candle flame. This is why the first result can often be a huge release of emotion, perhaps by copious tears or unexplained laughter. The normal constraints you place upon yourself in waking life are removed, allowing you to touch in on areas you normally suppress. Your thinking, rational mind has gone to sleep. You may, in fact, also surprise yourself by not feeling anything at all. It is as though all feeling has been suspended. These are only stages to be gone through until you reach the more subtle energies.

You have to turn off the thinking function by focussing your mind on something constant. Then, there is nothing to stimulate your thinking which normally tends to block out all other ways of operating, such as sensing, feeling and, ultimately, just being. It is only when you start trying to turn off this thinking function that you realize what a large amount of data we have to deal with each day. We are literally bombarded from all sides with information – some subtle and some not so subtle. When we learn to 'tune out', the mind can stop 'thinking' and can begin feeling and sensing the finer energies. When this happens, you are then free to enter a whole new world.

At first your awareness on this level may be very suspect and you will be unsure whether to trust what you are feeling, but gradually your ability to feel and to sense will increase. You will be able to accept your subjective experience as being right for you. Eventually you will become so proficient at this process that you can turn off your thinking mind at will and simply sense whatever is there, no matter what kind of practice you undertake. (It is important to remember that the practice is just the means by which you discover your inner Self, so do not allow yourself to get caught up in the idea that one method is better than any other.) Experiment with different ways until you find one that suits you, or until you can synthesize a number of different types to give you a way that is uniquely yours. Ideally, it is better to find a teacher who can take you through the initial stages of any meditation process, but we give examples of different types of exercises below which may start you on the path.

You will find meditation can be a help in all sorts of ways within your everyday life. It brings with it a sense of calm which often allows you to make decisions without the emotional baggage which you may carry. It can bring with it insights into peoples' motives which might not be available on a more conscious level and can allow you to tailor your responses accordingly. It can give you a strong sense of community and an awareness which allows you to act for the good of all.

Finally, meditation will allow you to reach a state of cosmic awareness – a state where perception includes an awareness of everything that is, in its vastness and in its detail. In this state there is no separation between you and anything else. It is all one, an enhanced perception of a state of integration and integrity you will already have experienced on a purely physical level as you learn about yourself.

MEDITATION TECHNIQUES

The aim in meditation is to keep the mind alert yet relaxed, and focussed upon a single subject, rather than to listen to the 'chatterbox' in one's head. A short period of meditation or creative visualization last thing at night gives you access to your rich, inner creative self while a similar period in the morning allows you to work with, and understand, the opportunities of the new day.

✦ Settle on a place where you will not be disturbed and make sure that the telephone is disconnected. To begin with, five minutes meditation is enough. Sit in an upright chair or cross legged on the floor with your back supported if necessary. It is important to be in as comfortable a position as possible although lying down is not such a good idea since you may fall asleep before you have finished meditating.

✦ Now, depending whether you are a beginner or not, you may choose to partially close your eyes to shut out the everyday world or to close your eyes completely. Do whatever feels most comfortable for you. If you are an experienced meditator you may find it easier to focus your eyes on the bridge of your nose or the middle of your forehead. This latter is the point of the Third Eye, or Ajna, which is traditionally considered to be the point of visioning.

✦ One technique which allows the mind to quieten down considerably is to begin to breathe evenly and deeply, 'watching' the breath as you do so. First of all, breathe in for a count of four and out for a count of four. When you have established this rhythm, breathe out slightly longer than you breathed in. A rate that is comfortable for you might to be to breath in for four and out for six counts. Become aware of the breath itself. Imagine that the energy from the breath is travelling around the whole of your body, cleansing and clearing it of the difficulties and worries of the everyday. As you breathe in, breathe in peace and tranquillity – as you breathe out, breathe out negativity. You might then attempt to lengthen the out breath even further to a count of four and eight. You should soon be able to achieve a deep state of awareness of your own body and its various systems. For instance, in one meditation you might concentrate on the skeletal system of the body, while in another you might look at the organs. Often this will allow you to recognize an imbalance which gives an early warning of a health difficulty. Any stray thoughts can be noted and dismissed; if meditating at night, this enables you to move straight into the sleep state. You may also use this period prior to sleep to visualize creatively something that you desire, so that this may be carried over into your dreams. (Problems as well as desires can also be dealt with in dreams.) If you are meditating in the morning, the concentration may be focussed on the solution to the problem or the realization of one's desire.

So, practising meditation begins by simplifying everything, reducing everything to a very basic level. Relaxing and being who we are, we sit in our own particular spot, follow our breath and watch our thoughts. As your practice improves so you will find the period of meditation tending to extend of its own free will to anything up to twenty minutes. When you complete the meditation on the breath, try to keep the mind in the same calm and tranquil state. Keep your physical movements unhurried so they flow in harmony with your consciousness.

Unless we are able to deal with the simple things, we cannot begin to think about raising consciousness to a high level. What we are actually doing is taming our minds, trying to overcome all sorts of concerns and worries, patterns of thinking, so that we are eventually able to sit in a kind of dynamic stillness. This mind-taming is, in fact, a complete attention to detail – experiencing the present situation as it really is. Life is a series of moments joined together and it is up to us to enjoy those moments as the gifts they are.

When you sit down to meditate, you perhaps should think of that place as the centre of the universe. From that point everything radiates, and ultimately the idea is that you control your own destiny from that point. As you carry that centre within you, you may like to have your own prayer rug or cushion which is sacrosanct and signifies your contact with the earth on which you sit and is your gateway to the spiritual, no matter where you happen to be. Others may feel that the act of preparation – sitting cross-legged with a relaxed posture with hands on thighs – sanctifies the spot. Some people will wish to use a traditional practice from the East and place the thumb and third finger together to show that they are willing to suppress the ego and help the energy circulate. In this way we are in contact with ourselves, the earth on which we live and the spiritual universe which nurtures us.

In sitting in this way, you will need to ensure that you are comfortable and do not feel that your physical energy is blocked in any way. If you get pins and needles then just move! Tuck your chin in slightly and focus on a point some six feet in front of you. If you find your gaze wavering it does not matter, simply close your eyes and begin again. Allow your mouth to fall slightly open, and if you wish place your tongue just behind your front upper teeth. This helps you to allow the energy to flow around the body in some of the later exercises.

Rather than watching the breath, you may like to concentrate on a candle flame. Here you place a lighted candle at the point mentioned above, approximately six feet in front of you. Now just watch quietly. Initially you will find that all sorts of thoughts intrude. These may be anything from everyday concerns to thoughts about meditation to questions about your own validity. Do not try to complete the thoughts or deal with them at this stage, just acknowledge that they are there and bring your mind back to the candle flame. When you feel you have sat still for long enough and completed your meditation, just sit quietly and allow the everyday world to come back into focus again. Try to ensure that you retain the sense of tranquillity which arises from doing this method of meditation before plunging back into your everyday world. Do not forget to extinguish the candle when you have finished. You can choose an alternative to a candle on which to concentrate. Any kind of object can be used – a flower or fruit perhaps, something belonging to the natural world.

An extension of this method is to take one of the concerns which arose from the intrusive thoughts and to contemplate it quietly by concentrating on it to the exclusion of all other concerns and just being aware of what pops into your mind as you do so. You may find that you receive an answer to a problem, have an insight as to what is causing a difficulty or even give yourself a symbol which helps you to gain extra courage or strength. The possibilities are endless.

At this stage it is important to reiterate that we are still not talking about trying to get into some kind of altered state of consciousness. You are simply learning how to bring your mind under control. This means that the circumstances you find yourself in, in their entirety are available to you and you are now beginning to see where you may be bringing a situation towards you or are at the mercy of events. Such awareness allows us to live life mindfully.

Yet another way to bring the mind under control is to use visualization. Here you imagine yourself surrounded by a midnight blue sky. This is because midnight blue is easier to visualize than straightforward black which can often seem oppressive. Let this sky be as full of movement or energy as you like. Gradually begin to slow it down until such time as you feel comfortable and feel that you are calming down. See each thought as a star in the sky and gradually bring one star into focus, holding it steady within the centre of your visual field. For the moment continually remind yourself that it is just a symbol and contemplate it as such. Gradually you will find your mind slowing down to the point where you have few, if any, thoughts, even about this particular representation or symbol.

There are only a few recommended guidelines for meditation, for you will very quickly find your own preferred routine:

✦ It should be done every day, preferably at the same time. This is good for self-discipline.

✦ For reasons of comfort, it should preferably be done before a meal rather than after. Many people prefer to meditate before going to bed and on rising.

✦ A spot should be set aside for meditation, which should be a quiet place and usually used for nothing but meditation. Your own sacred space or in front of your shrine would be ideal.

✦ Try to sit with the spine straight and vertical (whether you are sitting on the floor or a chair). This will help when you come to deal with kundalini and other energies later on.

The more we put ourselves in touch with our own 'inner landscape' and are comfortable with dealing with the insights which arise, the more we are able to access powers and energies which in former times were termed 'supernatural'. We have seen how, even in simple societies, shamans and priests have been able to gain access to other worlds and it is now widely accepted that a trained meditator has similar access to these astral planes, as they have been called, albeit in a different fashion. It will depend very much on the training that has been undertaken how these planes are accessed and managed. Many schools of meditation recognize such levels of awareness as illusion while others will accept them as having a validity of their own.

As an analogy, the modern day drug taker's experience is often real at the time but recognized as illusion when he returns to his everyday reality, whereas for the shaman, whose culture uses peyote as a doorway to other worlds, both realms are real. So it is with meditation. The deeper one ventures into a state of being where the inner life becomes more real than the outer, the easier it becomes to reject the trials and tribulations of the outer life. These then are recognized as illusion in the same way as Buddhists have learnt to accept. However, for many, this is a negative attitude which bypasses the beauty of your given circumstances. If one or other of these inner or outer aspects dissatisfies, then the essential balance is lost.

Ideally, a balance needs to be reached where the inner life enhances the outer life and vice versa, and it is here that magic truly exists. By the correct use of energy and power, changes can be made from one level of existence to another – the spiritual can affect the physical and the physical the spiritual. As the individual embraces these ideas, he or she begins to realize that they can develop the power to exercise a degree of control in both worlds.

This leads us back very neatly to our definitions of thaumaturgy and theurgy – thaumaturgy including the idea of personal control, theurgy being supernatural control.

When you have begun to control your own mind, you are beginning to develop the ability at best to make things happen, and at the very least to take control of your own circumstances. While the concept of mind control smacks of aliens and 'ghosties and ghoulies ... and things that go bump in the night', control of mind means recognizing that an uncontrolled mind makes a poor master and an even poorer servant. Most of us find it all too easy to begin a train of thought and then find that we have gone off at a tangent and have forgotten what we were thinking about in the first place.

Meditation helps us to retain a focus, firstly within the ordinary everyday world and then within our inner world, which is as rich a source of information as the external world. We each have access to huge libraries of information and when we train our mind through meditation we have a kind of inner librarian which can fetch and carry the right knowledge for us when we request it. Having taught our minds to be free and spontaneous through the previous exercises, we now need to teach them to reveal the secrets which they hold.

One method of assimilating unconscious contents which are revealed through dreams, fantasies and the symbols thrown up in meditation is through some form of creative self-expression – painting, dancing, writing, poetry and so on. Another way of doing this is through what C. G. Jung called 'active imagination'. This aims to give expression to sides of the character (particularly the anima/animus and the shadow – the more negative side of the Self) to which we do not normally pay much attention. In this way, a pathway of communication between consciousness and the unconscious is established. A process is initiated between the individual and the images he creates which shifts his consciousness to a different awareness.

The first stage of active imagination is very akin to the process of dreaming and to the exercise you have already done with the star. Just as you previously contemplated the star in order to slow your thoughts down, now you take either an image which arises spontaneously or one which you have deliberately chosen and concentrate on it. Fix your attention on this image to the exclusion of everything else and just watch it. Most of the time it will change in some way, as the very act of contemplation gives it a life of its own. Try to remember what changes occur, but under no circumstances attempt to change it deliberately at this stage. This is because you are learning how your mind makes its own connections using images you have assimilated from your life experiences, your childhood and other such times. In other words, you are learning how your mind works when it is not forced into rigid pathways. It is the psychic processes which are revealed, the spontaneous connections which you as an individual make.

In the second stage, you move beyond simply observing the images and deliberately involve yourself in a conscious participation in them, asking what relevance they have to you and your particular situation. You then make an intellectually binding and moral commitment to act on the insights which come up. This is a transition from a merely perceptive, observing attitude to one of discrimination and active participation in your own internal processes. The question then is 'What does this mean to me?' You take part in your own personal internal drama and thereby produce a significance for yourself which makes life more meaningful. When you can bring this ability into the waking world, you are able to live within the moment.

A man can get to know his anima, his inner hidden feminine, through the process of active imagination. She is given a personality and a voice of her own, and by asking her questions and paying attention to her response, a great deal of information can be assimilated.

Jung himself recognized that this might be a difficult process when he said:

I mean this as an actual technique ... The art of it consists only in allowing our invisible partner to make herself heard, in putting the mechanism of expression momentarily at her disposal, without being overcome by the distaste one naturally feels at playing such an apparently ludicrous game with oneself, or by doubts as to the genuineness of the voice of one's interlocutor. ['Anima and Animus', CW 7, pars. 323f.]

Naturally, the reverse process where a woman can allow herself to become acquainted with her animus – her inner hidden masculine – may also be used to some effect. This technique can also be used to come to terms with those inner demons which beset the traveller on the path to reality. Often such figures will manifest in response to stress or some hidden trauma which has not been dealt with by other means.

With strong similarities to the way in which the practising shaman is taught to deal with his demons, the meditative state coupled with active imagination or creative visualization can be used to understand and exorcise troublesome aspects of the personality. During a meditation on such aspects you might try the following:

✦ Let the problematic aspect come alive for you, at the forefront of your consciousness.
✦ Describe the aspect to yourself physically as it appears in the meditation. For instance, you might see your anger as a petulant child or your fear as a dragon or monster.
✦ Do not let the symbol change, but consider its essential nature. Hold it steady so that you can really contemplate it in its entirety
✦ How do you feel with the symbol? Can you get to the point where you feel you can deal with it – confront it, make it smaller, or change it in some way?

✦ What does the symbol bring up for you? Does it remind you of anything? If you still have unresolved issues with it can you recall it so that you can work with it again?

When you have worked with it as far as you can on this occasion, let the image fade, acknowledging its presence or assistance as you do so. Because you have given this aspect in effect a life of its own, you are now almost honour bound to go through a debriefing exercise with yourself so that you can ground what you have discovered about yourself in the real world.

✦ List its characteristics and functions within the meditation. This is really a reprise of the second step above and allows you to bring the information through to consciousness.

✦ Register the characteristics of the image as it functions within your everyday life. Recognize where your behaviour may belong as much to this particular aspect of your personality as to the everyday you. Be aware of how often you will bring out this aspect, perhaps as a defence mechanism or in response to a particular set of circumstances.

✦ Reduce qualities to their essence. By taking everything back to either their basic cause or their essential nature you can have an appreciation of both who you are and why you respond to aspects of your life in certain ways. You are again beginning to live life mindfully.

✦ Compare, contrast and blend inner and outer characteristics. By living life in a more mindful way you are able to recognize, for instance, where you are not being true to yourself or where you might be able to act more appropriately according to the circumstances around you.

When you feel that you are beginning to understand the art of living mindfully, you can begin to enhance your meditations.

MEDITATION ENHANCEMENT

The use of incense is a very efficient way of enhancing the mind's ability to uncover information. Incense is dealt with more fully later in the book, but we suggest the following combination as a simple starting point. Burn just a small amount of this incense before meditating to relax your conscious mind.

Meditation Incense

1 part Gum Acacia (arabic)
1 part Sandalwood

Many people also like to have some music to accompany meditation – it could be said to be a language which transcends barriers. Though they are difficult to perceive, music does have its own mathematical formulae. These formulae can have a profound effect on the vibrations, both physical and spiritual, of which we are all made – indeed, in former times, people actually believed that mathematics was a form of magic.

Music can be inspiring, exciting, calming or motivating and it is important that you choose pieces not only that you like, but also ones which serve your purpose. If you wished, you could, for instance, choose an evocative piece of music to train yourself in the art of visualization. You simply play your music, settle yourself in a comfortable position and allow the music to generate mental pictures for you. Hold each picture steady for a few moments and note all the details before letting it fade away, just as you did with the star visualization technique earlier.

This generating of pictures is the beginning of the art of clairvoyance, in the sense of clear seeing, and it teaches you to trust your own abilities – later you can practice with the pictures generated by your perception of another person. Do not worry if this seeing of pictures does not develop immediately, it will with time. For the purposes of meditation, you will find that you develop certain favourite pieces of music and these may come from the classics, New Age, modern or ethnic music. The choice is up to you.

Earlier you learned how to watch your breath, so the next stage, with or without music, is to find your Point of Power or cosmic energy centre. For anyone who sees themselves working within the field of magic this is very important.

Locating and Using your Point of Power

It is from the Point of Power that you ultimately control your own energy and also that which you use in your relationship with the natural world. In this next exercise you will practice abdominal breathing and will be able to locate the seat of your life force or spiritual core.

METHOD

Place your hands in what is called the 'cosmic mudra'.

Your right palm faces up, with the side of your little finger against your lower abdomen about three inches below your navel.

Your left hand is placed on top of your right hand.

Your middle knuckles overlap one another.

Your thumbs are just touching directly in front of your navel.

Both hands now form an oval shape in front of your lower abdomen – this locates your seat of power just about three inches below your navel.

(If you were able to draw a line from the external point to your solar plexus, the internal point would be on that line.)

This line is called the Dantien in Japanese or Tan Tien in Chinese.

Your breathing should now continue only through your nostrils.

Become aware of your breathing as you did earlier in Meditation Techniques.

With each inhalation and exhalation begin to breathe slowly into your abdomen.

During abdominal breathing, your chest stays relatively motionless while your lower abdomen seems to expand like a balloon.

As you become more proficient, you can track your breath on inhalation to the cosmic mudra and the Dantien point.

Note: This abdominal breathing can initially be difficult. If you find that you are becoming tense, stop and come back to it at a later date.

Pause there for a moment and then begin to allow the exhalation to start from the Dantien point.

As you finish the exhalation, see the energy of it reaching to the top of your head.

Gradually you will begin to sense the energy beginning to spill over like a fountain around you.

You might like to think of this as your own protective device – your sacred space – should you wish, in due course, to send out healing or good thoughts to someone.

When you feel that your practice is complete, allow the energy to sink back to your Point of Power and sit quietly for a few moments, just appreciating who you are.

At the conclusion of the exercise, you may use this energy to strengthen and energize your own body, re-vivifying the tissue, sinking deep into the bone material, cleansing the marrow, and affecting every cell in your body. All the connections between the cells are complete and strong.

This meditation is a good one to start with and is a necessary preparation for the more complex Kundalini or Kabbalistic techniques. When you feel that you have mastered the exercise – which may take weeks rather than days – you can move on to the next stage; that of becoming aware of the ways in which to use this new energy you are tapping into. As you breathe in this fashion and become aware of your Point of Power, be very conscious of the life energy which is yours. You will find yourself feeling more and more empowered, aware of the moment in which you are living and ready to use the energy you are building up to achieve that which you have decided is necessary.

Always treat this energy with humility and respect. If you treat it as a gift, you may discover that you know instinctively how to use it to maximum effect. With the caveat that it should only be used for good, you can then stream it out into the universe in quite a dispassionate way, knowing that you have done what you can.

If you find yourself becoming distracted when doing this exercise, do not worry too much. Simply relax and go back to watching your breath. Do not worry either if you find yourself becoming sleepy. Sometimes this can be because there is something that you do not wish to face, but often it can simply be because you are tired and your mind will not stay focussed. Simply try again another day. For the time being though, do remember to close down and allow the energy to return to the Point of Power. You can then use any visualization which helps you to feel protected against the grosser vibrations of everyday life. You might like to put a hard shell around your fountain, to envisage the fountain itself as protecting you or to draw a cloak up from the ground behind which you feel safe. It is your own way of protecting yourself and will in time be a trusted tool.

KUNDALINI

You have just learned how to recognize your own Point of Power. To be able to use this power successfully you need to have a little understanding of the ideas and theories behind it.

In any training in the use of magic, or rather magical forces, it is important to understand, and be able to use, the energy which is probably the most potent one known to humanity. In the East, this energy is known as Kundalini, which literally means 'coiling, like a snake'. (In the classical literature of hatha yoga, Kundalini is described as a coiled serpent with two heads (polarities) residing at the base of the spine, and is a reservoir of untapped potential energy.) Kabbalists may call it 'The Serpent Fire' – the foundation of our consciousness, so that when Kundalini moves through our bodies our consciousness necessarily changes with it – or the 'Dragon' which awakens the sleeping Self. Most spiritual practices are to some degree focussed on awakening this energy, which lies dormant until specifically aroused. Generally in the West, there is an inconsistency in our awareness of such a potent energy and its role in esoteric practices.

Awakened
Kundalini
energy

Much is made in the West of the problems that can arise from the misuse of Kundalini, such as excruciating headaches, unbearable sensations of heat, fits, extreme anxiety and psychosis. These have been the price paid by many who stressed their minds and bodies in over-stimulating practices. (All of these afflictions may also occur during an intense Kundalini episode when there has been no interference, but are a temporary condition. The system rebalances itself more quickly when the practitioner has learned to respect the natural course of raising Kundalini.) In fact, common sense and a willingness to take things slowly may be the best protection against any unpleasant side effects of any such esoteric practices.

It is best to learn lessons thoroughly before moving on to new things. It is true that the use of this power has a profound effect on the subtle energies and physical being of the practitioner, but it is also true that the benefits of learning how to use it can be quite phenomenal. A balanced lifestyle is essential and it is probably wise to ensure that you have achieved this before commencing daily practice. This means, in effect, honouring your body as a temple and treating yourself and everything you do with respect.

The exercises in the following section are meant to assist in freeing the Kundalini in a controlled fashion. This takes regular practice as well as commitment and perseverance. It is through these qualities that virtues and powers develop which ensure the practitioner's acceptance as an adept or expert. As a part of development, at some point the adept is required to pass on his knowledge to someone else so it is very important that you keep a diary of your practices and experiences with the exercises. You yourself will be in a better position to judge your own progress if you do.

The amount of time given to the exercises should not exceed more than 15 or 20 minutes in the beginning – indeed, people with busy lifestyles will find this is quite sufficient. Daily practice can then later be stepped up to 30 to 45 minutes, either all at one time or split into two parts, one in the morning and one in the evening. It is much better to be thorough rather than trying to hurry the process. You will probably find that any change in your practice takes place spontaneously as the inner changes occur. Avoid becoming fanatical and rigid in your thinking because this will be counterproductive –

above all, ensure that you maintain a firm hold on the reality in which you have to live.

Working slowly and progressively, clearing more and more subtle channels of energy as you go, will do a great deal to bring about subtle changes in the way you relate to the outside world and will help you to have an easy passage through to realization. You may also like to harness your dreams to help you; a technique for doing this is given in the section on Magical Dreaming above.

Kundalini energy is perceived as lying dormant at the base of the spine. Our consciousness of it is through our point of power. To be honest, only a small amount of energy is actually used in day-to-day living and a child, as he or she grows, learns to use this energy only in response to its greater awareness of the world. It is not until we make a conscious choice to develop and use this energy that we receive the benefit of a greater power. Most people experience at least one, and more often several, of the following benefits the more they practice.

✦ You will probably find that the health of the physical body improves.

✦ You will gain control over your feelings, experiencing richer emotions and deeper sympathy for others.

✦ You are better able to concentrate. Thinking, wisdom and discrimination become both more reliable and more available to you.

✦ Your mind no longer follows its own well trodden path and does not create attachments. You are able to let go of the non-essential much more easily.

✦ You are able to be much more dispassionate and to see the truth behind a situation.

✦ You know what action to take to help you to fulfil your goals.

✦ Psychic abilities appear.

✦ You begin to develop a much more direct relationship with the divine, whatever you perceive that to be, in keeping with your own spiritual state.

✦ You are able to maintain the principle of enlightenment while living in this world.

If this development is undertaken from the right perspective, you will not attempt to do it purely to develop magical powers.

Rather, those magical powers will become part of you as you explore the potential that there is. We give more information on this shortly.

Often a Kundalini experience is triggered by a temporary weakening of the life energy in the physical body – great physical stress, times of illness, or near-death experiences. At that point we may experience the Kundalini energy as a luminosity. This is often described as a ball of light surrounding us.

When this happens the individual can also experience other phenomena such as:

Inadvertent physical movements – shaking, rapid breathing, swinging of the torso, uncontrolled giddiness, and sitting bolt upright apparently without the individual's own volition.
The sense of a holy presence – an angel, their Higher Self, 'Holy Guardian Angel', or perhaps a great spiritual teacher.
Astral projection or an out of the body experience – this is when people become aware of places or dimensions other than the one they are in, or become aware that they are watching the scene around their own body from a different perspective – for instance, from above their hospital bed.

If, during this spontaneous release of Kundalini or 'secret fire', the energy does reach the top of the skull and beyond, the environment is ripe for a true spiritual awakening. This clears the path for the descent and re-ascent of the spiritual energy. During this time the psychic centres can be spontaneously awakened, leading to the manifestation of psychic powers and related phenomena. In the early stages of activation and awakening of the spiritual centres, physical and mental states may be experienced which might be considered somewhat strange. These are only temporary however, and should not cause anxiety – without fail, such phases pass. After a period of time the energy descends and returns to the base of the spine.

The effects of any spontaneous awakening especially on the consciousness of the individual will take some time to adjust to, for they are not limited to the 'non-physical' realms. The physical body is also changed and its functioning is improved, so if you decide to continue with further development, there has to be a conscious decision to cooperate with this influx of power if more permanent changes in consciousness are to be made.

When this energy rises as a result of this decision, the influx of energy can often be concentrated on various areas of the body, creating physical and psychic disturbances as listed below. Again, many of these will pass as you become more proficient.

✦ Intense pains are suggestive of an illness, usually caused by blockages in the energy.

✦ Crawling sensations of ants or small bugs over the skin, as well as a 'jumping' sensation of the energy. This is simply an increase in the overall energy available.

✦ A feeling of crystal clear calmness and tranquillity, rising from spiritual centre to spiritual centre right to the top of the head. As the centres clear, the perception changes thus putting you more in touch with your own energy.

✦ The energy ascends in the famous 'zigzag' or Rising Serpent pattern, the lightning flash of creation.

✦ The energy can miss out a centre, often caused by an inability to understand the implications of that particular centre.

✦ The power can reach the top of the head in a flash of light – another manifestation of the lightning flash.

✦ There is a strong consciousness of the polarities which are part of one's character and sexual power is increased.

✦ There can be the illusion of a spiritual awakening, a kind of messianic 'save the world' complex. This is markedly different to the knowledge that one has a part to play in the evolution of mankind.

This last point is somewhat tricky because once you are able to hold the energy properly at the top of the head at the centre of cosmic awareness, then it becomes possible to work directly on the life force within your body. You can use this as a means of enhancing the psychic experiences and spiritual awakening. You have established a line of communication between your own point of power and your cosmic awareness, but you also become aware of the illusory nature of life itself and that it is, in fact, transitory. You have accepted responsibility for your own physical and spiritual well-being.

CHAKRAS

After completing the exercise on page 196 you should have a sense of your own Point of Power, and we are now going to move on to an appreciation of the seven spiritual centres or 'chakras' as they are known in Sanskrit. The word means 'wheel' and that is how you can envisage them initially – as wheels of light. You might also perceive them as spheres of coloured light or as spirals. If you are of a more artistic frame of mind, you will appreciate the image of them as lotus flower of varying numbers of petals which gradually open into full bloom.

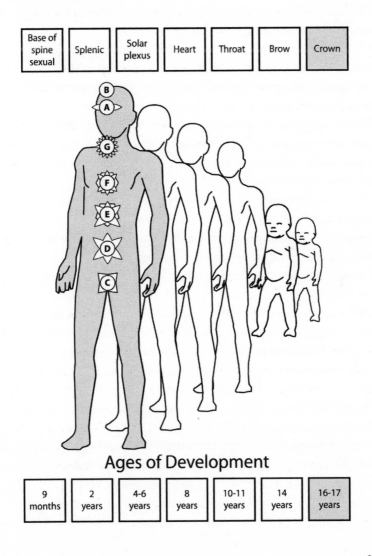

Base of spine sexual	Splenic	Solar plexus	Heart	Throat	Brow	Crown

Ages of Development

9 months	2 years	4-6 years	8 years	10-11 years	14 years	16-17 years

Chakra Development

This exercise continues with the opening of the spiritual centres and the various qualities associated with them.

METHOD

You should follow the same meditation procedure as before, but this time you will continue your meditation after you complete the fountain by working with and eventually opening up the chakra centres.

When you have successfully established the fountain, shift your awareness to the crown of your head and envision a pure white ball (flower, etc.) of light, just above your head. Start the ball spinning ready to move downwards through your body, and yet it still remains in place. (You will have two images to deal with, one the ball of clear light and the other the ball of energy which moves down the chakras.)

When you have this image clearly in mind, continue to the next chakra at the top of your head. This is normally seen as violet in colour and is much to do with how you perceive your place in the scheme of life – your cosmic responsibility.

Shift your awareness to the Third Eye area which is situated in the middle of the forehead. This governs perception and many of the aspects of clairvoyance and clairaudience – the psychic senses. The ball you perceive here is indigo in colour. Sometimes you may have some difficulty in separating out these first two chakras but be gentle with yourself and eventually they will become quite distinct.

When the indigo ball is spinning and stable, move to the throat chakra – the seat of right speech and wisdom. Here you should be able to visualize a beautiful azure blue ball. Think carefully about the wisdom that is needed within your own life and in the lives of others.

Next is the heart centre which can be conceived of as either a bright green or warm pink ball. The first denotes self awareness and the second love for others, so you can experiment initially with whichever particular one suits you. Do make sure that you also work with the concept and colour with which you are least comfortable.

Move down to your solar plexus, which is just above the navel, and see yellow as bright as a golden summer sun. This centre is the seat of the emotions and the point at which we receive a great deal of information from the outside world. It can sometimes be the most vulnerable point when working with the chakras but, if you bear in mind that it is very close to the point of power with which we have already worked, it is in fact easy to manage. Do take plenty of time to be sure that you have stabilized your visualization at this point as the gains in self-control are tremendous.

In the area below this, about half way between the navel and the sexual area, see your ball as an orange one. This centre is to do with relationships, not just sexual, but also your overall support structure and your relationship with yourself. By this, we mean the balance between the inner, private you and the outer worldly you.

The last chakra is normally thought of as being in the base of the spine and ties in with the concept of Kundalini. The ball you should see here is crimson red and is indicative of your self image and the way you think about yourself. As you work with this chakra you should become very aware of the energy of the 'secret fire' referred to previously.

From here, you can begin circling the energy upwards (using the spine as a conduit) until it comes back to the top of the head when you can let it sink gently back to the point of power.

Note: Take your time over this particular part of the exercise, since it is quite important that you become aware of the different energies at each level. You will use these perceptions as you begin to develop the siddhis. There are also small energy centres in the hands and feet, of which you will become more conscious as time progresses. Those in your hands will become part of your healing abilities and those in your feet will help you as you make your connections with the Earth's energy, as indicated in various rituals.

When you have successfully completed this part of the exercise, it is time to move on to the next. In this, once you become aware of the individual colours belonging to each chakra, you can allow them to flow back into one another, mingling and mixing as they do. They may stay somewhat separate or they may flow back into one another to become almost like mother-of-pearl, iridescent with all the other colours.

When you have finished these visualizations and meditations, sit quietly for a few moments and let your consciousness return to the ordinary. Initially, you should visualize each chakra being closed down in succession in accordance with your initial visualization until you are firmly grounded. You can check this by placing your hands on the ground or by touching a tree or even with the help of your personal stone as mentioned in Crystals and Stones later. Breathe deeply and appreciate your body as the temple it is for your essential energy.

As time goes on you may find that you become happy to remain aware and energized. So long as you do not become overly sensitive to conditions around you, that is perfectly alright. You may prefer to dedicate a special time for using the energy in magical practices.

Now that energy can be used as you wish in meditation and rituals. You might allow it to flow out and away from you to effect some kind of healing; you might use it to call on the divine energy or you might use it to become more aware of other dimensions and other worlds. You need to feel that it is yours to share in whatever way seems appropriate. In this way you will truly be creating magic.

Throughout the book in all of the rituals, techniques and spells we have suggested certain forms of words which might be suitable – these are suggestions only to get you started. As time goes on and you become more proficient, you will discover that you become more fluent and often words which you feel are more appropriate will come of their own accord. This means that you have truly made a connection through your inner self – the essential you – to the Divine source, whatever you believe that to be.

Some of you will wish to acknowledge God the Father, some Mother Earth. Use whatever form makes you feel comfortable. Others, who have followed the Christian teachings, will also acknowledge Christ – both as the Son of God and as the light of the world. Yet others will wish to work with the deities and energies or forces which seem to be more pagan or primitive. To work with natural magic, you do need to have a sense of connectedness and the feeling that you are using the energy and power correctly. Words are a potent way of doing this and prayer is an efficient use of words.

PRAYER

By and large, prayer can be structured very simply and generally consists of acknowledgement, thanks or dedication or promise. Thus, for instance, on waking in the morning you might begin the day by saying something like:

Father God/Mother of all, I thank you for your gift of this day and dedicate it to your greater good.

Working with this basic form, you may find that you are led to emphasize one particular part of the formula more than another. Thus you might say:

Father God, creator of all things and giver of life, we/I thank you for your many gifts and the opportunity to use them in your service. I promise to use them wisely and well.

An important part of any prayer or ritual is the request. Broadly speaking, in working magically, you are making a request in one of two ways. Either you wish to use the power and energies which you are accessing – i.e. you use the power and accept responsibility for that, or you ask for the power to be used on your behalf. Practice will tell you which you prefer. A Christian based prayer might be:

Let us come in humility to the fount of all life, our originator Father – Mother and to the son, the Cosmic Christ, who teaches us to use that life with respect. We now open our hearts and minds in thanks and adoration for our being, for all the good fortune which is ours, for the blessings which come to us. I ask that ...

A more nature-based prayer would consist of something like:

God of nature, God of life we thank you for the warmth of the sun and the soft light of the moon. Together they give the harvest of the earth and the bread of life which feeds man in all his needs. As we learn we grow and, asking your help, we desire to use thy gifts wisely and well. Help us to nurture our talents that we too may take part in The Great Harvest at the end of life's journey.

You may perhaps be motivated to ask for the power and the energy to carry out a task which is difficult. This requires that you call upon, not just the power of God, but of other deities/spirits and your form of words might then be something like this:

O God we pray that those who have gone before us, the heavenly hosts and those beings who have charge of us on the earthly realm help us as we try to achieve peace on earth [or whatever is your purpose]. May we receive a blessing on our endeavours and feel thy power and thy glory as we set about our task.

As time goes on and you find yourself more at ease with working in the spiritual realms, you will come to accept that the magic which you have been looking for comes about through cooperation with the Greater Powers. Hopefully, you yourself will be much more powerful and more able to use the siddhis or powers inherent in all of us. For this you might use a prayer such as the following:

Let us now acknowledge the spiritual realms where those who have gone before us now reside. May those we have loved reveal themselves to us, those who are our guardians and guides protect us and those who are to teach us step forward to be acknowledged. Beyond even those are the angelic ones, the masters and the saints. We approach with awe, knowing that, free of the constraints of the physical, these beings can assist us in our task. We ask that, like them, in due course we may achieve constant union with the divine. May we learn to use the power that is available to us in dimensions which are not of this earth for the good of all. May we learn to see, to sense and to feel with honesty and integrity. We would undertake never to use the power for evil, for such use brings its own punishment. We ask this, as always, in the name of the Creator.

The prayers above have all been examples of those addressed to God in the form of Father or Mother, Giver of life, creator and king of the spiritual realms. With these last prayers you will have become aware of a wider spiritual dimension; it is this awareness which will allow you access to other aspects of the power which we call the Ultimate.

Our forebears prayed to their ancestors just as we pray to those who have gone before. They called upon their Gods as they perceived them to be, perhaps giving them specific tasks to perform

– for instance, Mars being the God of War, Demeter Goddess of the Earth. We are perhaps fortunate nowadays in that we can have access to these gods and goddesses as part of a greater whole, but can also go, if we wish, to a specific 'department' for information and help. With a sufficiently open mind, we can also access the deities of other faiths and can use the power and energy to help us in our chosen tasks. The form of prayer will still be the one discussed above – acknowledgement, thanks, request, dedication or promise.

So, for instance, if you were praying to Athene as the Greek Goddess of Strategy, you might say something along the lines of:

Athene, Goddess of Wisdom and of Strategy, I thank you for your presence. I ask that you show me the best way of achieving my task. [You might then state your task as simply as possible.] I dedicate the outcome to you and believe that whatever the result it will be for the best.

Later you may wish to give thanks and might say something like:

Athene, wise Goddess of the Greeks, you helped me when I called. I offer thanks to you now and open myself to your knowledge and perception.

If you choose to work in this way, as you become more confident in your approaches you will probably find yourself drawn to particular gods and goddesses. Part of the relationship between you and these aspects of the Ultimate Being (or One God) is to get to know them better. You can do this through the act of prayer, so take the time to learn about them and to communicate with them just as you would a good friend. Treat the gods and goddesses with respect and love, just as you would someone on the earth plane and you need not fear anything which might occur.

The next stage is that you might begin to put some rhythm into your prayer. In some ways, rhythm is more important than rhyme because it has a hypnotic effect which can help you to change consciousness. Done properly, it can become a chant which allows you to turn inwards and make a connection in a way that is different from simple prayer. To petition the Horned God you might say:

Lord of the Forest
Horn-ed One,
Come to my aid
Your help I seek.

Lord of the Forest
Horn-ed One,
Come to me now
In my hour of need.

Lord of the Forest
Horn-ed One,
My spirit is low
And I crave your peace.

To petition the Goddess you might say:

Silver lady, lady of night,
Watch over me and mine I pray,
Keep us safe within your sight
Till once again we see the day.

This prayer might be used to encompass the spirit realms:

Those Beings who surround us tonight as we pray, bring with them their own
light, the light of the spirit. Often we falter, but always that light is before us
guarding and guiding us. It illuminates our darkness and bathes us with
compassion, for they too have suffered as we have. From that compassion we
draw strength and we stand tall, able to cope with all that life brings. Let us
now acknowledge their presence with heart and mind. Let us enter the silence
for a few moments so that, refreshed, we return to the everyday world and bring
back with us a little of that light that others may share. May the love of the
eternal spirit shine through and enfold you.

If the group considers their sacred space to be a temple, this is a suitable prayer.

Great architect of the universe, High and perfect spirit, we pray thee, guide us in all your ways. May we give expression through form to thy beauty, may we manifest it in the work of our minds and hands as a fit offering to thee. May our lives, every thought and every action be inspired by your wisdom. May we undertake life's journey with courage and humility and create a sanctuary for thy glorious presence.

Here are two blessings which are suitable for use in an ecumenical way:

To the eternal God, let us give thanks in silence and in peace! May our lives be the gift we offer and our hearts a dedication full of joy. Let us express our love in joyous living and our caring in compassion for others, that their needs may be met.

We bless and thank the great white spirit for his presence. We take deep within ourselves his love, his wisdom and his power. May we become ever more worthy to walk in his path.

Should you feel that it is appropriate, the incense below is specifically designed to bring about divine intervention in whatever form you perceive that to be necessary. Experiment with small amounts until you feel you have created your own balance with your gods.

Divine Intervention Incense

½ part Dragon's Blood Resin

½ part Frankincense Resin

¼ part Angelica

¾ part Galangal

½ part Bay

½ part Sandalwood

¼ part Cinnamon

Meditation helps you, as you have already seen, to bring your mind under control. As this happens it becomes a willing servant rather than a despotic master, a tool rather than an engine. As such, it is able to fetch and carry images which will be useful to you in understanding the world around you and your own internal world. Often it will present you with pictorial representations of ideas, rather than with the ideas themselves.

SYMBOLS AND SHAPES

One aspect of meditation that is common to all types is the use of symbols. As the mind begins to free itself, it plumbs the depths of archetypal (basic) awareness and you will find that many representations float to the surface which can be interpreted very easily if you give them a little thought. A flame, for instance, is a fairly universal symbol for fire as well as for power. Dream symbolism and the images which occur in meditation have many similarities and you may well discover that you are able to learn your own internal language and way of interpreting it through the use of both.

However, there is another universal language which is recognizable in magic and that is the symbolism of shape. Before people could count they recognized patterns and used those patterns and shapes to represent ideas and concepts. Unity and duality (one and two) can be represented by a point and a line and out of that arises geometry which might be defined as the appreciation of space. We give here some of the symbols used in this way:

Dot

The dot, or very small, filled circle, is one of the most common Western symbology marks. It has been in existence since the time of rock and cave carvings, and represents a point of being or awareness. It is perhaps worth remembering that a line is simply in essence a series of joined up dots. It also signifies identity.

The point or dot seems to denote something that is small or focussed, immediate in its impact or, more esoterically, The One. It also seems to enhance or intensify the meaning of other signs and sigils. The dot can also denote a beginning – a starting point – or an end, a goal.

LINE

A line is the unification of two points or dots and in magical terms suggests the energy which unites them. For this reason, the horizontal line — is a symbol for the feminine submissive, sympathetic, materially based dimension of the universe. It represents the base, the earth, the land. When it is combined with another sign placed over it, it increases or broadens that sign's meaning i.e. it raises its vibration. When placed below, it emphasizes it and gives it solidity and reality.

The straight vertical line – | in unifying the upper and the lower – stands for oneness as well as the positive, active, warm and masculine dimensions of the universe. It can also represent the self, personal power and influence. In magical terms, it can be divisive if combined with other symbols – i.e. it separates them, indicating that what is represented by those other signs may be treated separately.

When three lines are represented in the form of the arrow, ↑ they indicate a direction to be taken. This sign also represents masculinity.

Horizontal line   *Vertical line*   *Arrow/Masculinity*

TRIANGLE

By and large, the triangle does not seem to have been used much in prehistoric times – or rather, there is little evidence to suggest that it was. The equilateral triangle is used to suggest the number three and later, by association, in Christianity the Holy Trinity. It is also a symbol for power and, even today in universal signs, can also signify danger or a warning of such.

In magical terms and in alchemy by the Middle Ages △ had come to signify the element of fire, with its up-rush of power. When a line was added, ⌂ it was used to signify the alchemical symbol for the element of air. When the triangle was reversed to suggest power moving downwards and became the symbol for the element of water ▽ and then the symbol for the element earth ⩝ .

This is, of course, in line with the theories behind emanation and subsequent thought which we consider on page 72.

The triangle of manifestation is a simple way of bringing about a magical manifestation. It is a metaphysical belief that, in order to manifest something, the three components of time, space and energy must all come together. If energy is directed into a time/space continuum there must be some kind of manifestation. (By forming a triangle you mentally bind three aspects together, in this case, time, space and energy.)

To give yourself an easy way of directing the energy, you can use a triangle formed by placing the tips of the index fingers of both hands together while placing both thumbs tip-to-tip, and using the resultant space between as a focus for your energy.

Since the mathematical symbol for change is the triangle, in this movement it signifies the intent to change something and can therefore be used as flamboyantly or unobtrusively as necessary.

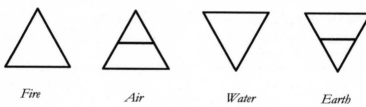

| Fire | Air | Water | Earth |

CROSS

The cross ┼ is one of the most common structures in Western cultures. The stem of the cross, the vertical line, | stands for the heavenly or spiritual, whereas the transverse beam — represents the material plane of existence. Before the time of Jesus, the cross represented, among other things, the staff of Apollo, and appeared on ancient coins. The sun wheel, ⊕ the inaugural cross, is identical to the ancient symbol found in the Bronze Age. It has been used by most cultures. The Maltese cross ✖ is one of the best known equal armed crosses whose eight points symbolize the eight virtues of the Knights of the Order.

The diagonal cross, with arms of equal length, ✕ is an extremely old sign. It has been found engraved on the walls of prehistoric caves of Europe. As an Egyptian hieroglyph, it meant 'divide', 'count' and 'break into parts', and thus can be used in the making of amulets and talismans. It is also a rune used in some of the old Nordic Rune alphabets, named *gif* or *geba*, and signified a gift from a chief to a loyal warrior or subject.

This sign has a wide spectrum of meanings and it will depend on the context in which it is used which meaning is relevant, particularly in talismanic work. It can signify anything from confrontation, annulment and cancellation, to opposition, obstruction and mistake. It can also mean 'devoid of sense or meaning', 'unfamiliar', 'undecided or unknown' and 'unsettled', and therefore should be used very carefully. When the diagonal cross appears white on a blue background, it stands for the cross of St Andrew, Scotland's patron saint; when red on a white background it represents St Patrick, patron saint of Ireland.

The Latin cross ┼ is chiefly associated with the cross on which Jesus Christ was crucified. This cross turned upside down ┴ is known as St Peter's cross after Peter, the disciple of Jesus who is believed to have been executed by crucifixion on an upside down cross since he did not consider himself worthy of the same treatment as the Lord Jesus. It also signifies the warrior. The cross of the patriarch ╪ is somewhat similar. The second crossbeam is said to be a representation of the cross of crucifixion and the temporal power exercised by an Archbishop. The cross of the Pope, ╪ thus signifies spiritual authority and is in turn, related to the cross of the Russian Orthodox Church ╪.

The Christian Church has often adopted cross-like ideograms from earlier ideologies that have had a positive meaning. The Egyptian cross ♀ for instance, is an adaptation of the ancient Egyptian hieroglyph ankh, ♀ a symbol for life and rebirth.

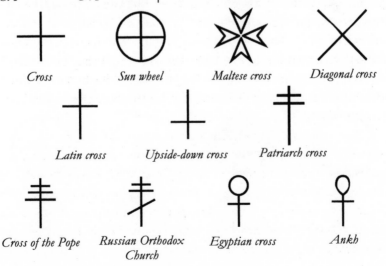

Cross   Sun wheel   Maltese cross   Diagonal cross

Latin cross   Upside-down cross   Patriarch cross

Cross of the Pope   Russian Orthodox Church   Egyptian cross   Ankh

CIRCLE

Both the empty ◯ and filled circles ● are extremely ancient. The former often represents either the sun or the moon. The filled circle, the disc or the globe, seems to be older than the empty. It is found virtually worldwide: among the Egyptian hieroglyphs, in Japanese Buddhist symbolism, in India as well as in Nordic rock carvings.

The circle with a point at its centre as a symbol (●) is ancient and seems to have been used almost universally. It always represents the sun, power or something very akin to the sun. It can also suggest the conscious self or the spark of divine consciousness, the life force. The scholars of the Middle Ages used as a sign for the Earth as the centre of existence surrounded by the great ocean.

⊕ The sun cross or Odin's cross is a structure which belongs to the Bronze Age. It is common on rock carvings and it appears in ancient Egypt, China, pre-Columbian America, and the Near East. In earliest times it was a symbol for the highest power, for the sun and its counterpart, the king. It also signifies the wheel of the sun and represented power and control. In the Catholic church it is known as the Gamma cross. At the consecration of a church, the bishop, using blessed water or oil, draws the wheel cross at 12 different places on the church walls. Said to represent the disciples, this also echoes the signs of the zodiac and may be associated with the wheel, in the sense of the turning of time and the raising of new opportunities.

The circle is a symbol of wholeness and completion. In magical terms, it is drawn to signify enclosure, but is also meant to show equality, particularly in group work such as in the Arthurian Round Table. It is thus almost a magical tool in its own right. Visualizing a person in a circle of light signifies protection or healing, while the creation of a circle of power has the effect of stabilizing and bringing under control an energy which might not otherwise be usable.

Empty circle   *Filled circle*   *Circle with point*   *Sun cross*

SPIRAL

The clockwise spiral – that is one which starts from a single point in the middle ⑨ represents power, water and independent movement. The spiral seems to have been included in drawings on cave walls somewhat later than circles, crosses and other such simple forms. It is seen as a symbol for potential power in Tibet, and is seen in Crete from around 2000 BC where it later evolved into the labyrinth.

In prehistoric rock carvings and paintings found in Northern Europe, the spiral seems to indicate the potential for movement, and by definition came to mean the migration of communities. The Vikings used it to represent independent movement – particularly against the sun, waves and wind. It also means eventual return for them, whilst in Greece the double spiral ⑨⑨ signified water and, more importantly, the sea. This particular representation was common on vases and amphorae.

In later times a version of this, two circles interconnected and two spirals rotating clockwise and anticlockwise, came to represent infinity ∞.

The spiral is also related to the swastika which is actually a very old structure. Its arms were angled in a clockwise direction (starting from a central point) – it therefore also bears similarities to the triskele, which is much beloved in Celtic imagery. In India, the swastika was given its name *su* – 'good' and *asti* – 'to be', with the suffix *ka*. The reverse rotation however, far from being good, is said to bring bad luck and difficulty.

In magical working the spiral can be used to represent the raising of consciousness which is used by the practitioner. It can also be used as a protective device against negativity.

Spiral

Double spiral

Infinity

217

Protection Visualization

Visualize a seven-ringed spiral of light descending over you from a point above your head, enclosing you in a very powerful force field which will repel any ill-wishes or misfortune which is directed towards you. The spiral can either be of white light or, from top to bottom, the reverse colours of the rainbow. This visualization is, of course, an extension of the circle used in rituals.

Now try it the opposite way round, visualizing the spiral of rainbow coloured light rising from the ground (Mother Earth), finishing up above your head in a circle of white light. This is the halo representation seen in many old paintings.

PENTAGRAM

If the planet Venus' movements in the zodiacal sky as seen from the earth were plotted on a chart, the shape of a pentagram would be revealed. Venus was probably first discovered as a results of astronomical research in the Euphrates – Tigris region about 6,000 years ago. It appears both as the morning (in the east before sunrise) star and the evening (in the west after sunset) star. As the morning star ★ Venus was the deity of battle, hunting and physical activity. As the evening star ☆ it was, and for many people still is, representative of the goddess of beauty, sexuality and fertility.

The pentagram was a common symbol among the Sumerians around 2700 BC, most likely as a cosmic symbol representing the four corners of the earth and the vault of the heavens. Because it can be drawn in one continuous line, it represents the interconnectedness of all things. However, during the Middle Ages the pentagram became much associated with magic and in popular belief the Antichrist – the Devil. In the process it was often drawn reversed ⛧ and even today many remain afraid of it in this form, since they still believe it represents the Devil and all things evil.

Today when the symbol of the morning star is used, it is often related to matters of war and military power, whereas the evening star appears as a sign to denote feasting, happiness, festivities and all sorts of favourable opportunities. In magical terms, the pentagram represents the Spirit ruling over the Elements.

Morning star

Evening star

Reversed star

The symbolism of the pentagram is thus:

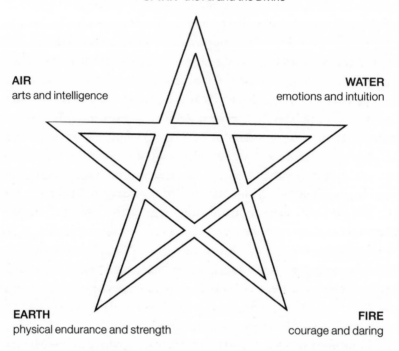

SPIRIT the All and the Divine

AIR
arts and intelligence

WATER
emotions and intuition

EARTH
physical endurance and strength

FIRE
courage and daring

This symbolism is used in the Lesser Banishing Ritual of the Pentagram previously.

There is one further way in which the pentagram is used in magical working and that is in the pentacle – the symbol of a circle surrounding the five-pointed star. The circle represents the power of the God and/or the Goddess and helps to focus and enhance the pentagram. The whole symbol is often used as a point of power to consecrate tools and other sacred objects or as a focus for meditation in order to ground any stray energy if necessary.

For many people the pentacle is a simple representation of the perfect human body surrounded by nature or the God and the Goddess and therefore, when worn as personal jewellery, is worn as a protection against negativity and as a reminder of one's potential. It forms a powerful link with others of like mind.

We give below two very simple rituals which make effective use of the pentagram's protective powers.

The Protective Power of the Pentagram

METHOD

With the first and middle fingers of your power hand (or your athame, if you have one),
trace the shape of a pentagram over the object to be protected.
Visualize electric-blue or purple flame streaming from your fingers (athame)
to form the pentagram.
Following the large diagram above, trace from Fire to Spirit to Earth to Water to Air and
finally back to Fire.
As you are doing this, envisage the article being totally protected from theft, breakage
or harm of any sort.

Note: Louis Claude de Saint Martin, the founder of Martinism (see page 67) probably used such a technique to protect himself and his followers.

Another way of using the power of the pentagram is to use it to banish an evil or
malign spirit. Here is how you do so.

METHOD

Take five dark coloured candles and place them in the shape of a pentagram around
you. You can anoint each candle with a suitable banishing oil.
Light each candle and as you do so visualize the flames joining together to create a
wall of protection around you.

Sit at the centre of the pentagram.
Concentrate on your wish to banish the evil spirit, then repeat at least three, and
preferably nine, times:

Ashes to ashes
Spirit to spirit
Take this soul
Banish this evil

Then snuff out the candles starting from the upper right point of the pentagram
(Water), so that the last one to snuff out is the one that symbolizes the Spirit.

You have now learned to understand and use geometric and magical symbols as tools, so it is time to learn creative visualization and the use of symbols to help you to handle some of the ordinary day-to-day problems which might arise.

CREATIVE VISUALIZATION

Creative visualization is the art of allowing the mind sufficient freedom to produce a symbol or picture which is meaningful to nobody else but you. It does not have to be ornate – indeed you will find the simpler the better. Sometimes the image will come to you in meditation, sometimes in dreams and sometimes will arise spontaneously apparently of its own volition.

As a general rule there are seven stages of creative visualization. These are as follows:

1. Setting the scene in as much detail as you can.
2. Visualizing objectively yourself and others taking part in your scenario.
3. Refining the detail, rejecting things that are obviously not feasible or are over the top, and accepting and adding additional detail where possible.
4. Seeing, feeling and sensing yourself participating in your visualization.
5. Testing your doubts and fears. These may range from 'Have I the right to expect this?' to 'Someone will stop me....' and taking in a huge range of similar such statements in between – even down to 'Do I really want this?'
6. Accepting that whatever you are visualizing can happen for you in the here and now. You are giving yourself an acceptable present.
7. Taking responsibility for allowing your visualization to happen. You have, and can have, a sustainable future.

You can often gain tremendous insight into your own and other people's motivation through this process and it is, of course, an invaluable tool in making things happen in a positive way. Here we use it to remove problems, but it could equally be used to create good things for yourself and others.

To Get Rid Of Fear

This is a good technique using herbs, visualization and relaxation to deal with difficulties. Though we have made suggestions for your visualization, try first of all to allow your own mind to create an image for you. Ask yourself 'What does my fear look like?'

YOU WILL NEED

Some herbs for courage
(such as Basil, Garlic, Mullein, Nettle, Thyme)
A red candle

METHOD

Construct your sacred space; spread the herbs around it.

Put the candle in front of you, then
Say the following three times:

Hear me, I call upon courage
To relinquish the holding ties of fear,
Break them, leave me, far away,
Let them not be near.

Now lie down quietly for 10 or 15 minutes, breathing deeply and concentrating on fear fading away into the atmosphere (cosmos).
You might use a symbol to represent fear. For example, you could use a visualization of a heavy weight which becomes lighter or the word 'Fear' itself in large letters which either breaks up into its individual letters and disappears or becomes smaller the more you concentrate on it.

Let the candle burn out on its own.

Collect up the herbs and candle and bury them in the earth.

Try to do this as far from your home as possible.
(This will help you stave off your fears and doubts.)

Creative visualization can be used in many different ways. In the section entitled 'Tree Personalities' (page 261) it is suggested that you 'become' the nature spirit of a particular tree. While this is in many ways an exercise in feeling, we have seen that creative visualization works best if you can visualize yourself participating in your most desired scenario. So, 'becoming' something is the next step to imagining a result. In previous times, it was this art that allowed the old magicians to shape-shift and become a being other than themselves. Today we would not necessarily use this ability, because scientific belief precludes the carrying out of this act.

However, to be truly magical is to believe in your own power, so you can certainly try to sense what it is like to be a tree or a flower, or even your own power animal. How far you decide to take this exercise is up to you. It will certainly give you a different perception to the one you normally have in the hustle and bustle of everyday life. Do remember, however, that this involves a change in consciousness and you should take time when you have been working in this way to ensure that you are firmly grounded afterwards in the everyday world.

This next ritual helps you to see the patterns in nature. As you learn how to do this you will begin to appreciate the beauty in form and how everything can be allowed to fall into place of its own accord. In the same way that you could see pictures in flames or 'stories' in rock patterns when you were a child, with practice you can do so again and will learn to be able to understand the wider picture rather than just what is immediately in front of you.

To Get Rid of a Difficulty

Nemesis is the Greek goddess of destiny, but also represents divine anger against mortals who break moral laws or taboos. She is often pictured as pitiless and unrelenting, signifying the need to submit to a will greater than one's own. She was often shown with a wreath on her head, an apple in her left hand, and a bowl in her right. There is, when working with her, always the need to bow to the inevitable, to accept a greater wisdom than our own limited vision allows.

When we are really troubled by our own intransigence or that of someone else, Nemesis gives us the space and the wherewithal to work things out, and do what must be done. She allows us to accept responsibility for our own actions.

YOU WILL NEED
Black candle

Patchouli/orange oil

Apple

METHOD
Empower the candle by rubbing it with the oil.

Light the candle.

Slice the apple across the middle in order that the pentagram seen in the arrangement of the pips is revealed.

Rest the apple next to the candle.

Explain everything about the problems you have to the goddess in your own words.

Then say:

The sign of justice is the scales.
Goddess of destiny, I ask that you take this problem
And weigh it in those scales.
If I be lacking, correct me and show me the solution.
If I have created it, unravel the dilemma.
If there is no blame then cleanse the record.

If the solution is not in my hands, then show me what must be done.
If there can be no resolution, then free me from the pain.
Work now thy wisdom and give me peace.
This I ask of you.

Now take time to meditate on the ritual you have just carried out.
Pick up the apple and contemplate the perfection of the arrangement of the pips.
Take note of all the thoughts which go through your head and any decisions that you may come to.

After the meditation, put the thoughts and decisions in order and then think about them logically.
The answer should soon become apparent, but only act when you are ready.

Allow the candle to burn out then bury the apple, bearing in mind that all things are cyclical and that the world consists of growth, decay and regeneration.

So far, we have looked at actual objects and personal qualities which will help us to become magical practitioners. One thing we must do is to learn how to use the energies which are available to us. This requires being able to use the energies of the elements. We have already ascertained that there are four basic elements. These are Fire, Air, Earth and Water.

THE ELEMENTAL KINGDOM

For those who are sufficiently sensitive to perceive them, within each of those four elements are nature spirits which are often pictured as being similar to humans. They are actually composed of etheric energy – a concept of power which is much more subtle than gross physical energy – and so can sometimes be perceived as coloured lights. Their world is that of their own element, so it will take some imagination and practice for you to experience this. All you need to remember is that they are living entities and you are, like them, part of the rich pattern of life energy.

There are many and varied beliefs as to the way that these elementals, as they are known, work. They operate primarily on the mental plane translating thought-forms into physical forms by altering mental patterns into etheric and then physical patterns. They lay down a matrix, or framework, for manifestation. Each of them seems to have the ability to create a specific form, whatever that might be.

Even though they are capable of creating form, they do not start off by having a definite character or appearance. Usually though they will manifest as an easily recognizable form appropriate for the element they represent. When you see a face in a flower, a shape in a raindrop or a damp area in the road, take time to look for you may be seeing an elemental. Usually elementals will show themselves when you least expect it and often when you are sitting quietly. They have a reality all their own, so do not try to invest them with human qualities. Once you realize that it is the interaction and relationship between you and them which enables them to be seen, you will appreciate that they should be treated with respect.

In essence they are like thought forms. Just as fear (an emotion) can generate a psychic black cloud, so elementals (patterns of basic energy) can produce a force field that is recognizable; they materialize whatever they pick up from the thoughts and feelings of mankind. Initially this relationship was intended to be a creative force in the rebuilding of a paradise here on Earth; as mankind becomes more and more divorced from Nature, so that creative force is weakened.

Perhaps the easiest way to think of the etheric energy is as the interface between the spiritual and physical realms. In the chapter on

Creation we speak of emanation. Each element, when manifesting from the 'world' above it, requires a degree of denser energy around which to have a physical reality. When the physical reality is no longer necessary (i.e. on death) the last thing to dissolve will be the somewhat finer energy, the etheric. Elemental energy might therefore be thought of as the spark of manifestation clothed in an appropriate image for each element. It depends upon the frequency of the vibration which image and which way of working is appropriate. Nature spirits are particular images and manifestations of elemental energy. We shall deal with them in order of element.

EARTH

The nature spirits of the Earth are called gnomes. This comes from a word invented by Paracelsus. This name was given to them because it was said that they knew the power of the earth and the exact location of its riches. They are said to live underground and guard the earth's treasures. Usually depicted as gnarled old dwarves wearing tight-fitting brown clothes and monastic hoods, they exhibit the qualities of the earth in which they live and seem to be capable of dissolving into the trunks of trees to hide from humans. Other groups within the Earth's nature spirits are brownies, dryads, earth spirits, elves, pans (ruled by the god Pan) and satyrs.

FIRE

Without salamanders, the spirit of fire, it is said that physical fire cannot exist. There are many families of salamanders, differing in size, appearance and behaviour. They have been seen as sparks or small balls of light, but most often they are perceived as being lizard-like in shape and about a foot or more in length. They are considered the strongest and most powerful of all the elementals. Salamanders have the ability to extend, or diminish, their size as needed. It has also been said that salamanders (and the other elemental beings) can be mischievous at times. As nature spirits they are greatly affected by the way that mankind thinks. Out of control, salamanders can be considered dangerous.

AIR

The sylphs are the air spirits; their element has the highest vibratory rate of the four. They are said to live on the tops of mountains and are volatile and changeable. They work through the gases and winds of the world and vary in size. They are usually perceived with wings and look like cherubs or fairies. They can assume human form but only for short periods of time. One of their tasks is said to be to help humans receive inspiration, so when there is a creative block it is worth finding a high, perhaps windy, place in which to think.

WATER

The undines are the elemental beings connected with water and are beautiful and very graceful. Often seen riding the waves of the ocean or by waterfalls and lakes, they are usually clothed in a shimmery substance which looks rather like water. The nymph is frequently found in a fountain and the mythical mermaid belongs to the ocean. Some undines inhabit waterfalls, others live in rivers and lakes. The undines also work with the plants that grow under the water and with the motion of water. Closely resembling humans in appearance, their size depends on the energy available to them, for they are emotional beings, friendly and able to work with human beings. Sometimes smaller undines are often seen as winged beings that people have mistakenly called fairies.

The more we learn about nature spirits, the more we are able to utilize opportunities to welcome them into our lives. Below are just a few examples of how nature spirits and plants interrelate.

PLANTS

Agrippa, in the 17th century, set out the way plants are thought of in regard to the elements, so you may wish to consider this when working with them in a magical way. He said:

In Plants also, the roots resemble the Earth, by reason of their thickness: and the leaves, Water, because of their juice: Flowers, the Air, because of their subtlety, and the Seeds the Fire, by reason of their multiplying spirit.

BERRIES

Berries, particularly strawberries, are often included in offerings to the gods and goddesses. Their rich ripe colour is considered to be particularly appropriate. In nature rituals, they can be left also as offerings to the nature spirits and the birds.

BLUEBELLS

Traditionally, bluebells planted outside the door are supposed to ring to warn witches that they have a visitor coming. It is said that as the world becomes more psychically polluted, bluebells will disappear. Because of their association with witches, people refused to have them growing in their gardens during the time of the witch persecutions, which is why they were – and indeed still are – often found in wooded glades.

EYEBRIGHT

One of the magical uses of eyebright is to help to develop clairvoyance (clear-seeing). For this, you can make an eye wash:

YOU WILL NEED
Boiling water
Two handfuls of eyebright herb
Heatproof bowl
Bottle

METHOD
Put the herbs in the bowl.
Pour sufficient water over the herbs to cover them.
Stir and leave to infuse for about 10 minutes.
If you wish, invoke your particular deity or nature spirit.
Let the liquid cool to room temperature.
Strain and bottle for future use.

GINGER

This pungent root is used, quite literally, to spice up spells and rituals. The root of the plant is dried and ground ready for use. A pinch placed on your pentacle or sprinkled on food or drink offerings seems to make results happen quicker.

MUGWORT

This herb is often an ingredient in dream pillows and is also used in divinatory incenses. Used as an infusion it can help develop clairvoyance. It should be used sparingly.

When you choose as part of your magical practice to work with objects from nature, one of the most rewarding aspects is working with stones – not necessarily gemstones but ordinary ones which you have found.

CRYSTALS AND STONES

Often a stone will 'speak' to you and will attract your attention in some way, either because of its shape, its appearance or, as you become more used to trusting your intuition, the way it feels. Ideally, it should fit comfortably and unobtrusively into your hand and your pocket so that you can work with it wherever you are. Strictly, you should not go searching for your stone, though there is a fine line between searching and recognizing a need.

When you do find your stone there are several things that you need to be aware of while you learn its story and learn how best to use it.

1. First you need to have some concept of how it became what it now is. Ask yourself was it once large and has now become weathered? Is it a piece of a larger stone which broke off somewhere? What has it experienced to get to you? Use your imagination to begin with, but as you develop a greater rapport with your stone, you may be quite surprised at some of the information you receive. Think now about how you can apply the concept of a journey to the way your life is at the moment.

2. Secondly, you need to have a concept of how you and it became connected. See it as energy and power, as it was in the beginning – a mass of gaseous material gradually becoming compact and manageable as an energetic force. Then see how the vibrations that it consists of reached out to you and made a connection, just as you did to it. Put yourself, through those connections, in touch with Earth and all its power.

3. Begin to use the stone as an energizer. When you are tired, rub the stone; when you are sad, hold on to it and use it to gain a sense of permanence, when you feel out of touch, use your own sense of touch to re-establish links. Initially you may feel a little silly doing this sort of thing but gradually you will become more at home and will gain much benefit.

4. Next, the stone brings your head out of the clouds and makes you realize what is important to you. As life's journey starts in earnest, we all have grand ideas about where we will end up. Using the stone as a foundation, and always having it around you, gives the grounding necessary to successfully complete the journey. It makes you realize that no matter what, we are all of this earth and should be grateful simply for that. This gives the stone more power than is first realized, for it has the ability to attract us towards it again or to be magnetic. This is powerful indeed and should make us aware of our own magnetism and the ability to attract.

5. Then the stone can link you in to eternal wisdom. Just as it has come to you through aeons of time, so also you are composed of many different experiences – not just yours but also those of your forefathers. It can give you a sense of continuity, of belonging and of being nurtured – indeed of belonging to a much wider family. Your experiences have a validity all of their own, and you need never be totally alone when you have your stone to remind you of who you are.

6. There are times when you need to feel protected from harm, from the hard winds of reality which can buffet you in many ways. Your stone will remind you of your ability to weather those storms, to stand firm in the face of adversity and to come through unscathed. You are – and always have been – unique and can make use of those unique qualities as you journey through life.

7. You can also use your stone as a meditative aid. Just as a child uses a comforter, so your stone can help you to be at peace, to be contemplative and to get back to simplicity. In a place of silence, perhaps in front on your shrine, by holding the stone and focussing your mind you can marshal your thoughts, plan for the future and let go of the past. Here you are using your stone as a 'worry stone'.

8. Your stone can remind you that you are part of a greater whole, that small as you are there is much to understand and much to appreciate in this world of ours. Finally, if you wish, you can make your stone a repository for your dreams and desires and, as you sit quietly with it, remind yourself of all you can and want to be.

USING STONES IN MAGICAL WORK

Crystals and stones are gifts from nature and can be used to enhance your rituals and magic. They can become sacred, magical tools in their own right. When consecrating a circle, creating your sacred space or making a shrine, you may like to search out stones which can represent the elements, so here are a few suggestions:

Air

When looking for stones to represent air, you need to think of crystal-clear stones or yellowish tinged ones. A quartz crystal point can often be picked up quite cheaply and, of course, it does not matter if it is flawed because, with a little imagination, these flaws can often look like clouds. Quartz pebbles are often found on the seashore weathered by the water.

Fire

Stones to represent fire should be red or orange or sometimes black. Any stone which has the feeling of passion or fiery emotion will do very well – carnelian or red jasper work particularly well. Volcanic rocks, or other very hard ones, often signify fire since they are the outcome of fire from the earth.

Water

Blue or blue-green stones are good if you wish to represent water and if you are near the sea you might find a piece of salt or sand-blasted glass which is ideal. Although glass is man-made, nature has done its work. White or greyish pebble stones actually found in water are also very useful whilst a piece of stone with seaweed attached is also good. Some agates are very pretty and can echo some wave patterns.

Earth

The colours for earth are green and brown, and many of the stones associated with earth are green as well. All stones are the product of earth so almost any stone will do, particularly if you have got to know it as we suggested above. Use it wisely and it will always repay you. Remember that you do not need polished stones for this – the more natural they are the better.

Spirit

Most clear crystals can be used to represent the fifth element of Aether, or spirit, as can the purple hued ones. Amethyst is particularly good as it is both a transmitter and a receiver of psychic and spiritual energy. Mostly, those stones which are capable of representing spirit will 'speak' to you and if you choose more than one you will have to use your intuition so that you choose the right one for your purpose.

We set out below some of the different ways in which such stones can be used.

PREPARING THE CIRCLE

If you wish to use stones and crystals when laying out your circle, you can use a mixture of both. You might mark each quarter with a large stone, particularly if you are outside, and then place other appropriate stones on top. Even if you use candles to mark the four quarters of the circle, you could surround or circle, each candle with any or all of the following gems, either rough or polished:

North: Moss Agate, Emerald, Jet, Olivine, Salt, Black Tourmaline
East: Imperial Topaz, Citrine, Mica, Pumice
South: Amber, Obsidian, Rhodochrosite, Ruby, Lava, Garnet
West: Aquamarine, Chalcedony, Jade, Lapis Lazuli, Moonstone, Sugilite

Over time, gather a number of appropriate stones together. Beginning and ending in the North, lay out 7, 9, 21 or 40 stones of any size to define your circle. (These are magical numbers and will enhance the power, so always bear in mind the purpose of your circle.) If you normally use ribbon or cord to mark out your circle your stones can be placed either inside the cord or ribbon or in place of it.

If the ritual to be conducted within the circle is of one which is sending the power outwards, place any stone with definite points facing outward. If the magic is of a protective nature, place them with points facing inward.

You must use your good sense when constructing your circle. If it is outdoors, is somewhere you use often and think of as your sacred space, you may wish to leave the larger stones in position and carry the smaller stones and gems with you. This way, no matter where you are, you can mark out a circle with the small stones and have available the power and energy of the larger space available to you.

Stone Altar

If you decide to use a stone altar it will depend on how simple or complex you prefer your rituals to be and whether you wish to leave your altar set up permanently. Ideally you should be able to find in the open a fairly flat stone which will give you the working surface you need. It can be as large or as small as you like or one which just feels right for your purpose.

YOU WILL NEED

Variety of smoothly-shaped stones flattish but of pleasing shape as follows:

At least three for the altar proper.

Stone to represent the female principle

Stone to represent the male principle

Small stone as candle holder to represent fire element or as mentioned previously

Small cupped stone to hold water

Small stone to represent earth as above

Stone to act as incense burner for charcoal or herbs

A flat offertory stone (optional)

Red candle

Water

Soil (optional)

Suitable incense for your purpose

METHOD

Create the altar itself from three large stones.

Two smaller ones of almost the same size are used as the base, while a longer, flat stone (such as a piece of slate) is placed on top of these to form the altar itself. Make sure that the structure is stable.

Place one stone on the left of the altar to represent the Feminine principle or Goddess. If there is not enough room on the altar proper, place the stone on the ground to the left.

Note: You can use a stone with a hole, a natural, river-rounded stone, or any of the gems appropriate to the Goddess. These include all pink, green and blue stones; those related to the Moon or Venus and Water and Earth-ruled stones, such as aquamarine beryl, blue quartz, emerald, kunzite, peridot, pink tourmaline, rose quartz and turquoise.

To the right of the altar, place a stone to represent the Masculine principle or God. This might be a piece of volcanic rock or a long, thin, club or hammer-shaped rock. Again if your altar is small, these can be placed on the ground on the right.

Note: Generally, all orange and red stones, stones related to the Sun, Mars and Fire and Air-ruled stones can signify the God. Gemstones such as such as bloodstone, carnelian, calcite, diamond, garnet, sunstone, orange ruby, tiger's eye, topaz and tourmaline can also be used.

Between these two stones place a smaller stone to represent the element of Fire. Affix the red candle to it to represent the unified energy of the masculine and feminine principles – the union of the God and Goddess.
In front of this, place a flat stone to receive offerings of wine, honey, cakes, semi-precious stones, flowers and fruit appropriate for the ritual you are performing.

A small, cupped stone (if one can be found) should be set to the left of the offering stone. Fill this with water to represent that element.
To the right of the offering stone place a stone to signify earth. If you like, you can place a small quantity of earth on this stone.

Additionally, another flattish stone can be placed in front of the offering stone to serve as a place on which to burn your incense.
This is an ideal opportunity for you to use your travelling tools.

Most of us have a particular place which means a great deal to us – somewhere which has touched a chord within where we feel safe. This might be the home that we buy, a particular grove of trees, a waterfall or simply a corner of the garden that is special to us. There is a resonance between us and the place. This is why we feel inextricably drawn to particular places.

SHRINES AND SACRED SPACES

In shrines and sacred spaces, we are closer to our own centre and close to our own inner teachers, our own power and often as close as we can get to our own concept of God or the Ultimate. Our helpers and spirits work closely with us if we will allow them to, in everything we do, and it is often they who have led us here in the first instance.

Something deep in the place and something deep in us unites together to become greater than either of us. Some would say that the spirit or essence of the place touches the spirit in us. At that point we may find the universe co-operates with us in almost miraculous ways. It becomes possible to spend more time in the place, we are enabled to look after it in our own particular way or perhaps we find that our lives adjust so that we can become guardians of that space on a full time basis. What may have seemed to be pure luck or chance initially, later is recognized as a life-changing circumstance and we find ourselves making a commitment beyond the call of duty.

If one is open to such ideas, the place speaks to us and demands a relationship with it which truly enables it to become a sacred space. Any such vocation first requires understanding of ourselves and the environment or place. So, we must always begin by making connection with the place, remaining open and listening to what information the place and its spirits has to give us. (A method of doing this in the open air is given in a previous book, *Spells, Charms, Talismans and Amulets*, by the author, and is repeated briefly overleaf.)

If approached with respect, Nature may give you many pleasant surprises; nature spirits, as we have seen, often will channel tremendous amounts of power into the area you choose to use. When entering an area in order to find a site for a ritual or quiet contemplation, first find a place that feels right. Then let Nature channel her power in her own way and do not consciously try for specific manifestations. You are attempting to make contact not only with nature spirits but also with the essence of the place. Try not to have any preconceived ideas, and remember if you attempt to command nature spirits or indeed any other type of spirit rather than listening to them and inviting them to work with you, they may take flight, resist, or turn on you.

Then try the following, either individually or, if in a group, as a guided meditation:

✦ Affirm that you are at one with nature and wish to communicate with the spirit of the place and with the life forces associated with it. (This opens up the possibility of communicating with nature spirits in the open air or with house spirits and guardians indoors.)

✦ Remind the universal energy – and yourself – that you are a magician, a medicine person, or shaman who respects it and wishes to work in harmony with it. Let this inner self emerge into full awareness.

✦ Let the beat of your heart and the rhythm of nature awaken that part of yourself that naturally communicates on a very subtle level with other life forms.

✦ This means that you become aware of your own telepathic senses.

✦ Now send out signals of love and light to any entities present to be aware of your presence and make themselves felt.

✦ Say why you have come, and then invite them to join with you.

✦ Visualize the light and love energy you are channelling extending out and merging with the influences from distant places.

✦ Feel the power of the Earth flowing up through your body and feet.

✦ Feel the power from the sky, and allow this energy to flow through and out from you to the forces around you.

✦ Perceive the light expanding and merging with the other energies until one seems to become separate and ready for consideration.

✦ Continue to send out telepathic signals and communicate with this entity in whichever way seems appropriate.

✦ Open your eyes a little. You may sense light coming from certain areas that are receptive. You may get other signals, such as a feeling of power or love being returned from a certain direction. Perhaps the type of response to this work will be unexpected; follow your intuition in your interpretation of it.

Shamanic practice – or indeed any process which reconnects us with Nature – alerts us to how we play our own part in her complexities and simplicities. Just as we can be calmed by the atmosphere and ambience of a place so buildings and constructions can take on the feelings of the people who use them. Places as well as people can have an individual aura about them. A Catholic

Church will have a very different 'personality' to a Buddhist temple, yet both are spiritual places, while a busy bank again will feel totally different to a busy supermarket.

Environments can heal, inspire, protect, and teach. Conversely, we can do the same for a place or building. We might, for instance, come across somewhere which seems very bleak, and which cries out for personal attention. Perhaps someone has died in the building or been very sick. We have the ability to cleanse and clear that building and to make it a place of happiness and joy once again. One method of doing this is shown below.

Purification of the Home

Sometimes unwanted entities in our homes prove extra difficult to get rid of, but they can often be cleared out by using a specific ritual to effect a spiritual cleaning and purification. Think of it as though you were moving through your home gathering up the negativity and ushering it out of the door.

✦ Plan your route through the house so you end up at an outside door. Put everything you need on a tray to carry it from room to room. If you have someone to help you might find it easier, but it does not really matter.

✦ Use a banishing incense (See section on incense further on) either in a burner or as a stick.

✦ Have a chalice of water with a little salt in it (which you have blessed) to use as a seal; also a bell or rattle to use the vibration of sound.

✦ Beginning at the farthest end of your home from the outside door, circle each room three times clockwise, keeping the incense smoking as you go. You can often judge how negative the atmosphere is by the amount of smoke produced. Waft the smoke into all cupboards and corners.

✦ Next ring the bell or shake the rattle. This is said to scare away the demons.

✦ Finally, take the chalice of water and with your forefinger, touch each window and door with the water. Do the same with all mirrors, to prevent any re-entry of negative entities.

Move to the next room and repeat the technique. Work through every room in your home, including the basement and attic if you have them, ending up at the exterior door. Before marking the sides of the door with water, open it and wave the smoking incense toward the door. Say out loud if it feels right to do so, if not direct your thoughts:

> *Mean and troublesome entities,*
> *Leave now this place.*
> *You are not welcome here!*

As you do this you should feel a lightening of the atmosphere as the negativity clears. Close the door and mark the sides with water. Use whatever sign feels appropriate – a cross, circle or line, all of which have their own symbolic meaning.

Now you must call on the positive energies to take up residence, lest the negative ones re-enter. Lay aside your tools and raise your arms. Say something like:

> *Welcome to all beings of Light and love.*
> *Fill this place always with your life and goodness.*
> *Keep out all aspects of Darkness,*
> *And bring my [our] life back into proper balance.*

Many people would pooh-pooh the idea that relationships can develop between a human being and a place or house, yet how many of us have, when moving, wandered around 'saying a last good-bye'? This ritual is comforting for us and allows us to release the energy of the memories, joys and sadnesses that are part and parcel of the nurturing and caring which has gone on during the time we have lived in this place. We are, after all, severing a tie into which we have put a great deal of energy. As magical practitioners we must always do our best to maintain the vibration of our environment and personal sanctuary.

Deep loving relationships can develop between people and a place that becomes imbued with the vibrations of that relationship. As we can sometimes find ourselves drained of energy, so also places and areas can become depleted and need to be reconnected into what might be called the grid of natural power that is constructed and renewed within the earth plane. However, the most common reason healers are requested to do a house clearing is the suspicion that the building itself may be subject to geopathic stress; i.e. changes in energy due to tension in the Earth's surface.

One of the problems we investigate when dealing with 'sickness of place' is indeed the debilitating effects related to geological abnormalities and underground water courses in or about buildings. There are shamanic techniques and related spiritual practices which aim to keep the environments in which we live and work as free from hidden stress as possible. Often such practices – perhaps the placing of crystals or natural objects in the home, the cleansing of the atmosphere with a sagebrush or with incense, or the placing of an effigy of a beloved deity – connect us with traditional systems and customs which give us insight and understanding in our work with sacred space.

When we are called upon to rebalance energies which disturbing the peace of a place or building our first focus will be on identifying any underground water courses, misplaced holes and rocks or lines of energy which exist under the premises, and dealing with them. Obviously it is not always possible to excavate to verify ones suspicions, but it is often possible to use ones intuition, divining rods or pendulum to identify difficult areas. The subsidence caused by an over-dry summer, for instance, might be counteracted on a more esoteric level by the use of stone inside the building, though obviously something practical would have to be done as well. Any infilling might be accompanied by the placing of crystals in the foundation, which would have the effect of changing the vibration in the whole house.

Moving or dispersing the 'inappropriate energy fields' associated with such areas is often done by means of metal rods (usually iron) inserted in locations dictated by the energy paths. Once the paths or concentrations have been established and marked, we can proceed to work in the same manner through the individual rooms inside. Each room's purpose will have an effect on how it reacts to the various geopathic stresses.

The following home blessing is in some ways more elaborate than the simple clearing technique above. It consists of three steps: cleansing, blessing and protecting.

Home Blessing

This blessing uses several techniques; colour candle magic, herb magic, crystals and sound. It is assumed that there will be more than one person to perform this ritual, although it can be done alone.

YOU WILL NEED

Hand bell (one for each member of the group is nice)

Salt water

Rosemary herb or oil

Light blue candles

Nightlights and holders

Large quartz crystal

Several pieces of onyx or obsidian

Two pieces of rose quartz

Home blessing incense (see below)

METHOD

The group should assemble at the heart of the home, often considered to be the kitchen.

Remain quiet for a few moments, linking with the energy of the group for your common purpose.

Proceed through every room.

Ring the bells as you go and sprinkle the salt water carefully in each room, not forgetting the corners.

Choose a route which means that you finish up back at the heart of the home.

Repeat the process, this time using the lit candles, sprinkling some rosemary in every room. You may like to leave a lit nightlight in a holder in each room. Make sure that it is left in a safe place.

Repeat a blessing, hymn or chant as you go appropriate to your belief. Perhaps something like:

Bless this home Gods above,
Keep it safe and filled with love.

Return to the centre of the home and, sitting down with linked hands, form a circle.
Use a chant that can reach a crescendo such as 'Om' or 'Evohay' or even perhaps the name of your favourite deity.
Feel the sound swelling until you can sense a circle of sound enclosing the home and grounds if you have them.

Process through the house a final time with your oil and stones.
(The large crystal remains visible at the heart of the home, or an equally safe place, where it becomes a power source for the other stones.)
A piece of the dark crystal (onyx or obsidian) is placed in each room, though if you like you can choose a crystal appropriate for the occupancy of each room.

You should now draw a protective sign such as a pentagram or rune over each opening with the ritual oil.
Remember to include all doors, windows, fireplaces, central heating vents etc.
The rose quartz is placed either side of the main entrance.
You may then wish to burn a house blessing incense, such as the one below, as a final gesture.

It would be appropriate to hold a housewarming party at this point.

Note: You have not closed the circle. This is deliberate since you will wish to leave a circle of protection in place.

Home Blessing Incense

YOU WILL NEED

1 part Lavender

1 part Basil

1 part Hyssop

Few drops of Cucumber or Melon Oil

Having blessed and protected your home, you will want to prevent any unwanted intrusion. This next incense is a good one to use after you have completed the above ritual.

Lock Incense

YOU WILL NEED

3 parts Frankincense Resin

2 parts Juniper berries

1 part Vetivert

$\frac{1}{2}$ part Cumin

METHOD

During the day burn this mixture in your burner in front of your front door. Move in a clockwise direction throughout your home wafting the smoke over any entrances. Remember to include windows, basements etc through which thieves may enter.

Visualize the smoke forming an invisible but impenetrable barrier.

Repeat monthly at the time of the Full Moon or use as needed.

Do not forget to lock your doors and windows as well!

Within the home, any concentration of sacred objects will raise the vibration of that particular area in significant ways. Continual usage of a space maintains its energy whether that is chaotic or still and you will always be able to reconsecrate it by a simple prayer each time you use it. A kitchen might be rededicated each morning to be a warm loving centre for the home perhaps, and the principles of feng shui utilized in order to keep an atmosphere focussed in the correct way. Following the same principle of emotional imprinting by constant use, a group of family photographs will trigger memories, ideas and concepts to do with both good times and bad within the family.

Specific symbols of belief systems will also concentrate the mind on those beliefs and allow them to be used in a spiritual way. When you decide to dedicate an altar or a shrine to a specific purpose you may wish to have some of the symbols mentioned elsewhere on or near that space.

Outdoors, truly sacred spaces are most successful when they are marked by concentrations of natural energies. Shinto shrines for instance were traditionally near natural energy points, such as waterfalls, caves, rock formations, mountain tops, or forest glades which displayed Nature at her most powerful. This of course echoes the earlier natural shrines which paid homage to spirits and deities belonging to nature. Rituals were usually held outdoors, among natural surroundings, with a structure appropriate for the occasion. In the aforementioned Shinto religion in Japan, the purification ritual ('harai') is done with natural flowing water sources such as hot springs, rivers and waterfalls. We can make use of this awareness in our own everyday lives by creating concentrations of energy by rock formations or waterfalls in our personal space.

Rather than having an altar, you may wish to have a shrine to your own particular belief system, deities and so on. From the earliest times, almost every culture has set aside small areas in their homes, temples, or work places and have put an article there as a focus and reminder of a spiritual presence in that place and in their own lives. In Mediterranean countries small wayside shrines commemorate the Virgin Mary whereas previously they would have been dedicated to Hecate as goddess of the crossroads.

Hecate

We have many ways to honour 'spirit of place' or actively to encourage a particular type of energy there. The real secret of a powerful shrine lies in our working partnership with the place where we build it. We should first seek intuitively the best spot to erect the shrine – this goes for both indoors and outdoors as shown previously. Then allow your intuition to guide you towards what needs to be placed there. Use found objects, things you have been given, or articles which have particular significance for you. Be as imaginative as you like and always have a good reason for including an object. If it feels right to do so, place it within the sacred space and see whether the object is acceptable. You will usually get a strong sense of whether it is right or not – you may well discover that the object is better placed in another part of the building or space and yet belongs to an overall design.

In other instances, we might be aware of an overwhelming energy or atmosphere belonging to a specific item of clothing, jewellery or furniture. Sometimes, items which have become charged with an emotional imprint generate an energy which requires acknowledging. We may need to place them within the atmosphere of a shrine – or in close proximity – lest they cause discomfort in a room, or indeed throughout the whole house. This is as a direct result of their own 'held' memories of the past. It is as though the very strong energy is protected by being placed within a shrine's environment.

Emotional imprints can be examined and interpreted very easily using simple techniques of touch. By holding an object and allowing it to 'speak' to us, we are able to decide what needs to be done. Often this will give a sense of knowing, this is a way of sharing with the spirit or energy of the object. Where problems in rooms are caused by specific items, these might be cleansed perhaps by leaving them in moonlight, in sunlight, in running water or by saying a prayer over them, depending on their composition. Using our own preferred ritual methods we may decide to dispose of them altogether.

Shamanic training builds strong relationships with guides, spirit helpers, animals and teachers as does any other form of spiritual discipline. We are privileged to share with those spirits, creating greater understanding and awareness between various places on Earth itself and the people who live there. This enables us, when an area has become depleted, to choose to clear stagnation and difficult atmospheres from rooms and sacred spaces using the drum, rattle or voice – the use of sound vibration. We can also use these instruments to draw spirit towards us to enhance the use of our shrine. This method must be according to our own individual training and practice though certainly you can experiment until you find a method right for you. Never simply imitate the rituals, methods or practices of another person, no matter how impressive they seem to be.

Rituals are personal and what works for someone else may not necessarily work for you – and vice versa. You can always use a basic ritual, but it is your own personal touches which are important. Working with sacred space of whatever kind carries with it a great responsibility (and an ability to respond) and is much enhanced by your own simple reverence for what you do. This way of working requires a degree of genuine respect and personal honesty which leads to a discipline and clarity of perception. Each person's personal practice grows from within which enables us to reach out to the whole of Creation in whatever form it manifests. We thus become in our own right a kind of sacred space. When you build a shrine and dedicate it in your own way you reflect the heart of the place where it is built, the being of the person who built it and the relationship between them. A cairn, a carefully constructed mound of stones, can be such a place.

CAIRNS

Used from time immemorial as markers, cairns can also become magical places charged with the energy – both of the stones of which they consist and with the magical energy of the rituals performed there. They are firmly based upon the earth but raise themselves upwards, signifying the interconnectedness of the physical and spiritual realms.

When working in the outdoors, you could ritually mark each of the four directions with a small cairn of appropriately chosen stones rather than just a single stone. You could then, if you wished, leave these small markers in position either to maintain the sacredness of the space, or as an offering to the nature spirits. Though fashioned by human hand, these markers are indicative of your partnership with nature.

Building A Cairn

Building a cairn can be an opportunity for you to use your new-found ability to appreciate and understand stones. When you are able, find yourself a sufficient number of stones – just ordinary, everyday ones that take your fancy – and spend some time with them as suggested above.

When you are ready, do the following:

METHOD

Identify a magical need, perhaps something you want to change, to make better, to develop or to get rid off.

As you visualize this need, hold one of your stones.

Feel the energy beating within it – the power of the Earth, the power of nature.

Place it on the cleared ground.

Pick up another stone, still visualizing your need, and put it next to the first.

Still visualizing, continue to add stones, building them into a small pile.
You might put them in the shape of a circle, a triangle or a square.
Keep adding stones until you feel your pile beginning to pulse and vibrate.
When it feels right, place the last stone at the top of the pile and state your purpose in the form of an affirmation – a positive statement.

Now sit quietly and place your hands on either side of the pile without disturbing it.
Allow your energy to flow into the cairn and feel the energy of the completed cairn coming back to you.
Make it a real interchange and then leave it alone to do its work.

GEOMANCY

Rather than being the building up of stones and a concentration of energy, geomancy is a system of divination that uses the scattering of stones, grains of sand, or seeds on the earth followed by an interpretation of their shape and position. It would seem that this Western form of divination has its roots in feng-shui (the Chinese art of interpreting the movements of wind and water). It is thought that the final position of the pebbles responds to the subtle earth energies known in the Western world as ley lines (lines of power).

Developing your own Divination Tool

If you enjoy working with stones, you may like to develop your own divination tool. Here is how to do it.

YOU WILL NEED
Cloth on which to cast stones

Note: You can prepare this cloth on one of several ways. It can be without markings, which allows an open and varied interpretation, you can mark it with the four elements or directions or you can draw a circle divided into 12 segments in accordance with astrological timings.

Your own selection of polished or unpolished stones (Your choice of and the number of stones should be according to your own intuition.)
Velvet pouch to keep the stones safe

METHOD

Take each stone and familiarize yourself with it as suggested above.
Decide what each stone is going to represent (family, relationship, career etc.)

When you wish to work with the stones, sit quietly holding the bag in your hand
bearing in mind your main concerns.
Shake the stones out onto your cloth.

The direction in which the stones fall will give you the information with which to make
your interpretation.
Pointed stones may give you direction, coloured stones may be interpreted
according to the list of elements above, stones grouped together may be interpreted
as 'group' situations. The possibilities are endless.

The art of using stones is a very ancient one and worth further separate study.

TREES

Any magical practitioner claiming to use natural objects will probably also need to develop their knowledge of trees in rituals and magic. We can have a clear picture of the role of trees in the sacred life of the people of ancient Europe by looking at the myths and stories dealing with mystical states of consciousness. The following quote, from the ancient Scandinavian Poetic Edda, refers to the archetypal journey into shamanic knowledge undertaken by the god Odin. The story is that, in order to acquire eternal wisdom, Odin hung for nine days upside down on the tree of knowledge:

I know that I hung on the windswept tree.
The wisest know not from whence
spring the roots of that ancient tree.

To the peoples of the old world, the trees around them provided support for them as a fuel for heat, cooking, building materials and weaponry. Many woods, however, also provided a powerful spiritual presence. Those believed to be 'sacred' shared certain traits though different cultures accorded their trees varying significances. The great oak, the mystical yew and so many others are reminders of the power that trees have on our lives – the power of the tree's spirit could grant that tree a central place in the folklore and mythology of a culture. Even today we find that certain trees capture our imagination and our thoughts. Once we accept that trees are living things, filled with the essence and energy and of the Elementals and of Mother Earth, we sense power which is often visible to those who have taken the trouble to see.

The lore which surrounds particular trees or woods often reflects the power the old ones sensed and drew from their presence, and this can be seen in the combination of Oak, Ash and Thorn.

All three trees are counted as sacred in the Druidic tradition and are part of the Celtic Tree Calendar (as is Elder). They are often called the 'Fairy Triad' because groves which include all three of them are truly magical places where it is said you can spot fairies. Traditionally, if you take wood from a tree for magical purposes make sure you ask the tree for permission to do so and leave a gift in its place.

Alder

This tree was sacred to the Druids. To this day, some diviners in search of water hidden underground still use its forked branches, traditionally called 'Wishing Rods'. It is still considered a crime to cut down a sacred Alder tree and the individual who does so is considered to be the cause of any trouble in the community.

The alder is associated with courage and represents the evolving spirit. It commemorates Bran who was a mighty warrior of ancient Britain. In one battle, Bran fights the Ash King on behalf of the Alder King – though he loses the battle, he is still recognized as a great warrior.

Alder wood is used in dairy vessels and to make whistles as the pith is easily pushed out of the green shoots. Several of these shoots can be bound together and trimmed to the desired length for producing the notes wanted – this whistle can be used to entice Air elementals. The old superstition of 'whistling up the wind' began with this custom.

Apple (Domestic)

This is another tree sacred to the Druids. There are several magical uses for the apple. An apple wood wand is the appropriate one to use if you want to make shamanic journeys, since the apple is used as a calling sign to the Otherworld. The wand will help you physically, mentally and spiritually connect to the Apple tree. You might use apple cider in any spells calling for blood or wine.

If you have warts try cutting an apple into three pieces, then rub the cut side on the warts, saying: *'Out warts, into apple'*. Bury the pieces and as the apple decays, the warts will disappear. Apple indicates choice, and is useful for love and healing magic. When choices are offered, the biggest test is to choose only one and not to waste energy in vacillation.

Ash

Since ancient times, some have believed that the first man was created from the branches and flesh of the Ash tree. Druid wands were often made of ash for they were good for healing and general and solar magic because of the wood's straight grain. It is said that you should put fresh ash leaves under your pillow to stimulate psychic dreams.

One mythological belief focuses on when Christianity was brought to Northern Europe. The Scandinavian gods of the North were obviously affected by this new belief of Christianity and transformed themselves into witches. The ash became their favourite tree since it contained a good deal of knowledge. In Celtic mythology the ash is known as the tree of enchantment as the Celts believed that they came from the Great Deep or the Undersea land of Tethys.

Birch

Known as Lady of the Woods, Paper Birch and White Birch, the birch tree, being symbolic of fertility and new birth, is closely associated with the waxing phase of the moon. Girls would often give their lovers a twig of birch as a sign of encouragement to indicate that they no longer wished to be maidens. The 'Besom Wedding' was, for a long time, considered legal and jumping the broomstick – usually made of birch – is still part of pagan ceremony. In Norse mythology, the birch is dedicated to Thor. Emotionally, the birch is all about being nurtured and cared for; spiritually we are cleansed and made ready for the future.

The following love charm uses, in birch, the recognition of the change from maiden to mother and is an indication to the universe that you are ready to take on the responsibility of partnership.

A Love Charm

YOU WILL NEED

Strips of birch bark gathered at the New Moon

Red ink and pen

Love Incense 9, as shown in the Incense section

METHOD

Write on the birch strip

Bring me true love

Burn the strip along with the incense and say:

Goddess of love, God of desire,
Bring to me sweet passion's fire.

Alternatively, cast the bark into a stream or other flowing water, saying:

Message of love, I set you free,
to capture a love and return to me.

Blackthorn

Blackthorn is a winter tree with a black bark and truly nasty thorns, which are sometimes used negatively in poppet magic. The thorny hedges symbolize the idea that you may discover new opportunities or direction if you are prepared to deal with a chaotic situation first. Blackthorn indicates outside influences that must be obeyed and may well appear when a negative challenge is presented. This tree teaches its lessons well and will help to create a psychic barrier to protect you against similar situations arising in the future. The white flowers are seen even before the leaves in the spring. The wood is used for the shillelagh, a protective staff.

Broom

Also known as Scotch Broom or Irish Broom, it can be substituted for furze (gorse) at the time of the Spring Equinox. Sweep your outside ritual areas with it to purify and protect them; burning the blooms and shoots is said to calm the wind. Broom multiplies profusely if there is a need for its protective powers. The Irish called it the 'Physician's Power' because of its diuretic properties.

Cedar

Also known as the Tree of Life, Arbor Vitae and Yellow Cedar, this tree grows to a great height and has a very imposing spread. The wood is reddish-white, fragrant, and close-grained, particularly in older trees. Size made a tree important, but this is only part of the reason that it was much revered by the Ancients. The oil that it produces is highly preservative and the tree's longevity is part of its sacredness.

To draw Earth energy and ground yourself, place the palms of your hands against the ends of the leaves. It is often used in incenses to honour the gods.

Elder

Also known as Ellhorn, Elderberry and Lady Elder. The Druids used elder to regulate their communities and to bless. Elder wands can be used to drive out evil spirits or thought forms. Music played on panpipes or flutes of elder has the same power as the wand. As a protection against evil (and later against witchcraft), its branches were hung in the doorways of houses and cowsheds, buried in graves and its twigs were carried. Ancient folklore states that you put your baby at risk if its crib is made from elder wood; you run the risk of the fairies coming to take your baby away. In German-Scandinavian folklore the Hydermolder is a particularly malign nature spirit associated with elders.

Sacred to the White Lady and Midsummer Solstice, it is said that standing under an elder tree at Midsummer will help you see the fairies. The Elder is also the Old Crone aspect of the Triple Goddess, and her protection and blessing is powerful.

A Blessing

METHOD

Scatter elder leaves and berries to the four directions, and over the object or person to be blessed. Say:

Goddess of Wisdom, Goddess of Mystery,
Third of the Threefold,
Bless now this [person/object]
As transformation comes to pass.

At Samhain (31 October), the last of the elderberries are picked with solemn ceremony. The wine made from these berries was considered to be the last sacred gift of the Earth Goddess. Elder flowers have many magical uses. You can keep some on your altar to use with any spell which uses the energy of the fairies or nature spirits. They are particularly useful when performing rituals for prosperity, healing, binding, banishing and protection.

Elm

A slightly fibrous, tan-coloured wood with a slight sheen, elm wood is valued for its resistance to splitting. The inner bark was used for cordage and chair caning. Elm is often associated with Mother and Earth Goddesses, and was said to be the abode of fairies. Elm adds stability and grounding to a spell. Once known as 'Elven', its nature spirit is the elf – when carried by humans it will ensure a new love.

Fir

Fir is a very tall slender tree that grows in mountainous regions on the upper slopes. Its cones respond to varying weather conditions by opening and closing. Symbolically, fir indicates high perspectives with a clear vision of what is beyond and yet to come.

Known as the Birth Tree, the silver fir needles are burned at childbirth to bless and protect the mother and baby, and to clear the environment. According to Scandinavian folklore, the spirit or Genii of the Forest is traditionally depicted as holding an uprooted fir tree.

It is believed that the fir tree has strong connections with the owner of the land where it stands. Should a fir tree ever be struck by lightning, begin to wither or be touched, it is said that death is present, and the owner will die.

Hawthorn

Also known as May Tree, White Thorn, Haegthorn and Quickthorn this is one of the most wild, enchanted and sacred of trees. It can live to a great age, becoming gnarled in the process. Hawthorn is traditionally used to make psychic shields for the innocent and vulnerable, particularly children – often at puberty when the youngster may be particularly sensitive.

The hawthorn tree is associated with the sacred as well as with inauspicious events. Because the hawthorn guarded the Celestial Fire, to destroy a hawthorn was to incur the wrath of the gods. Wands made of this wood are of great power. The blossoms are highly erotic to men. Hawthorn can be used for protection, love and marriage spells. You can make a charm ball which incorporates these at first light at Samhain.

Charm Ball

YOU WILL NEED
Hawthorn twigs
White ribbon

Note: The charm ball that you make represents your new self with all its dreams and aspirations. Each year, as you replace it a new one, it then becomes a representation of the troubles and difficulties of the previous year. You burn the old one on a bonfire of straw, ash twigs and acorns (see Ash and Oak above and below).

METHOD
As you fashion and weave the ball, visualize what you hope for for you and yours and how you wish the coming year to be.
Finish it off with the white ribbon.

Hang it in a window or doorway.

Hazel

The hazel tree has long been magical and is used to gain knowledge, wisdom and poetic inspiration and the art of communication. It is said that it was the nine magical hazelnuts which gave the Salmon of Knowledge its wisdom. Wands made of this wood symbolize white magic and healing, whilst forked sticks are traditionally used to find water or buried treasure.

If in need of magical protection, string hazelnuts on a cord and hang them up in your home or sacred space and carry them with you when out and about. When working with nature, a circle drawn around you with a hazel twig will enhance the energy.

Holly

A white wood with an almost invisible grain, holly is similar in appearance to ivory. Associated with death and rebirth, holly may be used in spells to do with sleep or rest and to ease death's transition. This symbolism is evident in both Pagan and Christian lore and holly is important at Yuletide. In Celtic mythology holly is the evergreen twin of the oak. It is called a kerm-oak. The oak rules the light part of the year while holly rules the dark part.

Holly suggests directed balance and the courage to fight if the cause is just. A symbol of luck and good fortune, a bag of leaves and berries carried by a man is said to increase his ability to attract women.

Ivy

Ivy is evergreen and represents the ever-present aspects of the human psyche. Traditionally regarded as the harbinger of death, the Celts associate ivy with their lunar goddess Arianrhod and her ritual which marks the opening of the portal to the Otherworld, but is also as a symbol of hope of better things to come.

Ivy was worn as a crown at the winter feast of Saturnalia, is associated primarily with fidelity and is a symbol of married love and loyalty and stable relationships. Houses with ivy growing on them are reputedly safe from psychic attack. Ivy represents all that is mysterious and mystical.

Juniper

An evergreen coniferous tree which has prickly leaves and dark purple berries, juniper is used in numerous incenses. Berries were used with thyme in Druid and Grove incenses for visions and manifestation, the smoke being helpful to the working. Also used for protection and purification, juniper can be grown by the door where it discourages thieves. A small bunch of twigs or a few berries in a pouch can also be hung in the rafters of a building or over the lintel of the doorway as a longer-term protection against accidents and also to attract love.

Mistletoe

Also known as Birdlime, All Heal and Golden Bough, mistletoe is probably the most well-known and sacred tree of the Druids. It rules the Winter Solstice when bunches of mistletoe can be hung around the home as an all-protective device. It is extremely poisonous and should only be used homoeopathically under strict supervision. It is used magically to combat despair, to bring beautiful dreams, to unlock the secrets of immortality and to protect the bearer from werewolves.

The wood can be used for wands and ritual items, or such items can be placed in a mistletoe infusion to strengthen their power.

Oak

Oak is such an all-purpose tree, providing food, shelter and spiritual regeneration that it is considered sacred by just about every culture that has encountered it. The oak was the 'King of Trees' and Druids and Priestesses 'listened' to the tree and its inhabitants to acquire wisdom. Acorns gathered at night hold the greatest fertility powers and oak galls, also known as Serpent Eggs, are sometimes used in magical charms.

The oak has the propensity to help you to find new understanding. This brings strength and courage in adversity. The oak tree nourishes our faith in ourselves and enables us to aim for what we most desire. Wands made from an oak which has been struck by lightning are considered to be particularly powerful, firstly since lightning does not strike twice in the same place and secondly because the wand is empowered by the blast of energy. When you burn oak leaves it purifies the atmosphere lending strength, success and stability to your magic.

Pine

The pine tree is an evergreen and is known for its ability to cleanse the personal environment. It is one of the seven chieftain trees of the Irish. There are numerous ways it can be used; to purify and sanctify an outdoor ritual area, brush the ground with a branch of pine wood. For the home or indoors, mix the dried needles with equal parts of juniper and cedar and burn (this leaves quite an exceptional odour). The cones and nuts can be carried as a fertility charm, whilst a cleansing and stimulating bath can be prepared by placing a few handfuls of pine needles in a loose-woven bag. To make things easier you could, of course, use a few drops of the essential oil in running water.

Pine is very efficacious when used with other herbs and incenses to accumulate wealth, as shown in the incense below.

Wealth Incense

2 parts Pine needles or resin

1 part Cinnamon

1 part Galangal

Few drops of Patchouli Oil

Rowan

Also known as Mountain Ash, Witchwood, Sorb Apple and Quickbeam, the rowan has long been known as an aid and protection against enchantment by beguiling. Sacred to the Druids and the Goddess Brigit, it is a very magical tree which is used for wands and amulets. A forked rowan branch can help find water; wands of rowan wood are for knowledge, locating metal and general divination. Indeed, this is the wood to use for making any magical tool which has anything to do with divining, invocation and communication with the spirit realms. The rowan has the ability, perhaps more than any other tree, to help us increase our psychic abilities. It has a beneficial energy which will increase our abilities to receive visions and insights.

In the past it was valued as a protection against enchantment, witches, unwanted influences and evil spirits. Sprigs of rowan were placed over doorways and fixed to cattle sheds to protect the animals from harm. Speer posts, magically protective house timbers inscribed with runes and magically charged patterns, were traditionally made of rowan wood. Rowan bushes were often grown near stone circles as protective devices.

Rowan will help you to discriminate between what will do you harm and good and help you deal with anything which threatens you.

Willow

Also known as White Willow, Tree of Enchantment and Witches' Asprin and one of the seven sacred trees of the Irish, the willow is a Moon tree sacred to the Goddess. There are legends and myths of willows being able to move around, to use their branches like arms and to communicate through their whispering leaves. One of the nature spirits, called a hamadryad, often makes its home in a willow tree and it is said that the willow gives an understanding of the feminine principle.

It is said that priests, priestesses and all types of artisans sat among these trees to gain eloquence, inspiration, skills and prophecies. The willow will always enhance inspired leaps of the imagination as it is known as a tree of dreaming and enchantment. It is recommended for use when seeking to assimilate the teachings of a wise woman or master or any oral tradition. Willow wands are used for any ritual associated with the moon and as a protection on deep journeys into the underworld and the unconscious since the willow tree has always been associated with death.

In Celtic mythology it is associated with the creation myth of two scarlet sea serpent eggs which contained the Sun and the Earth. These eggs were hidden in the boughs of the Willow tree until they hatched, thus bringing forth earthly life.

Yew

A smooth, gold-coloured wood with a wavy grain, the yew is an ancient tree species that has survived since before the Ice Age and, as such, as been revered and used by humankind throughout the ages. Because of its longevity and the way it regenerates itself by growing new trunks from within, it has come to represent everlasting life, immortality, renewal, regeneration, rebirth and transformation.

Many churches and churchyards once stood in a circle of yews – representing the passage from life to death – a belief based on old Druidic custom. The yew is sacred to Hecate (the Crone aspect of the Triple Goddess) and therefore the ancient wisdom of the feminine and is also a symbol of the old magic.

Considered to be the most potent tree for protection against evil, magically it is a means of connecting to your ancestors, bringing dreams and Otherworld journeys. This is one of its most valuable abilities, for it provides us with the opportunity face death, to progress further than fear and to establish communication through visions with what lies beyond. These all bring about an understanding and clear insight. It is thought by many to be the original 'World Tree' (Yggdrasil) of Scandinavian mythology.

TREE PERSONALITIES

A system has been worked out by which each day of the year has been assigned to a tree. People born on any particular day will have certain personal qualities which are common to everyone born under the rulership (connected to the vibration) of that tree.

Find your birth date in the list below and then find your tree. Decide for yourself if you think the description given subsequently is accurate or not. The list starts at Yuletide – after the winter solstice. In this list, the solstices and equinoxes come under a tree's rulership for one day only, although the purists would say that this one-day rule should only be correct for the winter solstice which was when the Lord of Chaos and Misrule held sway and no tree had rulership. It was as though the world and everything in it held its breath, before restarting Nature's cycle again.

A good meditation exercise using this principle of chaos is to choose a tree other than that associated with your own birth tree (perhaps one with qualities that you would like to have). Visualize yourself as the nature spirit associated with that tree and 'fit' yourself into a place within its trunk. How different does this make you feel?

23 December to 31 December	Apple Tree
1 January to 11 January	Fir Tree
12 January to 24 January	Elm Tree
25 January to 3 February	Cypress Tree
4 February to 8 February	Poplar Tree
9 February to 18 February	Cedar Tree
19 February to 28 February	Pine Tree
1 March to 10 March	Weeping Willow Tree
11 March to 20 March	Lime Tree
21 March	Oak Tree
22 March to 31 March	Hazelnut Tree
1 April to 10 April	Rowan Tree
11 April to 20 April	Maple Tree
21 April to 30 April	Walnut Tree
1 May to 14 May	Poplar Tree
15 May to 24 May	Chestnut Tree
25 May to 3 June	Ash Tree
4 June to 13 June	Hornbeam Tree
14 June to 23 June	Fig Tree
24 June	Birch Tree
25 June to 4 July	Apple Tree
5 July to 14 July	Fir Tree
15 July to 25 July	Elm Tree
26 July to 4 August	Cypress Tree
5 August to 13 August	Poplar Tree
14 August to 23 August	Cedar Tree
24 August to 2 September	Pine Tree
3 September to 12 September	Weeping Willow Tree
13 September to 22 September	Lime Tree
23 September	Olive Tree
24 September to 3 October	Hazelnut Tree
4 October to 13 October	Rowan Tree
14 October to 23 October	Maple Tree
24 October to 11 November	Walnut Tree
12 November to 21 November	Chestnut Tree
22 November to 1 December	Ash Tree
2 December to 11 December	Hornbeam Tree
12 December to 21 December	Fig Tree
22 December	Beech Tree

The keyword for each type of tree personality is shown in brackets.

Apple (Love) – These people are of slight build, are attractive and appealing with a pleasant aura. They can be enterprising and flirtatious, a sensitive and tender partner. They tend always to be in love, wanting to love and be loved. Faithful and generous, they live for the moment, can have a scientific bent, and a carefree attitude to life.

Ash (Ambition) – These are usually the centre of attention and they revel in it. They are often attractive and spontaneous but can also be brash and demanding. They hate being criticized, but are very loyal to those close to them. They can play mind games with people, but their reliability and trustworthiness usually means they are good friends to have.

Beech (Creative) – People born under the rulership of this tree have good taste but are also vain. They keep fit and make good natural leaders, making few risky decisions. Because they are well organized and economical, they also make good life partners.

Birch (Inspiration) – Lively and attractive, those born under the birch rulership are also humble but elegant and friendly. They do not like excess and hate garish, vulgar things around them. These people are calm, but coupled with that can be a lack of passion and ambition.

Cedar (Confidence) – These people are usually of special beauty. They are adaptable, have a tendency to be impatient but are able to make the right decisions quickly. Cedar tree people are hardworking and eager to please though they can also be a touch condescending. Their all-round abilities generally makes them popular to be around.

Chestnut (Honesty) – Usually striking and bubbly these people are something of a paradox as they also lack self-confidence and consequently can be irritable and sensitive in company. They are good to have on your side in an argument but can appear superior and they always feel as though they might be misunderstood.

Cypress (Faithfulness) – Cypress tree people are usually solid and dependable. They take what life throws at them and make the best of what they are left with. They are faithful but also petty and not easily satisfied. They are, however, very passionate and are rarely satisfied sexually.

Elm (Noble-mindedness) – Often good leaders but not good followers, they can be unforgiving but do not ask much of people. They are good to have in a crisis and will often see it as their duty to take charge. Generally cheerful and generous, they are honest and faithful but can be a little overbearing.

Fig (Sensibility) – Such a person loves life and everything in it but can be very lazy. Independent and stubborn, they hate losing arguments. They often have many 'mates' but not many close friends, often attracting others with their sharp sense of humour.

Fir (Mysterious) – Blessed with great dignity and sophistication, they have an appreciation of all things highbrow. People born in the shadow of the fir tree are usually arrogant and ambitious but talented and hardworking. Those close to them are held very dear but many friends also breed many enemies.

Hazelnut (Extraordinary) – Often making a good first impression, these people are usually sympathetic and considerate. They have a deep social conscience but are tolerant of others and try to see the good in all people. They can be moody and are not always faithful.

Hornbeam (Good Taste) – Liking to take care of their looks, these people are generally fit and naturally good-looking. They have good taste and try to make life as comfortable as possible; this is usually done by being undemanding and running to a well rehearsed, if somewhat erratic, routine. Often mistrusting of their own feelings they can be totally perplexed by others, constantly looking for approval.

Lime (Doubt) – Lime tree people accept what life dishes out in a composed way, hate fighting, stress and hard work but also dislike laziness. They will often make sacrifices for their friends, being very loyal. With many facets, they are not determined enough to go for broke and frequently complain about their circumstances.

Maple (Independence of Mind) – These are no run-of-the-mill people. Being a complex mixture of imagination and originality, they are highly motivated, upstanding and while on the whole self-confident, they can have a propensity to be shy and withdrawn. Such people have complex relationships, often wanting to be noticed.

Oak (Brave) – Of a very courageous manner, such people express the strong, sturdy qualities of their tree. Unyielding and not liking change, they are nevertheless doers and not talkers whilst keeping their strong sense of independence.

Olive (Wisdom) – The term 'sun worshipper' was invented for those born at the time of the olive tree. They are also warm and forgiving people who go out of their way to avoid a confrontation. They are excellent mediators and have a developed sense of justice. Often well read and educated, they like to be surrounded by sophistication of all forms.

Pine (Particular) – These people are good companions, loving pleasant company. They fall in love easily and equally easily fall out of love. Strong and very robust, they enjoy activities of short duration. Continually looking for an ideal relationship, whether personal or business, they can give up very easily when disappointed. They will have a passion for comfort and will set out to attain it.

Poplar (Uncertainty) – Not very self-confident, a poplar person needs congenial surroundings and lots of feedback. Often isolated, they are choosy by nature and take partnership very seriously indeed. Their artistic nature is coupled with a flair for organization and they can usually be reliable. They are capable of a passionate animosity towards others.

Rowan (Sensitivity) – Charming, cheerful and fun to be with, Rowans like to draw attention to themselves though often without self-centredness. They love life and sometimes seem to be in perpetual motion. They invariably have good taste and can be artistic. They do not forgive easily.

Walnut (Passion) – Completely spontaneous but with reactions which are completely unexpected, people in this group can be strange and sometimes difficult. Inflexible and uncompromising, they are often aggressive and are highly ambitious, developing strategies which are somewhat surprising. Admired rather than liked, they can make jealous lovers.

Willow (Melancholy) – Restless and beautiful but full of melancholy, willow people love anything beautiful and tasteful. Usually dreamers, they are erratic, though can be influenced if they trust the person concerned. Not easy to live with, they are demanding, albeit honest.

When you have read this list you may feel that you are not typical of your tree. As you do the Tree Meditation on page 129, or the group attunement, first imagine yourself to be your birth tree and see how that feels. You may simply have not yet developed some of the attributes.

Otherwise, particularly if you are looking to acquire some of the qualities of the other trees, sense the one which seems most appropriate within your being and work for a little while with the feelings that brings up. If you can find a piece of wood belonging to your tree, keep it near you or carry it with you in your wish sachet.

INCENSE

Woods are an important part of magical practice, particularly in the use of their resins, perfumes and significances. Perhaps the most efficient way of using them in this day and age is, along with other herbs, in the use of incense representing the Air element in the creation of sacred space.

The use of incense in magical workings can be quite a personal act of worship; the various blends can sometimes either appeal to your senses or smell absolutely foul, often depending on your mood. For this reason, we have gathered together a number of blends from numerous sources. We suggest that you experiment until you settle on your own particular favourites and then work from there.

There does need to be some clarification of the lists of ingredients, however. Where we have specified a 'part' this indicates one measure, which may be a teaspoon, a cup, a kilo or whatever. Fractions indicate portions of a part. Personal experience shows that making small quantities is best as the incense then stays fresher and is often more cost-effective. If you plan on making quantities of several types of incense, we suggest you procure or save a number of individual portion jars in which jams and honeys are packed. Such quantities are ideal for our purpose.

Unless otherwise specified, we use dried herbs, flowers, roots and resins since these are often both easier to get hold of than fresh and are packed in suitable quantities and compositions for incense making. The more unusual herbs, oils and resins used can usually be obtained from any good herbalist or 'new age' supply shop and we suggest that you research locally in directories; there are now also several suppliers who supply by mail order and will often blend their own mixtures. There are a number of excellent books available and the internet is a rich source of supply and information should you wish to take this area of your studies further.

We give below an accepted way of making incense, but would warn that you do need to be patient. The art of blending is highly skilled and your own experiments will show you the best methods for you. Initial purchase of the various ingredients is quite expensive so you may wish, if you work with other people, to share the cost in some way. If you work alone and would still like to experiment, when you are making incenses we suggest that you start off with the first ingredient, grind it small and then add each subsequent ingredient in small quantities until it smells and feels right. Most oils and binders such as the gums are added last. If you know your correspondences you can call on the various deities to help you in your task, or just simply bear in mind the ultimate purpose of your incense.

Incense have been used since time immemorial in religious rites and rituals, often in the hope that changes of awareness can be achieved through their use. Modern law is very specific in its classification of mind-altering substances, so we make no claims that incense can be used for this purpose. We would suggest, therefore, that you do not intentionally use them for this purpose, but use them as representatives of the Air Element in your rituals. In true magic it is the intent that is the important aspect, therefore we have divided our extensive list into what we feel are broad headings of appropriate purposes. The general method of preparation remains the same.

Incense Preparation

YOU WILL NEED
Pestle and mortar

Note: Your pestle and mortar can be of any material, though one that does not pick up the perfumes of the ingredients is obviously best. If you do not have a pestle and mortar, a chopping board and rolling pin will suffice, though it is messier this way.

Set of measuring spoons
Large bowl in which to blend your mixture thoroughly
Small containers with lids
Labels
Your chosen herbs, resins, oils etc.
Charcoal blocks for burning the incense

METHOD
Make sure that you grind each quantity of the herbs and resins as small as possible.
When each ingredient is ground place it in your larger bowl, reserving a small quantity in the right proportions of each ingredient with which to do a test run.
Mix each ingredient well in as you add it. Mixing by hand is probably most successful, since this allows you to introduce your own personal vibration.
(You could use a wand of sacred wood reserved specifically for the purpose if you wish.)
As you mix, say:

*May this herb [resin/oil] enhance the power
Of this offering for spirits of Air*

Add any oil last and make sure that this is thoroughly mixed in and not left in one place in the mixture.

When all ingredients are combined, spend some time thinking about your purpose and gently mixing and remixing your incense.
Remember that if you are making incense for a particular purpose, the herbs and resins used should correspond to that purpose; therefore your incense may not necessarily smell as pleasant as you would like.
If wished, ask for a blessing or consecration for the incense, as follows:

May this the work of my two hands
Be blessed for the purpose of [state purpose]

Now test your sample by lighting a charcoal block and burning it carefully in a safe place.

Incense often improves with keeping, so your sample may not smell the same as your stored incense. If it is to your liking and you feel it is suitable for your purpose, fill the containers, secure them tightly and label them clearly. They should be stored in a cool, dark place.

When finished, ask for a blessing on the magical process of blending.

Your incense is now ready for use. Many incenses blend, change and strengthen when stored correctly.

BANISHING, EXORCISM AND PURIFICATION

All of the following incenses work on the principle that certain energies need to be banished – got rid of – in order for the practitioner to work effectively. The creation of peace, purification of the area and, of course, exorcism of unwanted spirits all come under this heading. Do think very carefully about what you wish to achieve before deciding which incense is right for your purpose. Insofar as is possible, we have made certain suggestions or the purpose is clearly indicated in the title.

It is always possible when making incense to make substitutions in the ingredients. We give here a list of herbs which are traditionally known to be used for purification and banishing. They can all be mixed and matched ad infinitum, though you may have to experiment with the quantities until it 'feels' right (or until it smells right).

You need to be very conscious of the purpose of your protection or banishing incense, so here are a few specific suggestions.

Banishing: Hyssop, Lilac, St John's Wort
Cleansing: Cinnamon, Clove, Lovage (use the powdered root), Mullein (cleansing of ritual tools and areas), Pine, Thyme, Vervain (cleansing of sacred spaces)

Exorcism: Angelica, Basil, Birch, Frankincense, Juniper, Garlic, St John's Wort

Hex-Breaking: Chilli Pepper, Galangal, Vertivert

Peace: Aloe, Camomile, Gardenia, Lavender, Violet

Purification: Anise, Benzoin, Betony, Cinquefoil, Dragon's Blood, Fennel, Frankincense, Hyssop, Lavender, Lemon, Oak Leaves (of ritual spaces), Pine, Rosemary, Rue (of ritual spaces and tools), Sandalwood, Thyme, Valerian, Vervain

BANISHING AND EXORCISM

Banishing Incense

1 part Bay Leaves

2 parts Cinnamon

1 part Rose Petals

2 parts Myrrh Resin

Pinch of Salt

Clearing Incense

1 part Frankincense Resin

1 part Copal Resin

1 part Myrrh Resin

½ part Sandalwood

Burn this with windows open.

Ending Negativity Incense

1 part Marjoram

1 part Thyme

½ part Oregano

¼ part Bay Leaves

¼ part Cloves

Exorcism Incense

3 parts Frankincense Resin

1 part Rosemary

1 part Bay Leaves

1 part Avens

1 part Mugwort

1 part St. John's Wort

1 part Angelica

1 part Basil

Burn this incense with the windows open to drive out very heavy spiritual negativity from your surroundings.

Jinx Removing Incense

2 parts Clove

1 part Deerstongue

Few drops of Rose Geranium Oil

This incense can be used when you think someone is against you

Uncrossing Incense

2 parts Lavender

1 part Rose

2 parts Bay

1 part Verbena

Use this incense when you feel you or your home has been 'cursed' or you are under attack.

PURIFICATION

Purification Incense 1

2 parts Sandalwood

1 part Cinnamon

2 parts Bay

1 part Vervain

Pinch of Salt

Burn this incense with windows open to clear a disturbed home after an argument, for instance.

Purification Incense 2

2 parts Sandalwood

1 part Cinnamon

Leave windows open to clear an atmosphere quickly.

Purification Incense 3

3 parts Frankincense Resin

2 parts Dragon's Blood Resin

1 part Myrrh Resin

1 part Sandalwood

1 part Wood Betony

½ part Dill Seed

Few drops of Rose Geranium Oil

This is good for clearing your new home.

Domestic Tranquility Incense

¾ part Sage

¼ part Rue

½ part Ground Ivy

Few drops of Bayberry Oil

¼ part Bayberry

1¼ parts Linden (Lime)

Hearth and Home Incense

2 parts Dragon's Blood Resin

½ part Juniper

½ part Sassafrass

½ part Orange Flowers

2 parts Myrrh Resin

½ part Rose Petals

This incense should be burnt when you wish to create a safe, warm, loving home.

Peace and Protection Incense

4 parts Lavender

3 parts Thyme

2 parts Vervain

3 parts Basil

1 part Frankincense Resin

Pinch of Rue

Pinch of Gum Benzoin

Few drops of Bergamot Oil

Few drops of Jasmine Oil

This can be used both in Peace and Protection rituals.

PROTECTION

There are many ways of protecting both yourself and your own space by the use of incense. If you simply wish to protect against the intrusion of negative energies it is probably best to use those incenses which are based mainly on the resinous substances. This is for two reasons. Firstly, most resins are relatively slow burning, high vibrational energy substances so their effect is long lasting; secondly you have more opportunity during their preparation as you grind to introduce specific intents into the incense. Perhaps, for instance, you might wish to protect yourself against the jealousy of a former lover or against financial loss. Using substances which have a high vibration helps to build a 'wall' of protection, which means that neither the bad thought nor the subtle energies activated on a more spiritual level can harm you.

Some of the incense below are specifically to protect against not just negativity on a purely physical plane, but also malign energy deliberately directed at you and your loved ones. Incense such as the ones for Psychic Protection will give you the security you need to know that you can combat such gross intrusion.

Other incenses mean that you can react quickly to outside influences should you need to do so. We have offered many alternatives in this as in other sections so that you can decide for yourself which ones work best for you. A lot will depend on what is local to you, and so far as protection incenses are concerned, we are aware that the sensitivities can change depending on the environment surrounding the individual. Where the incense is for a specific purpose, we have given you that information.

It is always possible when making incenses to make substitutions in the ingredients. We give here a list of herbs which are traditionally known to be used for protective purposes. They can all be mixed and matched ad infinitum, though you may have to experiment with the quantities until it 'feels' right (or until it smells right).

Aloe, Angelica (Root), Anise, Balm of Gilead, Basil, Bay Laurel, Betony, Caraway, Camomile, Cinquefoil, Clove, Coriander, Dill, Dragon's Blood, Fennel, Fern, Garlic, Hawthorn, Holly, Hyssop, Ivy, Lavender, Lilac, Mandrake, Marjoram, Meadowsweet, Mistletoe, Mugwort, Mullein, Nettle, Onion, Pennyroyal (avoid when pregnant),

Black Pepper, Periwinkle, Rose, Rosemary, Rowan, Rue, Sage, St John's Wort, Sandalwood, Vervain, Witch Hazel, Wormwood.

Protection Incense 1

½ part Bay Leaves

½ part Cloves

¾ part Oregano

¾ part Sandalwood

Protection Incense 2

4 parts Verbena

1 part Galangal Root (ground)

1 part Peppermint

1 part Cinnamon

½ part Rue

Protection Incense 3

¼ part Basil

½ part Cinnamon

½ part Rosemary

1½ parts Thyme

½ part Sage

½ part Star Anise

Total Protection Incense

2 parts Frankincense Resin

1 part Dragon's Blood Resin

½ part Wood Betony

This incense creates quite a high vibration and protects on all levels of existence.

Iron Protection Incense

¼ part Iron Filings

1 part Galangal Root (powdered)

Few drops of Citronella Oil

This incense uses the ancient idea that iron will change a negative vibration.

New Orleans Protection Incense

2 parts Myrrh Resin

½ part Bay Leaves

1 part Cloves

1 part Cinnamon

This is an incense often used in Hoodoo work.

Sandalwood Protection Incense

3 parts Sandalwood

2 parts Juniper

1 part Vetivert

Pennyroyal Protection Incense

2 parts Verbena or Vetivert

1 part Galangal

1 part Pennyroyal

¼ part Rue

½ part Cinnamon

Rosemary Protection Incense

2 parts Rosemary

½ part Orris Root (ground)

1 part Basil

1 part Frankincense Resin

10 Herb Protection Incense

2 parts Frankincense Resin

2 parts Myrrh Resin

1 part Juniper Berries

½ part Rosemary

¼ part Avens

¼ part Mugwort

¼ part Yarrow

¼ part St John's Wort

½ part Angelica

1 part Basil

5 Resins Protection Incense

2 parts Frankincense Resin

1 part Copal Resin

1 part Myrrh Resin

1/2 part Dragon's Blood Resin

1/2 part Gum Arabic

Witch's Bottle Home Protection Incense

1/2 part Frankincense Resin

3/4 part Sage

1/2 part Basil

1/2 part Mistletoe

1/4 part Garlic (mix of dried and ground)

3/4 part Rosemary

1/4 part Rue

1 part Sandalwood

1/2 part Myrrh Resin

1/2 part Orris Root

1/2 part Yarrow

Note: The next two incense can be used if you wish to protect your surroundings against theft and burglary.

Prevent Theft Incense

1 part Ground Ivy

1/2 part Juniper

1 1/2 parts Rosemary

Stop Theft Incense

1/2 part Dogwood

1/4 part Caraway

1/2 part Rosemary

1/4 part Tarragon

1 part Willow

Few drops Honeysuckle Oil

Note: The next four protection incense deal specifically with protection on a psychic level, while the two after deal with the effects of an unwanted spiritual visitation. They could be considered equally to belong to the categories of Banishing and Exorcism.

Psychic Protection Incense 1

½ part Elder

1 part Cinquefoil

½ part Bay Leaves

⅛ part Valerian

Psychic Protection Incense 2

¼ part Broom

½ part Agrimony

½ part Basil

¼ part Cranesbill

1 part Vetivert

½ part Oregano

Psychic Protection Incense 3

¼ part Frankincense Resin

½ part Oregano

¼ part Lovage

½ part Cloves

¼ part Ginger Root (ground)

½ part Sandalwood

¼ part Star Anise

Psychic Protection Incense 4

½ part Benzoin Resin

¼ part Dragon's Blood Resin

½ part Frankincense Resin

¼ part Camphor Gum

½ part Cassia

¼ part Patchouli

2 parts Sandalwood

Each ingredient in this incense is a resin.

Note: These next two incense will help to keep your home clear of spirit interference unless you have specifically asked for spirit to be present.

Spirits Depart Incense

2 parts Fennel seed

2 parts Dill seed

½ part Rue

Spirit Portal Incense

½ part Cinnamon

½ part Lavender

Pinch of Wormwood

Note: The next six protection incense all have as their main ingredients resins, particularly Frankincense. If you dislike the perfume of Frankincense, experiment with the proportions of your other resins.

Protection Incense 1

4 parts Frankincense Resin

3 parts Myrrh Resin

2 parts Juniper Berries

1 part Rosemary

½ part Avens

½ part Mugwort

½ part Yarrow

½ part St. John's Wort

½ part Angelica

½ part Basil

This incense is so all enveloping that it will protect against almost everything.

Protection Incense 2

2 parts Frankincense Resin

1 part Dragon's Blood Powder or Resin

½ part Betony

This incense is particularly potent when attempting to visualize the source of your problem.

Protection Incense 3

2 parts Frankincense Resin

1 part Sandalwood

½ part Rosemary

Protection Incense 4

1 part Frankincense Resin

1 part Myrrh Resin

½ part Clove

Protection Incense 5

2 parts Frankincense Resin

1 part Copal Resin

1 part Dragon's Blood Powder or Resin

LUST, LOVE AND RELATIONSHIP (BEGINNING OR ENDING)
It is with some trepidation that we include this section. The idea of trying to influence someone else directly goes against the ethics of many practitioners and magicians. One must be very careful because incense prepared with the intention of trying to make someone do that which they do not want to, or which goes against their natural inclination, can possibly misfire and cause the originator of such a spell a good deal of difficulty.

Love incense really should only be used with the intent that the occurrence will only be in accordance with the Greater Good. That is, that you are helping something to happen, not forcing it. Apart from that, many of these incense have a beautiful perfume and can help to create a loving, supportive atmosphere. Needless to say, we cannot claim responsibility for the outcome or effect of any of these incense!

It is always possible when preparing incense to make substitutions in the ingredients. We give here a list of herbs which are traditionally known to be used for relationships or aspects of relationships. They can all be mixed and matched ad infinitum, though you may have to experiment with the quantities until it 'feels' right (or until it smells right).

Fertility: Acorns, Geranium, Hawthorn, Mandrake, Orange (dried and powdered peel), Pine, Poppy, Sage, Sunflower (seeds), Walnut

Friendship: Lemon, Rose, Passion Flower

Harmony: Hyacinth, Heliotrope, Lilac, Meadowsweet

Love: Apple, Balm of Gilead, Basil, Caraway, Catnip, Coriander, Cowslip, Dill, Dragon's Blood, Gardenia, Ginger, Ginseng, Honeysuckle, Jasmine, Lavender, Lemon Balm, Lemon Verbena, Linden, Marigold, Marjoram, Mistletoe, Myrtle, Orris Root, Rose, Rosemary, Valerian, Vanilla (the bean in love charms, the oil as an aphrodisiac), Vervain, Violet (particularly when mixed with Lavender), Yarrow

Luck: Apple, Ash (leaves), Daisy (wear when performing midsummer rituals), Hazel, Holly (for newly-weds), Ivy (for newly-weds), Mint, Rose, Rowan, Vervain, Violet.

Lust: Cinnamon, Lemongrass, Nettle, Rosemary, Violet.

To attract men: Jasmine, Juniper (dried berries), Lavender, Lemon Verbena, Lovage, Orris Root, Patchouli

To attract women: Henbane, Holly, Juniper (dried berries), Lemon Verbena, Lovage, Orris Root, Patchouli

There are many different aspects to relationships. In this section the individual titles of each recipe are self-explanatory.

Loving Friends Incense

½ part Acacia

1 part Rosemary

¼ part Elder

½ part Frankincense Resin

1 part Dogwood

Attract a Lover Incense

1 part Lovage

½ part Orris Root (ground)

1 part Lemon Verbena

¼ part Patchouli

Few drops of Lemon Verbena Oil

Attract Love Incense

½ part Cloves

1 part Rose

¼ part Saw Palmetto

½ part Juniper

Few drops of Musk Oil

Few drops of Rose Oil

½ part Red Sandalwood

Draw and Strengthen Love Incense

2 parts Sandalwood

½ part Basil

½ part Bergamot

Few drops of Rose Oil

Few drops of Lavender Oil

Love Incense 1

1 part Orris Root (ground)

Few drops Musk Oil

1 part Sandalwood

1 part Violet

Few drops Gardenia Oil

Love Incense 2

2 parts Dragon's Blood Resin

1 part Orris Root (ground)

½ part Cinnamon

½ part Rose Petals

Few drops of Musk Oil

Few drops of Patchouli Oil

Love Incense 3

1 part Patchouli

Few drops of Musk Oil

Few drops of Civet Oil

Few drops of Ambergris Oil

This incense makes the opposite sex more aware of you.

Love Incense 4

1 part Violets

1 part Rose Petals

½ part Olive leaves

Love Incense 5

2 parts Sandalwood

2 parts Benzoin Resin

1 part Rosebuds

Few drops of Patchouli Oil

Few drops of Rose Oil

Love Incense 6

2 parts Sandalwood

½ part Basil

½ part Bergamot

Few drops of Rose Oil

Few drops of Lavender Oil

Burn this incense to attract love, to strengthen the love you have and also to expand your ability to give and receive love.

Increase Love Incense

½ part Benzoin

¼ part Jasmine

1 part Rose

¼ part Patchouli

½ part Musk Root

½ part Sandalwood

Few drops of Musk Oil

Few drops of Civet Oil

Few drops of Rose Oil

Few drops of Jasmine Oil

This incense can be used in love rituals when you wish to strengthen the bonds between you.

Note: The next three incense are all thought to have an effect on the libido.

Fiery Passion Incense

¾ part Yohimbe

½ part Cinnamon

¼ part Ginger Root

2½ parts Damiana

Few drops of Ambergris Oil

Passion Incense

½ part Cranesbill

1¼ parts Cascara

½ part Savory

Few drops of Civet Oil

½ part Musk Root

Physical Love Incense

¾ part Damiana

½ part Yohimbe

½ part Musk Root

¾ part Cascara

Few drops of Bergamot Oil

Few drops of Ambergris Oil

Fidelity Incense

¼ part Basil

¼ part Dragon's Blood Resin

1 part Red Sandalwood

½ part Rosemary

1 part Dogwood

Few drops of Honeysuckle Oil

Marital Bliss Incense

1 part Vanilla Bean (ground)

2 parts Wintergreen

1 part Khus Khus

1 part Narcissus

Few drops of Wintergreen Oil

Burn this incense at night, just before you go to bed.

Virility Incense

½ part Holly

¼ part Patchouli

½ part Savory

½ part Mandrake

Few drops of Civet Oil

¼ part Dragon's Blood Resin

½ part Oak

¼ part Musk Root

Few drops of Musk Oil

Conceive a Child Incense

½ part Mistletoe

1 part Mandrake

1 ½ parts Motherwort

Few drops of Strawberry Oil

Fertility Incense 1

¾ part Allspice

½ part Fennel

¾ part Star Anise

1 part Sandalwood

Fertility Incense 2

½ part Basil

½ part Dragon's Blood Resin

¼ part Holly

1 part Pine

¼ part Juniper Berries

Note: The following five incense should be used carefully and thoughtfully because it is not wise to try to influence someone against their will. Your choice of words when performing the ritual is important.

Stay at Home Incense

½ part Clove

½ part Allspice

½ part Deerstongue

1 part Mullein

1 part Sage

Break Off an Affair Incense

¼ part Camphor

1 part Slippery Elm

1½ parts Pennyroyal

Divorce Incense

½ part Frankincense Resin

½ part Rue

½ part Allspice

¼ part Marjoram

¾ part Pennyroyal

½ part Yarrow

⅛ part Camphor Resin

½ part Sandalwood

End an Affair Incense

¼ part Menthol

1 ½ parts Willow

1½ parts Lavender

Love Breaker Incense

½ part Vetivert

1 part Patchouli

1 part Lemongrass

½ part Mullein

This incense can be used to aid the smooth break up of a relationship.

Release and Ending Incense

½ part Bay

½ part Lemon Balm

¼ part Yarrow

½ part Pennyroyal

1 part Willow

Few drops of Lemon Balm Oil

Few drops of Peppermint Oil

BUSINESS, MONEY, PROSPERITY AND SUCCESS

After love incense, incense that can be used to bring about success in business affairs and finance are the ones that intrigue people most. On the quiet many business people who use incense would concede that they have received assistance, but they would hate to admit it publicly. These incense are especially appropriate for those who value secrecy, because they can be used without fuss to create circumstances where the desired effect becomes inevitable.

Using these incense might be considered by some to be employing thaumaturgy – magic that is designed to have an effect specifically on the mundane world. Wherever possible, we suggest that you keep your intent as altruistic and as clearly in mind as you can when using incense. The 'higher' the intent, the more likely it is to happen because it can be said to be in accord with the Greater Good. We would also suggest that any prosperity, money or success you receive as a consequence is tithed; that is, a portion is dedicated to good causes – in old-style belief, 10 per cent.

It is always possible when preparing incense to make substitutions in the ingredients. We give here a list of herbs which are traditionally known to be used to bring success of various sorts. They can all be mixed and matched *ad infinitum*, though you may have to experiment with the quantities until it 'feels' right (or until it smells right).

Good Fortune: Ash leaves, Heather, Nutmeg, Rose, Vetivert

Luck: Apple, Ash leaves, Daisy (Wear at midsummer rituals), Hazel, Holly, Ivy, Mint, Rose, Rowan, Vervain, Violet flowers

Money: Camomile, Cinquefoil, Cinnamon, Clove, Comfrey, Fennel, Ginger, Mint, Poppy (seeds or the dried seed pod), Vervain

Prosperity: Acorn, Almond, Ash, Basil, Benzoine, Honeysuckle

Success: Cinnamon, Ginger, Lemon Balm, Rowan

BUSINESS

These first ten incense are burnt when you wish to increase your personal portfolio and business acumen. Burning the Total Confidence incense, for instance, will help you to gain confidence, but only if you have something to build on in the first place.

Business Incense

2 parts Benzoin Resin

1 part Cinnamon

1 part Basil

Confidence Incense 1

1 part Rosemary

¼ part Garlic

½ part Camomile

1 part Musk Root

Confidence Incense 2

1 part St. John's Wort

1 part Thyme

½ part Oak

¼ part Sweet Woodruff

Recognition Incense

2 parts Benzoin Resin

1 part Rue

1 part Sandalwood

This incense can be used when you feel your efforts should be recognized and rewarded.

Note: These next three incense should be used when you require a little extra 'oomph' to carry you along a chosen path.

Determination Incense 1

½ part Althea

½ part Camomile

1 part Thyme

¼ part Garlic

Determination Incense 2

1 part Rosemary

1 part Willow

1 part Musk Root

Few drops of Musk Oil

Determination Incense 3

$\frac{1}{2}$ part Allspice

$1\frac{1}{4}$ parts St John's Wort

$\frac{1}{2}$ part Southernwood

$\frac{3}{4}$ part Willow

Note: These following two incense can be used to encourage the flow of money towards you.

Financial Gain Incense 1

1 part Lovage

1 part Bay

$\frac{1}{4}$ part Cinnamon

$\frac{1}{2}$ Meadowsweet

Financial Gain Incense 2

$\frac{1}{2}$ part Star Anise

$\frac{1}{4}$ part Poppy Seed

$\frac{1}{2}$ part Mistletoe

$\frac{1}{2}$ part Juniper

1 part Cherry

Financial Increase Incense

$\frac{1}{4}$ part Cucumber

$\frac{3}{4}$ part Allspice

1 part Sunflower

$\frac{1}{4}$ part Saw Palmetto

$\frac{1}{2}$ part Marigold

This incense can be used when you are deliberately wishing to increase what you already have; i.e. make a profit, rather than simply gain money.

Note: These following two incense may be used when additional information or insight is needed either in specific circumstances or on a day-to-day basis. They are good incense to burn in a training situation.

Gain Knowledge and Wisdom Incense 1

¼ part Angelica

¼ part Vervain

1 part Sage

½ part Solomon's Seal

Knowledge and Wisdom Incense 2

1 part Solomon's Seal

¼ part Benzoin Resin

½ part Vervain

½ part Cloves

½ part Bay

Money Incense 1

1 part Basil

1 part Cinquefoil

½ part Hyssop

½ part Galangal

Money Incense 2

1¼ parts Lavender

¼ part Camomile

¼ part Comfrey

1 part Red Clover

¼ part Acacia

More Money Incense 1

¾ part Cinnamon

½ part Dragon's Blood Resin

1¼ parts Cascara

Note: These next seven incense are good for accruing more than your immediate needs. The last two enable you to call in, and give, favours when necessary.

Prosperity Incense

1 part Frankincense Resin

¹/₂ part Cinnamon

¹/₄ part Nutmeg

¹/₂ part Balm

Wealth Incense

1 part Nutmeg

¹/₂ – 1 part Pepperwort

1 pinch Saffron

Increased Wealth Incense

2 parts Frankincense Resin

1 part Cinnamon

1 part Nutmeg

¹/₂ part Clove

¹/₂ part Ginger

¹/₂ part Mace

Gain Wealth Incense

2 parts Pine

1 part Cinnamon

1 part Galangal

A few drops of Patchouli Oil

Riches and Favours Incense 1

2 parts Benzoin Resin

¹/₂ part Clove

¹/₂ part Pepperwort

Riches and Favours Incense 2

2 parts Benzoin Resin

1 part Wood Aloe

¹/₂ part Peppermint

¹/₂ part Clove

Note: These next three incense are used to pull success towards you, whatever you may perceive that to be.

Success Incense 1

½ part Basil

½ part Bay

1 part Cedar

½ part Oak

Success Incense 2

¼ part Mistletoe

½ part Marigold

½ part Sunflower

¼ part Onion

1 part Sandalwood

Success Incense 3

¼ part Frankincense Resin

½ part Sweet Woodruff

1½ parts Vetivert

¼ part Angelica

1 part Sandalwood

Note: This following incense can be used when you wish to build on success you have already had.

Greater Success Incense

1½ parts Sandalwood

½ part Sarsaparilla

½ part Motherwort

½ part Quassia

Few drops of Jasmine Oil

LUCK INCENSE

These next four incense are all designed to bring good fortune. Your intent is very important when you use a first-rate Luck incense. The incense open the way to winning, rather than actually winning for you.

Good Luck in Life Incense

½ part Musk Root

1½ part Rose

½ parts Red Clover

½ part Galangal Root

Few drops of Rose Oil

Good Luck Incense

½ part Dragon's Blood Resin

½ part Mistletoe

1 part Cascara

1 part Linden

Improve Luck Incense

1 part Rosemary

½ part Dragon's Blood Resin

½ part Musk Root

½ part Sandalwood

Few drops of Rose Oil

Few drops of Musk Oil

Games of Chance Incense

½ part Dragon's Blood Resin

2 parts Gum Mastic Resin

1 part Frankincense Resin

This incense could be used, for example, when you wish to try your luck and have a flutter.

PHYSICAL AND EMOTIONAL HEALTH AND HEALING

Any incense used for the purpose of health and healing should only be used as an adjunct to other methods. If you are prepared to use incense in this way, you will probably have an awareness of alternative healing methods anyway, but they cannot – and should never – be used as substitutes for proper medical advice. Many of the herbs used are those which have been used for centuries to alleviate certain conditions, but bearing in mind modern laws and thought, you must make your own decisions as to their effective use. None of the mixtures given can, to our knowledge, harm you in any way. Indeed those given below have, through experience, had the stated effect. We suggest you seek the help of your herbalist or medical practitioner as to the nature of the ingredients and what form they should take (root, powder, etc).

It is always possible when preparing incense to make substitutions in the ingredients. We give here a list of herbs which are traditionally known to be used for health and healing matters. They can all be mixed and matched ad infinitum, though you may have to experiment with the quantities until it 'feels' right (or until it smells right).

Courage: Basil, Garlic, Mandrake (root), Mullein, Nettle, St John's Wort, Thyme, Wormwood, Yarrow

Healing: Aloe, Ash (wood), Camomile, Cinnamon, Comfrey, Eucalyptus, Fennel, Garlic, Hops, Marjoram, Mint, Nettle, Onion, Pine, Rosemary, Rowan, Saffron, Sage, Sandalwood, Thyme, Willow, Yarrow

Happiness: Anise, Catnip, Lily of the Valley, Marjoram, Saffron

Mental powers: Caraway, Lily of the Valley, Rosemary, Vanilla, Walnut

Wisdom: Peach (fruit), Sage, Sunflower

PHYSICAL HEALTH

Cold Healing Incense

1 ¼ parts Pine

½ part Cedar

⅛ part Camphor

⅛ part Menthol

½ part Spruce

Few drops of Pine Oil

Resins have always had their part to play in incense. This particular incense will help ease the symptoms of a cold – you can see from its ingredients it is as much medicinal as magical.

Healing Incense 1

2 parts Myrrh Resin

1 part Cinnamon

1 pinch Saffron

Healing Incense 2

1 part Rose

1 part Eucalyptus

1 part Pine

1 pinch Saffron

Healing Incense 3

1 part Rosemary

1 part Juniper

When used in oil form – i.e. on a tissue placed on a radiator or in a burner – this incense is easily used in a hospital environment.

Regain Health Incense

3 parts Myrrh Resin

2 parts Nutmeg

1 part Cedar

1 part Clove

½ part Balm

½ part Poppy Seeds

Few drops of Pine Oil

Few drops of Sweet Almond Oil

This incense acts as a good 'pick-me-up'.

EMOTIONAL HEALTH

All of these incense help to alter the state of mind and increase the ability to think positively.

Courage Incense

2 parts Dragon's Blood Powder or Resin

1 part Frankincense Resin

1 part Rose Geranium

1/4 part Tonka Beans

Few drops Musk Oil

Ease Emotional Pain Incense

3 parts Bay

3/4 part Allspice

1/4 part Dragon's Blood Powder

3/4 part Frankincense Resin or Gum Arabic

End Negativity and Give Hope Incense 1

1 part Thyme

1/2 part Rue

1/2 part Sweet Woodruff

1/2 part Cloves

End Negativity and Give Hope Incense 2

1 part Dittany

1/2 part Camomile

1/4 part Patchouli

Happiness Incense 1

1/2 part Myrrh Resin

1/4 part Marjoram

1 part Dittany

3/4 part Sandalwood

3/4 part Oregano

Few drops of Spearmint Oil

Happiness Incense 2

1 part Oregano

1 part Rosemary

1 part Marigold

'Poor Me' Incense

½ part Cloves

¼ part Juniper

2 parts Willow

⅛ part Menthol

Few drops of Eucalyptus Oil

Few drops of Wintergreen Oil

This incense can be used for when you feel the whole world is against you.

Tranquillity Incense

1 part Sage

1½ parts Rose

¼ part Benzoin Resin

½ part Meadowsweet

Few drops of Rose Oil

This incense induces a sense of tranquillity which allows you to rebalance and recharge your batteries.

Note: These next two incense give strength and integrity in a chosen task.

Strength Incense 1

½ part Dragon's Blood

½ part Musk Root

1½ parts Vetivert

½ part Cinquefoil

Few drops of Musk Oil

Few drops of Ambergris Oil

Strength Incense 2

½ part Cinnamon

¼ part Dragon's Blood Powder or Resin

¼ part Frankincense Resin

½ part Musk Root

¼ part Patchouli

1 part Vetivert

¼ part Yarrow

Few drops of Musk Oil

Study Incense

2 parts Gum Mastic

1 part Rosemary

Burn this incense to strengthen the conscious mind for study, to develop concentration and to improve your memory.

PSYCHIC POWERS, DIVINATION AND PROPHETIC DREAMS

Having indicated that the use of mind-altering substances should be very carefully considered, this section sets about indicating what we would consider to be substances which alter your sensitive vibrational rate. Each one of us consists of at least a physical body, an astral body and a spiritual aspect. These subtle energies can be successfully adjusted to connect us with other subtle vibrations – it is a little like logging on to a computer and connecting with a particular programme.

The incense below help us to do this and enable us to work without interference from other less manageable energies. They put us in touch with those inner powers which we use to penetrate other dimensions and help us to develop them without disquiet. Their specific purpose is, by and large, stated in the name of the incense.

It is always possible when preparing incense to make substitutions in the ingredients. We give here a list of herbs which are traditionally known to be used for enhancing the power of the mind. They can all be mixed and matched ad infinitum, though you may have to experiment with the quantities until it 'feels' right (or until it smells right).

Meditation: Camomile, Elecampane, Frankincense, Vervain

Psychic powers: Ash leaves, Bay Laurel, Bay leaves, Cinnamon, Cowslip (induces contact during sleep), Elecampane, Elder, Eyebright, Hazel, Hyssop (when this is burnt as an incense, it is possible to draw upon magical dragon energy), Lavender, Marigold (also use for prophecy), Mugwort, Nutmeg, Oak, Rose, Thyme, Willow (this can be used to bind together witches brooms, forked branch is ideal for use in water dowsing), Wormwood, Yarrow
Spirituality: Cinnamon, Clover (associated with the Triple Goddess), Frankincense, Myrrh, Sandalwood

DIVINATION

The following six incense can be used as part of divinatory rituals.

Divination Incense 1

1 part St John's Wort

³/₄ part Wormwood

³/₄ part Bay

¹/₂ part Frankincense Resin

Divination Incense 2

³/₄ part Cinquefoil

¹/₈ part Valerian

¹/₂ part Deerstongue

¹/₂ part Frankincense Resin

1 part Sandalwood

Divination Incense 3

¹/₂ part Cinnamon

¹/₂ part Chickweed

1 part Thyme

1 part Sandalwood

Divination Incense 4

1 part Yarrow

1 part St John's Wort

¹/₄ part Frankincense Resin

¹/₂ part Bay

Divination Incense 5

1 part Lavender

1 part Rose

½ part Star Anise

½ part Sandalwood

Divination Incense 6

2 parts Sandalwood

1 part Orange Peel

½ part Mace

½ part Cinnamon

PSYCHIC POWERS

These next four incense are particularly good for enhancing the psychic powers during magical rituals.

Psychic Power Incense

1 part Frankincense Resin

¼ part Bistort

Psychic Incense 1

2 parts Sandalwood

1 part Gum Arabic

Psychic Incense 2

2 parts Sandalwood

1 part Gum Acacia (or Arabic)

Psychic Incense 3

1 part Frankincense Resin

1 part Sandalwood

1 part Cinnamon

1 part Nutmeg

Few drops of Orange Oil

Few drops of Clove Oil

PAST LIVES

These next two incense can be used when you wish to find out about past lives

Recall Past Lives Incense

1 ½ parts Sandalwood

½ part Water Lily

½ part Holly

½ part Frankincense Resin

Few drops of Lilac Oil

Remember Past Lives Incense

1 part Sandalwood

½ part Cinnamon

½ part Myrrh Resin

Few drops of Myrrh Oil

Few drops of Cinnamon Oil

Few drops of Cucumber Oil

SPIRIT PRESENCE

These next three incense are good when you wish to invite positive energies to be present during magical rituals.

Spirit Incense 1

1 part Sandalwood

1 part Lavender

Burn on your altar or in your sacred space.

Spirit Incense 2

2 parts Sandalwood

1 part Willow Bark

This incense is a good one to use (particularly outdoors) when performing rituals during the Waxing Moon.

Open Eyes To Spirit World

1 part Gum Mastic

1 part Amaranth

1 part Yarrow

VISIONS
The next five incense can all be used as part of rituals where you wish to make a connection with other realms

Psychic Vision Incense
3 parts Frankincense Resin

1 part Bay

½ part Damiana

Second Sight Incense
1 part Parsley

½ part Hemp Seeds

½ part Frankincense Resin

Sight Incense
2 parts Gum Mastic

2 parts Juniper

1 part Sandalwood

1 part Cinnamon

1 part Calamus

Few drops of Patchouli Oil

Few drops of Ambergris Oil

Vision Incense
3 parts Cinquefoil

3 Parts Chicory Root

1 Part Clove

Gypsy Sight Incense
1 part Mugwort

½ part Clove

½ part Cinquefoil

Gypsies, in particular, use this incense when they wish to strengthen their psychic visions.

CELESTIAL INFLUENCES

This section is probably for those of you who have chosen to travel a little further on your voyage of discovery. The incense again are used to make a link or to enhance a specific purpose. It will depend on your own personal belief whether, for instance, you wish to use a specific incense to link with planetary energy or to use a specific incense at the times of the various sabbats and moon phases.

Accepted use has meant that certain woods and herbs are associated with days of the week, seasons of the year and lunar cycles. Here we have an easy to consult listing to enable you to get the best out of your rituals. There is nothing to stop you from mixing and matching as you so wish. You may find certain aromas more pleasurable than others.

DAYS OF THE WEEK

The following incense and oils may be used alone or combined for your daily rituals for maximum effect. They have been recommended according to the planetary ruler of the days of the week.

Day of the Week	Planetary Influence	Aroma
Monday	Moon	Jasmine, Lemon, Sandalwood, Stephanotis
Tuesday	Mars	Basil, Coriander, Ginger, Nasturtium
Wednesday	Mercury	Benzoin, Clary Sage, Eucalyptus, Lavender
Thursday	Jupiter	Clove, Lemon Balm, Melissa, Oakmoss, Star Anise
Friday	Venus	Cardamon, Palma rosa, Rose, Yarrow
Saturday	Saturn	Cypress, Mimosa, Myrrh, Patchouli
Sunday	Sun	Cedar, Frankincense, Neroli, Rosemary

AROMAS OF THE SEASONS

The following fragrances, either as plants or – where appropriate – essential oils, can be used to welcome each new season in your personal rituals.

Spring: All sweet scents, particularly Daffodil, Jasmine and Rose
Summer: All spicy scents, particularly Carnation, Clove and Ginger
Autumn: All earthly scents, particularly Oak moss, Patchouli and Vetiver
Winter: All resinous and woody scents, particularly Frankincense, Pine and Rosemary

The following seven incense are suitable for the various seasons and can be used either to honour the turning of the year or the ideas inherent in seasonal worship.

Spring Incense

¼ part Primrose

1 part Cherry

1 part Rose

½ part Sandalwood

Few drops of Lilac Oil

Few drops of Rose Oil

Few drops of Strawberry Oil

Summer Incense 1

1½ parts Lavender

1 part St. John's Wort

½ part Mistletoe

Summer Incense 2

1 part Cedar

½ part Juniper

1 part Sandalwood

Autumn Incense

¼ part Oak

½ part Pine

¼ part Frankincense Resin

¼ Cinnamon   ·

¼ part Cloves

½ part Rosemary

¼ part Sage

½ part Pomegranate

Winter Incense

1¼ parts Lavender

½ part Cloves

½ part Cinnamon

¼ part Benzoin Resin

¼ part Patchouli

¼ part Mistletoe

¼ part Orris Root

Few drops of Bergamot Oil

Winter Incense 2

½ part Mistletoe

¼ part Holly

½ part Bay

½ part Oak

1 part Pine

½ part Cedar

Few drops of Pine Oil

Few drops of Cedar Oil

AROMAS OF THE LUNAR CYCLE

Incense and perfumes can be utilized during the phases of the Moon to put yourself in line with lunar energy.

Sandalwood is particularly appropriate for the First Quarter when the Moon's waxing enhances spirituality.
Jasmine has the full-blown energies of the Full Moon.

The more ethereal lemon is symbolic of the lessening of the Moon's influence as it wanes in the Last Quarter.
Camphor signifies the similarly cold New Moon.

Below is an oil blend that can be used to anoint your altar, if you use one, or to diffuse around your sacred space at regular intervals, before you undertake any ritual, to purify and empower the space.

Altar Oil

4 parts Frankincense

3 parts Myrrh

1 part Galangal

1 part Vervain

1 part Lavender

ELEMENT INCENSE

Tradition dictates that you honour the four 'directions' and their appropriate Elements. The following four incense are suitable for honouring the four directions or cardinal points before moving onto the ritual proper. You can then use any of the other incense for their appropriate purpose.

Air Incense

2 parts Benzoin Resin

1 part Gum Mastic

½ part Lavender

¼ part Wormwood

1 pinch Mistletoe

Earth Incense

1 part Pine

1 part Thyme

Few drops Patchouli Oil

Fire Incense

2 parts Frankincense Resin

1 part Dragon's Blood Resin

1 part Red Sandalwood

1 pinch Saffron

Water Incense

2 parts Benzoin Resin

1 part Myrrh Resin

1 part Sandalwood

Few drops of Lotus Oil

PLANETARY INCENSE

The following incense can be used when you wish to call particularly on the power of the planets in your rituals. We have deliberately omitted incense suitable for use with Neptune, Uranus and Pluto. For these, you would be better served using your own intuition.

Sun Incense 1

3 parts Frankincense Resin

2 parts Myrrh Resin

1 part Wood Aloe

$\frac{1}{2}$ part Balm of Gilead

$\frac{1}{2}$ part Bay

$\frac{1}{2}$ part Carnation

Few drops of Ambergris Oil

Few drops of Musk Oil

Few drops of Olive Oil

Burn this incense to draw on the influences of the Sun and for spells involving promotions, friendships, healing, energy and magical power.

Sun Incense 2

3 parts Frankincense Resin

2 parts Sandalwood

1 part Bay

1 pinch Saffron

Few drops of Orange Oil

Sun Incense 3

3 parts Frankincense Resin

2 parts Galangal

2 parts Bay

$\frac{1}{4}$ part Mistletoe

Few drops of Red Wine

Few drops of Honey

Egyptian Solar Incense

3 parts Frankincense Resin

1 part Clove

½ part Red Sandalwood

½ part Sandalwood

¼ part Orange Flowers

3 pinches Orris Root

Moon Incense 1

2 parts Juniper

1 part Calamus

½ part Orris Root

¼ part Camphor

Few drops of Lotus Oil

Moon Incense 2

4 parts Sandalwood

2 parts Wood Aloe

1 part Eucalyptus

1 part crushed Cucumber seeds

1 part Mugwort

½ part Ranuculus blossoms

1 part Selenetrope (you can substitute Gardenia or Jasmine if you cannot find Selentrope easily)

Few drops of Ambergris Oil

Moon Incense 3

2 parts Juniper berries

1 part Orris Root

1 part Calamus

Few drops of Spirits of Camphor or Camphor Tincture or ¼ part genuine Camphor

Few drops of Lotus Bouquet Oil

Moon Incense 4

2 parts Myrrh Resin

2 parts Gardenia Petals

1 part Rose Petals

1 part Lemon Peel

½ part Camphor

Few drops of Jasmine Oil

Moonfire Incense

1 part Rose

1 part Orris Root

1 part Bay

1 part Juniper

1 part Dragon's Blood Powder or Resin

½ part Potassium Nitrate (saltpetre)

Burn this incense when you wish to call on the power of the Moon while performing divination and love rituals. The Potassium Nitrate (saltpetre) is included to make the incense sparkle and glow. Do not add too much though – it will explode.

Earth Incense

2 parts Pine

1 part Patchouli

1 part Cypress

1 pinch Salt

Mercury Incense 1

2 parts Benzoin Resin

1 part Mace

½ part Marjoram

Few drops of Lavender Oil

Burn this incense to invoke Mercury's powers and qualities when performing rituals for such things as intelligence, travel and divination.

Mercury Incense 2

2 parts Sandalwood

1 part Mace

1 part Marjoram

1 part Mint or a few drops of Mint Oil

Venus Incense 1

2 parts Sandalwood

1 part Benzoin Resin

1 part Rose Petals

Few drops of Rose Oil

Few drops of Patchouli Oil

Venus Incense 2

3 parts Wood Aloe

1 part Red Rose Petals

Few drops of Olive Oil

Few drops of Musk Oil

Few drops of Ambergris Oil

You may find it easier to mix the oils together first. Burn this for help from Venus in spells for love, healing and rituals involving women and beauty.

Mars Incense 1

2 parts Galangal

1 part Coriander

1 part Cloves

½ part Basil

Pinch of Black Pepper

Mars Incense 2

2 parts Dragon's Blood Powder

or Resin

1 part Cardamom

1 part Clove

1 part Grains of Paradise

This is a good incense to use if you need the assertive qualities of Mars.

Mars Incense 3

4 parts Benzoin Resin

1 part Pine needles or resin

Scant pinch of Black Pepper

Burn this incense to utilize the powers and attributes of Mars or during spells involving lust, competition of any sort and anything to do with the masculine.

Jupiter Incense

1 part Clove

1 part Nutmeg

1 part Cinnamon

½ part Balm

½ part Lemon Peel

Remember that Jupiter is the planet and god of expansion, so you need to be very specific in your intent when calling upon Jupiter.

Saturn Incense 1

2 parts Sandalwood Resin

2 parts Myrrh Resin

1 part Dittany of Crete

Few drops of Cypress Oil

Few drops of Patchouli Oil

This is the recommended Saturn incense formula. Remember that Saturn does put blocks in the way, but then also encourages from behind.

Saturn Incense 2

2 parts Cypress

1 part Myrrh

Resin

1 part Dittany

Few drops of Patchouli Oil

GODS AND GODDESSES

It would be impossible to give examples of incense for each individual god and goddess. Here we make some suggestions for those gods and goddesses most often honoured and suggest that you again do your own research should you wish to make an offering to any of the other deities.

Aphrodite Incense

1 part Cinnamon

1 part Cedar

Few drops of Cypress Oil

Apollo Incense

2 parts Frankincense Resin

1 part Myrrh Resin

1 part Cinnamon

1/2 part Bay

Mercury Incense 1

2 parts Benzoin Resin

1 part Frankincense Resin

1 part Mace

Mercury Incense 2

2 parts Sandalwood

1 part Gum Mastic

1/2 part Lavender

Few drops of Lavender Oil

Use this incense when honouring the god and his qualities of communication.

Kyphi Incense

1 part Myrrh Resin

1 part Frankincense Resin

1 part Gum Arabic

1 part Balm of Gilead Buds

1 part Cassia or Cinnamon

Few drops of Lotus Oil

Few drops of Musk Oil

This incense is based on an ancient Egyptian formula. The ancient Egyptians also added honey and wine to the mixture. You may do this if you like. Add only a little and let the incense dry prior to use.

Sahumeria Azteca Incense

2 parts Copal Resin

2 parts Frankincense Resin

1 part Rosemary

1 part Sage

1 part Lemongrass

1 part Bay

1/2 part Marigold

1/2 part Yerba Santa

The Sahumeria Azteca incense is still used in contemporary Mexican folk magic, and can also be used today in rituals based on ancient Aztecan practices. It is also used in purification rituals.

Hecate Incense

3 parts Sandalwood

2 parts Cypress

1 part Spearmint

Moon Goddess Incense

2 parts Benzoin Resin

1 part White Onion Skins

1 ½ parts Allspice

1 ½ parts Camphor

½ part Poppy

Sun God Incense

1 part Frankincense Resin

1 part Benzoin Resin

1 part Cinnamon

½ part Coriander

Note: The next two incense honour the Horned God.

Horned God Incense

2 parts Benzoin Resin

1 part Cedar

1 part Pine

1 part Juniper

Few drops of Patchouli Oil

Cernunnos Incense

1 part Pine

1 part Sandalwood

Pinch Valerian

½ part Cinnamon

Few drops of Musk Oil

Hermes Incense

1 part Lavender

½ part Gum Mastic

½ part Cinnamon

Hermes is the Greek counterpart of the Roman god Mercury.

Astarte Incense

1 part Sandalwood

1 part Rose

Few drops of Orange Oil

Few drops of Jasmine Oil

Isis Incense

1 part Myrrh Resin

1 part Frankincense Resin

½ part Orange Peel

¼ part Gum Arabic

½ part Vetivert

The Egyptian goddess Isis is one of the most important representations of a female deity.

Pele Incense

2 parts Frankincense Resin

1 part Dragon's Blood Powder or Resin

1 part Red Sandalwood

1 part Orange Peel

1 part Cinnamon

Few drops of Clove Oil

Burn this incense while honouring Pele, the Hawaiian Goddess of Volcanoes, when you need additional strength for any ritual, when you feel manipulated by others, or for Fire spells in general.

Medicine Wheel Incense

2 parts Sage

1 part Sweetgrass

1 part Pine Resin or Needles

1 part Osha (or Angelica) root

Scant pinch of Tobacco

Burn this incense during rites revering Native American deities and spirits and to attune with the land and its energy.

Offertory Incense

2 parts Frankincense Resin

1 part Myrrh Resin

1 part Cinnamon

1/2 part Rose Petals

1/2 part Vervain

Burn this incense while honouring the goddesses and gods, and also as an offering during rituals.

CEREMONIAL AND CONSECRATIONAL

Here we have put together some of the older types of incense. Some are suitable for consecrating your altar, your tools, your circle and other artefacts, while others will help strengthen the magic in the ritual itself.

Altar Incense

1 part Frankincense Resin

1/2 part Myrrh Resin

1/4 part Cinnamon

Consecration Incense

1 part Mace

1/2 part Frankincense Resin

1 part Benzoin Resin

1 part Gum Arabic

This incense can be used for consecrating your sacred space as well as any tools you may need.

Ceremonial Magic Incense

1 part Frankincense Resin

1/2 part Gum Mastic

1/4 part Sandalwood

Ritual Magic Incense

2 parts Frankincense Resin

1 part Wood Aloe

Few drops of Musk Oil

Few drops of Ambergris Oil

Circle Incense

2 parts Frankincense Resin

1 part Myrrh Resin

1 part Benzoin Resin

½ part Sandalwood

¼ part Cinnamon

½ part Rose

½ part Bay

¼ part Vervain

¼ part Rosemary

Sacred Space Incense

½ part Bay

½ part Camphor

½ part Lavender

½ part Broom

½ part Linden

½ part Ground Ivy

Crystal Purification Incense

2 parts Frankincense Resin

2 parts Copal Resin

1 part Sandalwood

1 part Rosemary

This incense is used when consecrating your crystals so that they work magically for you. The incense 'wipes' all other vibration and aligns the crystal with your purpose.

Talisman and Amulet Consecration Incense

2 parts Frankincense Resin

1 part Cypress

1 part Tobacco

½ part Ash

Talisman Consecration 2

2 parts Frankincense Resin

1 part Cypress

1 part Ash Leaves

1 part Tobacco

1 pinch Valerian

1 pinch Alum

1 pinch Asafoetida powder (smells horrible)

Temple Incense

3 parts Frankincense Resin

2 parts Myrrh Resin

Few drops of Lavender Oil

Few drops of Sandalwood Oil

Burn this incense in your sacred space or grove. You can also use this as a general magical incense or to consecrate your shrine.

Universal Incense

3 parts Frankincense Resin

2 parts Benzoin Resin

1 part Myrrh Resin

1 part Sandalwood

1 part Rosemary

Burn this incense for all positive magical purposes. If used for negative magical goals, it will cancel out the spell or ritual.

To Make Incense Cones

The use of incense becomes such a part of everyday life that you will often find yourself feeling quite bereft when you are not within your own personally enhanced environment. To complete this excursion into the perfumed world of incense, below is a way of being able to enhance your environment wherever you are.

These cones are useful for when you are travelling and do not have access to your normal sources of supply. You could, of course, pop them into your travelling tools bag (see page 173). We would warn that grinding charcoal is extremely messy and tends to fly everywhere. We suggest wrapping a few briquettes of barbeque charcoal in several layers of newspaper or old cloth and giving it some hefty thumps with a hammer. Think of Thor, whose symbol is a hammer, while you are doing it.

YOU WILL NEED

6 parts ground Charcoal

1 part ground Benzoin

2 parts ground Sandalwood

1 part ground Orris Root

(this 'fixes' the scent)

Pestle and mortar

Bowl

6 drops essential oil (use the oil form of one of the ingredients in your chosen incense)

2–4 parts incense according to any of the given recipes above

10 per cent by weight of Potassium Nitrate

Gum Tragacanth or Gum Arabic

METHOD

Mix the first 4 ingredients in the pestle until well blended.

Add the essential oil and mix again.

You will need to create a fine powdered mixture with a fine texture so use a good mortar!

Add 2–4 parts of your chosen incense mixture, grinding and empowering it thoroughly.

Place all these ingredients in the bowl and combine them well with your hands, thinking all the time of your intended purpose.

Now weigh and add 10 per cent potassium nitrate (which is a white powder).
Mix until thoroughly blended.
Never add more than 10 per cent, otherwise it will explode.

Next add the tragacanth glue or gum arabic.
Do this a teaspoon at a time, mixing with your hands in a large bowl until all ingredients
are dampened and the mixture is stiff and doughlike.

Now, shape the mixture into small cones and let it dry slowly for 2–7 days either in the
sun, a slow oven or an airing cupboard.

You now have available to you all the external tools which you will need to be able to become a magical practitioner. Incense in particular has always formed an intrinsic part of worship. Now you must learn to tap into the inherent powers which each of us holds within and use the rhythms and cycles that are both visible and sensed within the world. The first such cycle that we should consider is the lunar.

LUNAR MAGIC

The natural cycle of birth, life and regeneration is epitomized by the lunar cycle. The Moon for many aeons has represented the feminine principle and, for those who worked within an oral tradition, gave rise to many myths and stories which meant that people understood their lives just a little better. Her best personification is that of the Triple Goddess (Maiden, Mother, Crone) which is an image found in many early religions. The lunar phases (Waxing, Waning or Full Moon) can be made use of when planning your magical work.

It is always useful to have your rituals and spells coincide with the appropriate astrological influences. For example, spells and rituals calling on the Moon and involving the element of earth should be performed during a time when the Moon is positioned in one of the three astrological earth signs of Taurus, Virgo or Capricorn. Spells involving the element of fire should be done when the Moon is in Aries, Leo or Sagittarius; spells involving the element of air when the Moon is in Gemini, Libra or Aquarius, whilst spells involving the element of water should be performed when the Moon is in Cancer, Scorpio or Pisces.

You could also use the appropriate incenses for your rituals and there are other correspondences in the application of magic which might be utilized as shown below:

Moon in Aries
Magic involving anything to do with authority, leadership, rebirth, moving on or spiritual conversion should achieve success. Healing rituals for ailments of the face, head or brain are also best performed at this time.

Moon in Taurus
Work magic for love, security, possessions and money now. Healing rituals for illnesses of the throat, neck, and ears are also undertaken during at this time.

Moon in Gemini
This is a good time to work magic for anything to do with communication, including writing, sending emails, public relations, moving house or office and travel. Ailments of the shoulders, arms, hands or lungs also respond well to healing rituals done during this period of time.

Moon in Cancer
This is the best time to work magic for home and domestic life, and also any nurturing activities. Healing rituals for ailments of the chest or stomach should be carried out during this period of time.

Moon in Leo
Courage, fertility and childbirth are all ruled by Leo as is power over others, so this is the best time to work such magic. Healing rituals for problems of the upper back, spine or heart seem to have some success during this period of time.

Moon in Virgo
At this time magic worked for questions involving employment, intellectual matters, health and dietary concerns is much enhanced. Healing rituals for ailments of the intestines or nervous system are also best done during this period of time.

Moon in Libra

Magic involving artistic work, justice, court cases, partnerships and unions, mental stimulation, and karmic, spiritual, or emotional balance receive a boost when worked at this time. Healing rituals for ailments of the lower back or kidneys have additional energy now.

Moon in Scorpio

This is the best time to work magic involving sexual matters, power, psychic growth, secrets and fundamental transformations. Healing rituals for difficulties with the reproductive organs are also most effective during this period.

Moon in Sagittarius

This is the opportune time to work magic for publications, legal matters, travel and revealing truth. Healing rituals for ailments of the liver, thighs or hips are also done at this time.

Moon in Capricorn

This is an ideal time to work magic for ambition, career, organization, political matters and recognition. Healing rituals for the knees, bones, teeth and skin are best performed at this time.

Moon in Aquarius

This is the best time to work magic involving scientific matters, freedom of expression, problem solving, extra sensory abilities and the breaking of bad habits or unhealthy addictions. Ailments of the calves, ankles or blood receive benefit from healing rituals.

Moon in Pisces

Magic worked on the psychic arts involving dreamwork, clairvoyance, telepathy and music is enhanced at this time. Healing rituals for problems with the feet or lymph glands benefit from the flow of energy.

Rituals done according to the phases of the Moon make use of the energies of the cosmos in a particular way. It has long been known that the cycle of the Moon can instigate change, aid growth and be used to clear out old material. The following rituals come under one or more of these categories.

Drawing Down The Moon

We have talked elsewhere of changes of consciousness and of the trance state. One method of accomplishing both is to draw on the Full Moon's energy and make use of that power. This ritual is now known as 'Drawing Down The Moon' and is an accepted method used by many to empower the feminine.

Strictly, the ritual should be done within a cast circle but, in fact, the more proficient you become at performing it as a matter of course, the easier it is to feel protected by Moon's power anyway. It may be enough for you to envisage yourself protected by a shaft of light directly connecting you with the Moon as she shines in the sky.

This is a very powerful ritual, so make sure you use the energy wisely.

YOU WILL NEED

Creative visualization

Athame or wand if necessary

METHOD

Find a quiet spot, preferably in the open.

Spend a few moments centring yourself.

Breathe evenly and deeply and make a connection with the power of the Moon as you do so.

If not using an implement, raise your hands above you head and visualize yourself grasping one of the Moon's beams holding it safely in your hands.

If using your wand or athame, raise it above your head in both hands. (You should feel the power of the Moon as it connects with the wand or athame.) Say:

Moon above, source of power,
I now draw down that power into myself.
Pure essence of Goddess
Be with me now,
Your priestess.

3. PROCEDURES AND PROTOCOL OF RITUAL

As you say this, bring your hands level with your heart and visualize the energy passing through your hands, first into your physical body and then your aura, in waves of silver-blue light. If using the athame or wand, point the tip at your heart and feel the energy in the same way.

When you feel the power waning, bring your hands down to your sides and stand quietly for a few moments absorbing the energy.

When you have completed this, say:

I thank you for your blessings,
O powerful great Moon.

At the end of the ritual, ground yourself by touching the earth, or purposefully taking several steps away from the spot.

Solitary New Moon Ritual

This ritual, which signifies letting go the hurts of the past in a way that allows you to move forward with fresh energy into the future, can be performed at the time of the New Moon. By carrying it out every new moon you are gradually able to cleanse yourself of the detritus of the past, often as far back as childhood.

YOU WILL NEED

Cedar or Sage smudging stick (or cleansing Incense)

White candle

Athame or ritual knife

Bell

Cakes and wine or juice

METHOD

Cast your circle using the smudge stick or incense to 'sweep' the space as you move around the circle clockwise.

Think of your space as being dome-shaped over your head and cleanse that space too.

Ring the bell with your arms in the Goddess position (in a 'V' above your head, you should be standing with your feet apart) and say:

Great Goddess,
Queen of the Underworld,
Protector of all believers in you,
It is my will on this night of the new moon
To overcome my shadows and bring about change.
I invite you to this my circle to assist and protect me in my rite.

Hold your athame or knife with your hands in acknowledgement of the God (crossed over your chest, feet together) and say:

Great God,
Lord of the Upper realms,
Friend of all who work with you,
It is my will on this night of the new moon
To overcome my shadows to bring about change.
I invite you to my circle to assist me and protect me in my rite.

Light the candle and say

Behind me the darkness, in front of me the light
As the wheel turns, I know that every end is a beginning.
I see birth, death and regeneration

Spend a little time in quiet thought. If you can remember a time either in the last month or previously when times have not been good for you, concentrate on that. While the candle begins to burn properly remember what that time felt like.

Now concentrate on the candle flame and allow yourself to feel the positivity of the light. Pick up the candle and hold it high above your head. Feel the energy of the light shower down around you, the negativity drain away. Now draw the power of the light into you and feel the energy in every pore. Pass the candle around you and visualize the energy building up. If you wish, say

Let the light cast out darkness

You might then wish to perform the protective pentagram on page 221 to protect you from similar incidents in the future. Now ground yourself by partaking of the food and drink.

Thank the God and Goddess for their presence. Withdraw the circle.

The giving of new life can be fully celebrated at the time of the crescent moon, so this is a good time to welcome a new child with a suitable ritual such as this next one.

To Welcome a Child

This ritual calls upon the powers of the Egyptian deity Anuket who was called the Clasper, the Giver of Life, both of humans and animals, and was also the goddess of the Nile cataracts (waterfalls). Her symbol was the cowry shell, which is still used even today in various parts of Africa as a magical Great Goddess symbol and as a unit of exchange. Sometimes pictured as having four arms, Anuket represents the union of male and female principles and therefore family values. Her husband Khnemu was one of the few masculine Moon deities.

YOU WILL NEED

Lace or white cloth

2 silver and/or white candles

Clean water and bowl

Rose petals

Rose incense or essential oil

Ankh (Egyptian cross)

Sistrum or rattle

Goblet of milk or juice

METHOD

Set up a miniature altar using the white or lace cloth.

Place the two silver or white candles on it.

Pour water into a bowl and on it float a few rose petals.

Place this bowl between the candles in the centre of the altar and bless the water.

Lay your sistrum to the right, the ankh to the left.

Burn the rose incense.

(You can have a vase of colourful flowers to one side if you wish)

Place the goblet of milk or juice near the bowl of water.

Take the child to be blessed in your arms and hold him/her to face the altar and say:

Anuket, goddess of life, please bless the child of [parent's names]

3. PROCEDURES AND PROTOCOL OF RITUAL

Gently, with the ankh, touch the child's forehead and say:

Open his/her eyes and guide him/her on his/her right spiritual path.

Hand the child to one of the parents, the ankh to the other.
Raise the bowl of water with rose petals in it above your head and say:

Anuket of the sacred waters, please guide and protect the life of (name of child).

Place the bowl back on the altar.
Wet the tip of your forefinger and touch the child's heart, forehead and mouth.

[Name child], child of [name parents],
welcome to our mortal love and the love of the Goddess Anuket.

With one parent holding the child beside you and the other carry the ankh,
acknowledge all four cardinal points starting in the East.

Take the sistrum in your stronger hand, shake it three times in each direction. The
person holding the ankh should also present it to each cardinal point.

Go to the East. Say:

Keepers of Air, Spirits of the East,
Give this child insight and pure knowledge.

Go to the South. Say:

Keepers of Fire, Spirits of the South,
Give this child the powers of the ancients.

Go to the West. Say:

Keepers of Water, Spirits of the West.
Give this child inner calm and warmth.

End by going to the North. Say:

Keepers of Earth, Spirits of the North,
Give this child wealth and happiness.

Return to the altar and put down the sistrum and ankh.

Take up the goblet of milk. Give the child a drink of the milk and say:

Anuket, Giver of Life, feed this child,
Gently guide and protect him/her for ever more

Do you [name parents] swear before Anuket,
That you will give unconditional love to the miracle Anuket has given you?

The parents then answer:

We swear.

Take up the goblet of juice or wine. Say:

Rejoice, for Anuket gives her blessing to all.
Drink together and honour your promise to the little one.

First the parents, and then everyone else present, takes a sip from the goblet.

This ritual is dedicated to Anuket but can, of course, be dedicated to any aspects of the Great Mother. Rather than the ankh and the sistrum, symbols appropriate to your chosen goddess can be used.

Purifying Emotions

This ritual may be performed on any evening during a waning moon. It helps you to release negativity and distress that may build up when you do not feel that you are in control of your life. It has been kept deliberately simple so that you can spend more time in learning how to make your emotions work for you rather than overwhelm you. When you are using the chakras to accomplish self-development you might use this ritual to help you to clear the third chakra.

YOU WILL NEED

White candle

Bowl of water

Bowl of salt

Dried herbs (such as sage for wisdom) in a vessel in which it can be burned.

METHOD

Stand in your sacred space and say:

I call upon the elements in this simple ceremony
that I may be cleansed from the contamination of negativity.
I willingly release negative action in my fire.

Wave your hand over or through the flame and say:

I release stumbling blocks and obstacles in my earth.

Rub salt on your hands and say:

I clear my air of unwise thoughts.

Wave the smouldering sage in front of you, inhale the perfume as it burns and say:

I purify my water.

Dip your hands in the water and say:

Let this relinquishing be gentle.
Purified, cleansed and released in all ways,
I now acknowledge my trust and faith in my own clarity.

Spend a little time thinking about the month to come.
Recognize that there may be times when you need the clarity you
have just requested.

Now dispose of the ingredients immediately.
Put the salt in with the ashes then pour the water on the ground so that it mingles with
the ashes and salt.

It is helpful to find some sort of ritual or ceremony which enables you to let go of an old situation. It is now recognized that there is something called the 'transition curve' which most people go through in one way or another while making changes. We move from a first reaction of denial through apprehension and inertia to acceptance and enthusiasm for the new ways. A good time to do this is just before a New Moon, although it can be done at any time.

To Effect Change

This is a personal technique which can help you to move forward into a new situation. It reminds you on a very deep level what you are capable of and can often form the basis of a work plan. Choose a time when you will not be disturbed.

+ While you may use coloured candles if you wish I personally prefer to use all pure white ones.
+ 'Dress' the candle with aromatherapy oil which for you is evocative of the old situation and light it.
+ Using a plain, unlined piece of paper write on it those things you are moving away from or wish to leave behind. Think carefully about each thing as you write so that it has its own place in your mind.
+ When the candle is threequarters burnt through – most candles burn for 6 to 8 hours – burn the piece of paper completely to ashes while, either out loud or to yourself, stating the intention to be rid of the old. If you think the situation warrants it then allow the candle to burn out completely before lighting a new candle from a new match or light.

If there are elements of the old which you wish to carry forward into the new situation, light the new candle which you have dressed for the new situation from the old one.

+ This time write what you hope for from the new situation on a fresh piece of paper and place it under the candle as you allow the latter also to burn completely through.
+ Keep the paper on which you have outlined the new situation somewhere safe. Sleep with it under your pillow for three nights until you feel you have internalised the ideas.

You may experience a change in energy within yourself, for instance from apprehension to excitement during this time, and can go forward into the new phase of life with equanimity.

To Instigate Change

This spell is slightly more elaborate and is best performed on the night of a Full Moon.

YOU WILL NEED

A candle to represent yourself in your own astrological colour

An orange candle to denote sudden change and success

A silver or light grey one to embody the neutralization of bad luck

A black or dark candle to represent the bad luck itself

If wished, a magenta (deep red/purple) candle to speed up the luck-changing process.

METHOD

Anoint the candles with a good purification or blessing oil (Rosemary is ideal).
Use a stroking action with both hands.

Bear in mind that with the dark candle you are moving bad luck away from you, and should therefore work from the bottom up towards the wick as you rub in the oil.

Anoint the others, except for the magenta, but this time from the middle to the bottom and the middle to the wick to concentrate the energy within the candles.

With the magenta anoint from the wick to the bottom; this brings in what you desire.

Put them where they will burn safely.

Light the candle representing yourself and say:

This is me and everything that I am.

Light the dark candle (black if you are comfortable with it) and say:

This is my bad luck.
It must now leave me.
May it be transformed now and henceforth.

3. PROCEDURES AND PROTOCOL OF RITUAL

Light the grey candle and say:

This will counteract any bad luck which is left untouched.
It will dissolve into the void and become nothing.

Light the orange candle and say:

This represents the changes for good that are coming into my life.
I welcome success with open arms.

Light the magenta candle and say:

This is the energy to bring about the change.

Now sit for several minutes, repeating to yourself:

I welcome change.
I welcome the incoming good.

Leave the candles to burn out completely.

Be ready to let go whatever moves out of your life –
often changes start slowly and then escalate.
Whatever happens, be aware of the opportunities which may be
offered to you over the next little while.

DARK MOON

The Crone goddesses, representative of ancient Wisdom, are by and large connected in some way with the Dark Moon. When we choose to work with those goddesses who represent the Dark Moon, we are usually in need of change. The changes which are brought about when working with these deities are almost always far reaching and radical. While other rituals and techniques will largely have an effect on circumstances and events around you, this following ritual-meditation, in particular, will have an effect on a much deeper, more personal level. This means that you must be prepared to take responsibility for what happens. You must be very clear before you start that you will welcome those changes, for sometimes they can be unexpected and shocking.

It is best if you spend some time in careful consideration of what you truly desire. Think about what you want – perhaps a different life, a new way of working, a change of friends. Then think about what you need. In the examples given above perhaps you might choose a move to another area, a different job entirely or people who have similar interests to your own. Think now about what you require. To begin a new life, or rebuild, you must first get back to the basic you and understand yourself.

It would be no use moving to a new area if you are so painfully shy that you cannot make friends, for instance. You would have to work on yourself and understand why you have difficulty. This is truly the purpose of this particular ritual, to put you in touch with a source of energy which is both cleansing and revivifying. When you understand who you truly are, stripped of all pretence, change occurs naturally to accommodate this new knowledge.

Initially, you are working with an energy that the majority of people neither want or choose to handle. Rituals connected with the Dark Moon – the time when there is no light from the planet which signifies feminine energy – are more powerful, but more physically draining, than any others. This is because, by tradition, most of the rituals are cleansing ones – sweeping away the old and bringing in the new. They are based on the idea that it is at the time of the Dark Moon that we are most closely in touch with the ancient wisdom and with a kind of archetypal destructiveness which gives us opportunities for new beginnings.

Just as everything must eventually die so there are new beginnings, the sloughing off of the old must be endured first. Always it is we who must seek the deities of the Dark Moon who dwell in the void since, in the act of seeking, we signify our willingness to change. For this reason, so that no energy is squandered, you need to have definite ideas of what you want when working with aspects of the Dark Moon – it is not a journey to be undertaken lightly and is always a learning experience. It means being prepared to face some of the deepest spiritual mysteries and to understand the laws of spiritual balance.

Charge of the Dark Goddess

Working with the Dark Moon brings out the creative streak in us all and below is an example of what has become known as the 'Charge of the Dark Goddess'. The source is unknown, but it is particularly beautiful in its acknowledgement of the power of the feminine above and beyond the destructiveness that is normally so frightening.

I am the Darkness behind and beneath the shadows. I am the absence of air that awaits at the bottom of every breath. I am the ending before life begins again, the decay that fertilizes the living. I am the bottomless pit, the never-ending struggle to reclaim that which that which is denied. I am the key that unlocks every door. I am the glory of discovery, for I am that which is hidden, secluded and forbidden. Come to me at the Dark Moon and see that which cannot be seen, face the terror that is yours alone. Swim to Me through the blackest oceans to the centre of your greatest fears – the Dark God and I will keep you safe. Scream to us in terror, and yours will be the power to forbear. Think of me when you feel pleasure, and I will intensify it, until the time when I may have the greatest pleasure of meeting you at the Crossroads between the worlds.

When you have internalized the ideas within this, try writing your own version.

Dark Moon Ritual-Meditation

This ritual-meditation of cleansing and renewing should be done when the moon is completely invisible. For the maximum results it is best to repeat it for three nights. Begin on the actual night of the Dark Moon i.e. after the Full Moon and before the first quarter. You can double check when this is by referring to newspaper columns, diaries or an astrological ephemeris.

On the appropriate day for this ritual, eat lightly – preferably avoiding meat – to give your system a rest. Take a cleansing bath or shower using an oil which suits your purpose. Being conscious that you are washing away the old stagnant energy, you may wish to keep the water running to ensure a flow through of energy.

Do not speak to anyone between the time you take the bath and the time you begin the ritual, since this may disturb your concentration. Take notice of your emotions as you go into the ritual.

YOU WILL NEED

Chair, cushion or mat so that you can sit comfortably

Black or dark coloured candle

Patchouli incense

Black or dark coloured hooded robe, or a large towel or scarf to drape over your head.

If you meditate to music, choose instrumental music that is slow and heavy, yet pleasant to listen to. Drumming can also help you to reach the deeper realms.

METHOD

Light the incense (which represents air) and carry it counter-clockwise around the room visualizing yourself as a point of light.

See yourself spiralling downwards towards the beginning of life, unwinding your life and you experiences as you go.

Recognize that you will be reborn and reformed and can make a fresh start.

Place the incense within your sacred space, on your altar if you use one.

Light the dark candle and walk with it round the room in a counter-clockwise direction.

Replace the candle on the altar.

From now on you will be working only by candlelight.

3. PROCEDURES AND PROTOCOL OF RITUAL

Pull the scarf, towel or hood of the robe over your head.
Sit before your altar or in your sacred space so the room is obscured from view.
Start the music if you are using it.

Close your eyes, and sink deep into yourself – into your inner space.
Relax your body and sense yourself going deeper and deeper.
Don't push too hard, just let things happen – but don't fall asleep.

You should soon become aware of the entrance to a cave in front of you.
This is the door to your unconscious and the beginning of your introduction to the mysteries of the Dark Moon.
Move forward with confidence towards the dim light you will see in front of you.

Soon, you will find yourself at the entrance to yet another vast cavern.
In the centre of the cavern is a huge cauldron, surrounded by candles.
Behind the cauldron stands or sits a figure in a black robe.
Wait until this figure gives you permission to move forward.
Approach him or her with respect and dignity. (You may find that you wish to kneel in submission, such is the power you feel from this entity.)

Communicate the changes you feel are necessary but don't ask for specific ways of making those changes.
You will become aware of the responses given to your request – trust that the universe is ready to accept the Dark Moon's way of working.
Listen carefully to what is said to you.

Being asked to step into the cauldron is a major spiritual experience so be ready for whatever may occur; the cauldron experience differs from person to person – you may feel as if you are undergoing some form of initiation, see visions of the future or become extremely conscious of every part of your physical body.

Previous events in your life may re-emerge so that you can understand why you acted the way you did and to show you how to avoid the same thing in the future. Some experiences will bring up a great deal of emotion but be very cleansing. Re-experiencing a loss is immediately followed for instance by contact with the loved one to show you that nothing is ever totally destroyed.

Note: Should you decide to enter the cauldron, the Dark Moon deity will most likely indicate in some way that you are protected and assisted in your task.

When in your visualization you stand once more in the cavern, you may be shown symbols or objects by the Dark Moon deity which have personal meaning for you. Sometimes these symbols are clarified for you at a later date. It is as though you need time to 'decode' the information. Just remember what you have experienced.

The Dark Moon deity will acknowledge you and more than probably you will feel yourself spiralling upwards through the darkness back to physical awareness. You may be disorientated for a while and find that your breathing has deepened considerably, almost as though you are breathing from your abdomen.

Lower your hood and look round the room.
As you do so, you may well see or feel the presence of other-worldly beings.

Become conscious of your physical body and rub your hands together or touch your knees to reorientate yourself properly. This is because, for a short time, you have been working in what is called the astral body and need to become aware of the grosser vibration of the physical realm. This is called grounding.

Think about your experiences and thank the Dark Moon deity for their help.

During the next little while, it is best if you play close attention to your dreams – certainly until the next Full Moon. Because you have gone very deeply into the unconscious realms, you will have activated a number of what are called 'archetypal images'.

These are concepts which we all have, but which present themselves in different ways according to our experiences. When these images emerge through the sort of contact you have just made with the Dark Moon deity, it is a good idea to spend some time learning a little more about your relationship with them. You might take the symbols and dream images as a basis for a fresh meditation.

Simple Dark Moon Ritual

If you feel that the above ritual is a little too complex and theatrical for your taste, there is a very simple technique which can be used to achieve almost as good a result. This is a ritual for the dark of the moon which, through its invocation, draws both on all that 'is' and also on eternal wisdom.

YOU WILL NEED
Black robe with a hood
Bowl of water to act as a dark mirror
(To give a good reflective surface either the bowl should be black or alternatively add black ink to the water)

METHOD
Dress in the robe and cover your head with the hood.
Look deep into the bowl and say:

Deepest of the eternal dark, of fertility and final harvest,
This is the depth of powers beyond the reasoning of man.
Here, the well from which illumination pours forth.
This, the place, the pivotal growing place of knowledge around which we satellites revolve and glimmer meekly in silent reverence.

In this blackness we salute the dark of existence,
and grow from the strength that centres in that dark.
It shows us from its own completeness, our first journey.
O darkness, complete us in our secret selves.

In the nightly realms we bless the measuring of Father and Mother
That shows us the way through the darkness to the shining of the light,
And calls to us the revelation we crave.

In black, as in white, all salutations and blessings!

Now sit quietly and allow the images to come to mind.
When these images fade, ground yourself.
Pour the water on the earth as a blessing.

The phases of the moon can be used for many rituals and spells other than those necessary for working on oneself. Below are a few suggested ways of doing so. We also give information on perhaps one of the oldest New Moon rituals, that of the Jewish Sanctifying of the Moon.

Money Ritual

This is a ritual to help you come to terms with money and your attitude to it and should be performed around the time of the Full Moon. Most of us at some time or another have financial problems. We may not have enough, we may not manage it very well, there may be demands on us that we can't or don't feel we can meet.

There are two versions of this spell and you should choose the one you are most comfortable with. If you are really hard up you will find it simpler to use play money, however if you are very brave you may choose real money. Choose the largest denomination of money – either pretend or otherwise – that you are comfortable with.

YOU WILL NEED
Green taper candle

Mint or honeysuckle oil

Play money of various denominations or a single note of the largest denomination of real money you can afford.

METHOD
Two days before the Full Moon, take the green candle to your sacred space.

Carve several pound signs on the candle, thinking of a more prosperous life as you do so.

Anoint the candle with the essential oil.

Place it in the holder and set it in the middle of your sacred space.

Light the candle.

If using play money:
Spread out your 'money' in front of the burning candle.

Handle it, sort it, play with it.

Spend at least 5 to 10 minutes thinking about your attitude to money, how you would use it if it were real.

Then extinguish the candle.

The next night, light the candle again.
Play with the money again, thinking about how you might make it grow.
After 10 to 15 minutes, extinguish the candle.

The third night, the night of the Full Moon, do the same again; think about how you would help others.
Before the candle burns out completely burn a large denomination note of your play money after you have finished sorting it.
This is your offering to the Gods but it also represents your acknowledgement that money is simply an energy to be used.

If using real money:
The ritual is the same except that during your meditation on the first day you should think about how you wish to spend the money you are going to accrue.

During the second ritual visualize it growing and becoming more. See yourself going to the bank to put money into your account or some such action.

On the third night you have a choice.
You can either burn the money, place it somewhere safe, perhaps on your altar as a reminder of your good fortune or give it to charity. It is important that you do not use it for your own purposes.

Sometimes we become conscious that negative energy or power is present in our life but it is difficult to decide exactly where from.

This next ritual is best performed during the Dark Moon, the period between the Full and New Moon.

Reflection of Evil

The goddess Erishkegal was a deity of Mesopotamia, Babylonia and Assyria. She was called Queen of the Underworld and ruled over the seven hells (states of illusion). In her most well known aspect she is destructive and vengeful yet – as with many of the Crone aspects of the goddess – she is often a necessary part of the lessons we need to learn. Her sister Ishtar (Inanna), had to overcome Erishkegal's jealousy and terrible power in order to come to terms with her own task. Erishkegal ruled over dark magic, revenge, retribution, the waning and Dark Moon, death, destruction and regeneration.

YOU WILL NEED

Banishing incense

Two black or dark coloured candles

Mirror

Magic wand

Tarot cards or other divination method

Moon symbol (perhaps a circle of dark paper)

Herbs in a bowl (a mixture of blessed thistle, rosemary and bay laurel)

Incense burner

METHOD

Light the very black or dark purple candles.

If you use incense charcoal, the herbs can be slowly dropped on the lighted charcoal at the appropriate time in the ritual.

Burn the banishing incense first of all, in order to clear a space for your working.

Cast your circle or dedicate your sacred space as usual.

Call upon the four winds or Elements to guard the circle

When finished, stand facing the East.

Raise your arms in greeting and say:

3. PROCEDURES AND PROTOCOL OF RITUAL

Between the worlds I consecrate this space
Beyond time, this rite leads to the ancient way,
Come now, you gods of greatest strength
Deepest, Darkest, most omnipotent
I greet you.

Take your wand into your power hand (the one you project power with most easily)
Holding your arms outstretched, say:

The cycle of the Moon reaches her darkest place
Yet the wisdom of the Dark Mother is here within.
Only the uninitiated would use that power for wrong
At this darkest time is also power for good.

Tap the altar three times with the wand and say:

Hear me, Wise One
As I call upon you now.
Show me the paths that I must tread
Thus may we clear this sense of dread.

Mix the herbs lightly so that the perfume is released, then hold the bowl up over the
altar, and say:

I offer these herbs to cleanse and purify,
Accept them as both offering and token.

Regularly add small amounts of herbs to the burner. Often the amount of smoke
produced will show you from which direction the negativity is coming. Continue to
add small amounts of herbs throughout the rest of the ritual.

Take the Moon symbol in your power hand and the mirror in the other, the reflective
side away from you. With the mirror you will send the negativity back to source that it
has come from. It is wisest if you think of it going back to the source of evil rather than
rebounding on the perpetrator of your difficulty.

Go to the East, hold up the mirror and symbol then say:

I command you, all evil and unbalanced powers that come from the East,
Return from whence you came.

Go to the South and say:

I command you, all evil and unbalanced powers that come from the South,
Return from whence you came.

Go to the West and say:

I command you, all evil and unbalanced powers that come from the West,
Return from whence you came.

Go to the North and say:

I command you, all evil and unbalanced powers that come from the North,
Return from whence you came.

Stand in the centre of your sacred space and put the mirror down.
Raise the Moon symbol skyward, saying:

By the symbol of the Moon Goddess, I ask for protection
From all negative influences.
Lady of the Moon, I ask for new ideas and beginnings
And the wisdom and guidance to act upon them.
I believe that strengthened by your perception and skills
I shall be free.

Ask for guidance from the Dark Moon Goddess.
State as clearly as you can what is going wrong in your life and what changes you
would like to see happening.
Take up the wand, draw a circle in the air clockwise and say:

Goddess of dark and unlit places
I acknowledge you.
Within your secret realms
You change your form.
So seven times within each little hell
I beg for change
As complete as is this circle.

Sit quietly to receive inspiration and insight.

Follow this with divination with tarot or your chosen method to give you a clearer insight. You might do a ritual for binding or removing of problems. If you do carry out any other magical working, before you begin do not forget to thank Erishkegal for her presence.

When everything is completed, hold your wand over the altar and say:

Spirits of fire, earth, air and sea.
Circle of power now work for me.

Sense the energy of the circle being used to bind the negativity.
Close the circle in your normal fashion.

Feast of Divine Life

All agrarian societies celebrate harvest time – the time of abundance. The Egyptian Feast of Divine Life celebrated the moon and the belief that it provided the Waters of Life. Nowadays we recognize the cycle of life, the wheel of the cosmos, as it turns. We can still honour the triple goddess in all her forms – maid, mother and crone – as was done of old. At the time of the harvest she is honoured more as the fertile mother.

YOU WILL NEED

Green candle

Yellow candle

Cauldron

Wand

Three symbols of a fruitful harvest (e.g. bread, apples)

METHOD

Prepare your sacred space as usual, including your altar and say:

The harvest is now done.

A peaceful winter is before us.

Dark and light strike a balance.

Thanks be to the Triple Goddess.

Light the coloured candles.

Carrying the candles, move clockwise around the ritual area, commencing and completing in the East.

At each cardinal point, pause and say:

Triple Goddess, bless the year's harvest that I bring.

Place the candles safely and alight on the altar.

Tap the cauldron three times with your wand and place the symbols in the cauldron, then say:

Life brings death, brings life.
The wheel of the cosmos turns never-ending.
The negative is replaced by the positive.
I honour the Triple Goddess,
Harvesting my thoughts
I honour the Triple Goddess.

Meditate for as long as you wish then close the circle.

Dispose of the gifts to the Goddess by sharing them, not forgetting to leave some outside for the nature and wood spirits.

To Generate Opportunities

The Roman goddess Ops, a deity of prosperity, crops and fertility, used to be petitioned by sitting down and touching the earth with one hand. She was honoured during the Saturnalia festival in the month of December, when people exchanged gifts often in the form of wish dolls representing health and happiness. This, of course, is a form of sympathetic magic and is probably the precursor of Christmas gifts.

YOU WILL NEED

A bowl of sand (to represent the Earth)

Green cloth

Cinnamon/cedar incense

Dried chamomile, vervain or squill

Mint oil

Honeysuckle oil

METHOD

During the Full Moon, make a poppet (see page 165) out of the cloth while burning the incense.

While concentrating on the opportunities available to you, write your name on the cloth. Stuff it with the dried herbs to which you have added a few drops of the oils. Sew the figure shut.

Hold the poppet in the incense smoke and say:

Goddess of opportunity,
Bring good fortune now to me.
Guide me by your gentle hand,
For I am worthy as these grains of sand.

Let the sand trickle through your fingers to signify touching the earth.

Repeat this an odd number of times (seven works well).

Keep your poppet safe; you do not have to have it with you at all times, just with your possessions.

If the spell works for you then renew it every Full Moon, as necessary.

THE CEREMONIES OF THE JEWS

There is a ceremony or ritual which belongs to the Jewish heritage and which honours the New Moon in a very specific way. It is said that the Moon was unhappy with her apparently secondary position in relation to the sun, and that God placated her with her own special ceremony. While the ritual is addressed to the Moon, it also honours the renewal of the cycle of femininity and therefore it is an appropriate one with which to acknowledge the power of the matriarch. We give it here in the form of the old words since they are so meaningful.

Sanctifying of the Moon

After the third day of the New Moon every Jew should, either alone or along with their whole congregation, salute the Moon with a prayer. They should go together to a place where they can see the moon best and from there look up at the Moon.

The words to be repeated are:

Blessed art thou. O Lord our God, King of the World,
Who with his Words created the heavens and with the breath of his Mouth the
heavenly Hosts: A Statute and a Time he gave unto them, that they should not vary
from their Orders,
They were glad and they rejoiced to obey the Will of their Maker,
The Maker is true and his Works are true:

And unto the Moon, he said that she shall monthly renew her crown and her Beauty
toward the Fruit of the Womb
For they hereafter shall be renewed unto her,
To beautify unto their Creator for the Glory of his Name and of his Kingdom
Blessed art thou, O Lord, the Renewer of the Months.

Then say three times:

Blessed is thy Former, blessed is thy Maker, blessed is thy Purchaser,
blessed is thy Creator.

Next, rise up onto the toes and say three times:

As well I jump towards thee and cannot reach to touch thee, so shall none of mine
enemies be able to touch me for harm.

Then say three times:

Fear and Dread shall fall upon them,
By the Greatness of thine arm they shall be as still as a stone.
As a stone they shall be still by thy Arm's Greatness;
Dread and fear on them shall fall.

Then following words should then be said three times to each other:

Peace unto ye, unto ye peace, David, King of Israel liveth and subsisteth.

This acknowledgement of the validity of the moon was obviously an important part of ancient Jewish thought. Equally important was the way in which God was to be honoured for he could not be named outright.

In ancient writings, a description is given of the altar on which offerings of incense were to be made. The altar was made of Shittim (acacia) wood and covered with fine gold. It stood four square and had a crown of gold representing the symbol of 'endless glory, triumph, victory and all regal dignity'. There were horns on the four corners which were overlaid with pure gold. The power and honour of God was thus diffused far and wide over the face of the Earth – East to West and North to South.

It is here that we see the true meaning of incense, for it was considered to be a fit offering to God and was so highly regarded that it was to be handled only by the High Priest, who was also the one who had prepared it. It was considered that the smoke of the incense ascending and dispersing into the air represented the offerings of the prayers of the faithful as they procured blessings for the whole church. The prayers of the saints were thus carried on the incense and sweet odour.

The *qetoret*, the most holy of incense, is believed to have contained eleven spices. There were seventy parts each of balsam, onycha, galbanum and frankincense; sixteen parts each of myrrh, cassia, spikenard and saffron; twelve parts of costus, three parts of aromatic bark and nine of cinnamon. Other strictly controlled preservative substances were also added.

Looked at from today's perspective, it is interesting to see galbanum included since this is the one ingredient which has an extremely unpleasant smell. It is now thought to have been included to represent the evil that there is within the world. This particular incense (the incense of Aaron) was never to be used for mundane purposes; indeed if it was offered without due ceremony and respect or adulterated in any way, the perpetrator would suffer greatly – he may even have been put to death.

There were mundane daily incense rituals but the most important one wherein the High Priest entered the Holy of Holies (the inner sanctum) and penetrated the veil is described thus:

Afterwards they brought him a Golden Censer into which he put fire which he took from the outward altar. Then a Golden Shovel and a vessel of incense beaten very small.

Out of this he took two handfuls of incense and put it in the shovel. Censer in right hand shovel in left, he went to the Holy of Holies attended by two priests. As soon as he came to the veil, the two priests lifted it up and he entered the Holy of Holies and set the censer between the two Staves of the Ark.

When this was lost in the first Destruction he set it upon stone of 3 finger height. He then took the shovel and emptied all the incense into his clenched hands and poured it into the censer.

When the Inner sanctum was filled with the smoke he then went out backwards in a direct line between the ark and the gate.

GODS AND GODDESSES

Inherent in this ceremony and the Sanctifying of the Moon ritual above is the idea of there being both a masculine and a feminine principle. It is this duality which is acknowledged when we see Gods and Goddesses being worshipped. In order to understand unity, as with Manichaeism and Zoroastrianism, it is necessary to understand duality and polarity – two forces working in harmony.

It was believed there was a sympathetic connection between human and Divine conduct and the behaviour of the natural forces. The assumption came to be that the greatest of all sins was any form of illicit sexual intercourse because, by the law of sympathy, such transgressions caused similar irregular interactions between the male and the female elements of nature: droughts, floods or other natural calamities.

Known to rule over all carnal knowledge and often incorrectly seen and equated with Satan, we all have a need before enacting the sacred union to understand the Horned God, or Pan as he was known to the Greeks, without fear.

Communication with the Horned God

Known as Cernunnos by the Celts, he was called the God of Nature, God of the Underworld and the Astral Plane, Great Father and the Horned One. His symbols are a bull, ram, horned serpent and a stag. He is particularly connected with all things masculine and is obviously a Nature God of all growing things and thus of regeneration.

In this ritual, you will travel to meet the Horned God and gain knowledge from him.

YOU WILL NEED
Statues or pictures of wild animals

An animal mask

A drum

Blanket

Cernunnos incense (see below)

METHOD
First of all light the incense and spread the blanket on the floor and sit on it (if need be you can sit on a chair).

Lay the statues or pictures out on the floor.

Put on the mask and beat out a relaxing rhythm on the drum which is placed directly in front of you.

Completely relax and try to envisage allowing yourself to enter the realm of the Horned God.

With your eyes open, concentrate on each picture or statue you have before you. Think about that animal and, without being apprehensive, let the image become real in your mind.

Now be 'at one' with the mask and feel the energy of the animal it represents. This is akin to the totem animals seen in Native American shamanism.

The animal (for it is now a being) may wish to communicate. If it does, let it speak to you, note what is said and how it is communicated.

When you have identified with each animal, close your eyes and call upon the Horned God. You might say something like

Cernunnos, I call upon you now.

You may well find yourself on a natural path of some sort in your imagination, maybe next to a river or in a forest. Follow the path until you come to a grassy clearing.

Waiting for you, sitting by the biggest tree, should be the Horned God. If he is not there do not be disappointed – you should carefully allow yourself to return to the everyday world and start the ritual again, perhaps on another day.

If he is waiting for you, sit beside the Horned God and request the correct conduct for the problem you have.

When he has imparted his knowledge, he taps your forehead; you will find yourself returning to the present.

Keep your eyes shut and in your head slowly beat or count out a rhythm.

When you are comfortable, pick up the drum and begin beating the same rhythm. Slowly open your eyes and re-orientate yourself.

Cernunnos Incense

1 part Oak
½ part Sandalwood
½ part Allspice
½ part Coriander
Few drops of Cedar Oil

This need for correctness of conduct is epitomized in the concept of the Wheel of the Year as the God and Goddess come together in innocence and later part in the cycle of birth, death and regeneration. The natural order was believed to have depended not solely on the regular and precise performance of rituals, but also on the conduct of the people, particularly of its leaders, outside the sacred precincts. This meant that certain freedoms and restrictions were imposed at the times of the Sabbats (festivals). The Celtic year started with Samhain to encompass the period of rest before the God and Goddess became active. We still honour this concept today in the modern-day rituals performed at the times of the Sabbats. We give some examples of the rituals below.

Samhain – 31 October

Samhain is the third and final Harvest. The dark winter half of the year commences on this Sabbat. Now traditionally the door between the physical realm and that of spirit is open. At this time, the Dark Mother and the Dark Father – the Crone and her aged Consort – are paid due respect.

Food offerings are left on altars and doorsteps for the wandering spirits and a candle is often placed in the window to help the spirits and ancestors to come home. The coming darkness signifies a time of chaos and mayhem when often nothing is what it seems. For this reason, any ritual should always be performed within a consecrated and circle for your own protection.

YOU WILL NEED

Black candle to represent the dying God or a yellow one inscribed with the symbol of the sun

Grains, fruits and dried flowers as offerings to the Goddess

Runes, tarot cards and other divination tools

Corn or other suitable bread for the spirits of the dead

Samhain incense as shown below

METHOD

Cast your circle and build up your cone of protection.

Invoke the God and Goddess by saying:

I ask for your blessing Dark Mother and Father of Darkness,
As the veil between two worlds thins,
I greet my ancestors and loved ones who have gone before me.
May only those who wish me well enter within this circle.
We greet all those gone before us and who are free of Earth's ties.

Spend a few moments thinking of your loved ones,
then say:

We thank you for your presence here tonight.

Next, light the God candle and say:

Tonight, as all you dead souls walk amongst the living,
As we pass through into the shadow of darkness, we do so gratefully.
We know it is the wheel of the year turning.
We thank the Gods and Goddess for the glittering prizes of the summertime.
Tonight, the Lord of the Hunt, the Lord of the Sun, quietly moves from us.
It is the wheel-a-turning and it will turn again till the sun rises from the moon.
Here, this candle symbolizes the Lord of the Sun – its quenching, his passing.

Blow out the God candle, do not light it again until Yule.

You must now acknowledge the Crone aspect of the Goddess by saying:

The decreasing moon and stars are the gifts you gave.
Oh Goddess of wisdom and magic speak to us of your wisdom and power.
Understand it will be used wisely.
Pass on your energy and force so that our spells rituals and divinations will be enthused.
Understand again, oh Goddess, they shall bring no harm to your creatures.

Now dismiss the spirits of the ancestors by saying:

Aid us as we look beyond the long dark days of winter.
Go in peace.

Afterwards, use your divination tools to gain a perspective on the coming months, hold a simple feast, close the sacred circle then bury the offerings in the earth. Also, leave a plate of food for the spirits still at large.

Samhain Incense

1 part Dittany
½ part Pine
1 part Sandalwood
¼ part Patchouli
¼ part Benzoin Resin
Few drops of Pine Oil

Yule – 23 December

Yule is a celebration of rebirth and the renewing of the old. It is the start of longer, lighter days as the Lord of the Sun arises from his sojourn with the Goddess. Here, light becomes important as we use sympathetic magic to ensure the return of the sun. The Ancient Egyptians also watched and waited for the star Sirius to announce yet another birth, that of Horus as the son of Osiris from the womb of Isis at this time.

The Yule log symbolizes the idea of the continuation of light and this ritual honours that tradition. Before performing this ritual, you might want to decorate your home with evergreens, although mistletoe, which is sacred to both Druids and the Scandinavians, is still banned from Christian churches as being unholy. For the purposes of this ritual, consider that the Yule log is your altar.

Wish Branch

This next ritual is designed to be for a group, so there is some preparation necessary beforehand in order to get the full effect from it. You will need a wish branch to indicate your desires and wishes for the coming year. You should prepare this before you attend the group ritual. If you want to, you can spray the branch with silver or gold paint, but do not forget to ask permission of the nature spirits before you do so.

YOU WILL NEED

Branch of your chosen sacred wood

Ribbons and cords in various colours for decoration

Small representations such as cake or Christmas tree decorations or children's toys
of your most important aims and desires

(You might use one item for each month: be as creative as you like.)

Small wrapped sweets tied with coloured thread

Yule incense as shown below

METHOD

Light the incense.

Meditate on the coming year and what you would most like to see happen.

You might also include your wishes for your family and friends, or for your larger world.

When you have decided on your intentions, choose decorations or toys appropriate to your wishes.

Decorate the branch according to your own creativity.

(This is an intensely personal object and will be used later in the ritual).

Take the branch to your group ritual.

Preparation of Yule Log

So often nowadays there is nowhere to burn the Yule log properly but it is quite in order to substitute this method. This prepared log can then be used year after year and, of course, and becomes increasingly powerful the more it is used. The log can be of any of the sacred woods. The first time it is prepared, it should be done by the leaders of the group and strictly should be consecrated afresh each year with a simple prayer to the God and Goddess.

YOU WILL NEED

Red and green candles

(One candle for each member of the group, plus an extra green one for the leader)

Suitable log large enough to accommodate the candles

METHOD

In the log bore a hole large enough to hold each candle, plus 2 extra.

Line each hole with silver foil or a metal cake cup for safety so that the Yule log does not catch fire.

(Alternatively, you could wrap the end of the candle in silver foil.)

As you do so, ask for a blessing from the God and Goddess for the work you do.

Yule Celebration

YOU WILL NEED

Prepared Yule log

2 white candles

Black candle from Samhain (to represent the God)

Prepared red and green candles

Group's wish branches

A wreath (The wreath is symbolic of the Wheel of the Year and of the Goddess)

Yule incense (see below)

METHOD

Cast your circle and light the incense.

Place the Yule log in a prominent position.

Light the white candles at either end of the Yule log.

Place the God candle in front of the log and say:

Here this candle symbolizes the Sun God,
Its final flicker, His passing and here its flame once again lights His return.

Light the God candle from one of the altar candles.

The leader should then light their green candle and say:

Blessed be the maiden Goddess.
May this world be forever young in her presence.

From that candle a second candle is then lit. The words now used are:

Blessed be the mother Goddess, fresh and rosy with babe.
And so shall all that springs from her be strong, adventurous and bountiful.

Then light a third candle from the second and say:

Blessed be the deep-rooted Goddess,
Wise, powerful and temperate,
The keeper of wisdom and the ever-turning wheel.

Each member then steps up, lights their candle from the last and places it securely in the Yule log.

Finally the leader lights a last candle to complete the ritual and while facing towards the East says:

Tonight, the Lord of the Sun is born again.
The Goddess and the God are together in harmony.
The sun reaffirms as the wheel is a turning once again,
We praise the Goddess and the newly born God, our Father and Mother.

Now, if liked, each participant may talk about their wishes for the next year whilst placing their wish branches around the Yule log, or the wish branches may be placed in a large vase nearby.

Yule Incense

1 part Clove
1 part Juniper
1 part Cinnamon
½ part dried Orange Peel

Imbolc – 2 February

Imbolc, the festival of the Maiden, marks the centre point of the dark half of the year. It is the time of blessing of the seeds and consecration of agricultural tools, and the time when the ewes are brought down for lambing. As the world prepares for growth and renewal all maiden Goddesses, but particularly Brighid (also Bridget and Brigit) are honoured; the Crone of winter transmutes into the young Maiden of spring. Since Brighid is the guardian of the sacred flame as well as the Goddess of poetry, candles are lit.

On Imbolc in Ireland they make Brighid's Cross. Also known as Bride's cross, it is sometimes three-legged, a triskele, signifying the fact that she is in fact a Triple Goddess. Often it is an equal armed cross woven from reeds according to ancient patterns. This ritual is designed for group working.

YOU WILL NEED

Two white candles for the altar

White candle and holder for each person present

Reed cross

Corn dolly, if wished

White linen cloth to represent Brighid's mantle

Incense as shown below

Creative writings such as poetry or songs

Sheep's milk or fruit juice

Plain biscuits or shortbread

METHOD

Light the altar candles and the incense.

Invoke Brighid using words such as:

Lady of Light,

Maiden and Goddess,

Bless us with your presence here tonight

Wrap the corn dolly in the white cloth and say:

As you offered your mantle for sanctuary for the babe,
So we signify this tonight.
As bride we honour you also.

Place the dolly on your altar.

Now each person should take a candle and, in a clockwise direction starting with the leader, light them and place them safely at your feet so the lights form a circle. Share the creative writings with the group.

Afterwards, spend a few moments thinking of Brighid's power and say as a group:

As this flame burns,
So let it signify the eternal flame sacred to Brighid.

The leader should lift up the reed cross and say:

Protect us now as the light brightens.
We honour your symbol.

The cross may be placed either on the altar or at the front door of the meeting place. Afterwards, share the sheep's milk or juice and biscuits to reaffirm community. Your personal candles should be extinguished and may be taken home and relit in the main window of your home.

Imbolc Incense

3 parts Frankincense Resin
2 parts Dragon's Blood Powder or Resin
½ part Red Sandalwood
1 part Cinnamon

Ostara – 21 March

This ritual acknowledges spring's beginning, and celebrates the Goddess in her maiden form. Ostara or Oestra is the goddess of springtime. It is a time for fertility rites and the pruning of spring blossom. The ritual celebrates the glory of the coming of springtime and the banishing of darkness. It is the time when life quickens within the Goddess and she manifests her beauty in the pastel colours of springtime. The God reveres the process of constant renewal. Decorated eggs have been used to celebrate this time since the time of the Ancients. A group ritual can make use of the old customs.

YOU WILL NEED
Fresh flowers
Green and yellow candles
Cauldron
Hard-boiled eggs (one for each member of the group)
Ostara incense (see below)

METHOD
Light the candles and incense and cast your circle.
Fill the cauldron with the eggs (any remaining eggs should be placed in the circle).

Note: The filled cauldron here represents the womb of the Goddess.

If the cauldron is small enough, raise it in both hands or, if not, place both hands on it and say:

Hallowed be the Great Goddess, our Mother and our provider.
The bleak winter storms subside leaving life to flourish outward.
It peeps out quietly, refreshed by the God and Goddess's power.
We feel you. We thank you for all your gifts.

Now concentrate on the flowers and say:

May we carry within us a total understanding of all living creatures, both great and small.
Mother Goddess, Father God, show us how to worship the earth and all it holds.

Now is the time to decorate your eggs and perhaps hold a simple feast.

Ostara Incense

1 part Jasmine

1 part Rose

1 part Violet

Beltane – 1 May

Beltane (meaning 'Fire of Bel') was a Celtic Sun God whose coronation feast is celebrated on 1 May. Beltane has long been celebrated with feasts and rituals – as summer began, the weather became warmer and young people would spend the entire night in the woods. It was a time when married couples were given permission to be unrestricted in their behaviour without censure and when marriages of a year and a day could be undertaken.

The Maypole was a symbol of the sexuality that abounded at the time. The weaving of the ribbons symbolized the sacred marriage of the God and Goddess. For this reason any ritual performed at the beginning of May takes on the symbolism of a marriage feast. This is the time for youth and vitality.

This fertility ritual celebrates the union of the God and the Goddess. By now the Goddess is moving into her Mother aspect and her life energies are becoming more abundant. For this ritual each participant will need to bring a white flower, preferably with five petals to represent the elements plus Spirit. The cauldron represents the fertile mother.

YOU WILL NEED

White ribbon

Red ribbon

(about 1 metre of each per participant)

Flowers as mentioned above

Cauldron filled with flowers

Beltane incense (see below)

METHOD

Light the incense.

Wearing a flower garland if you wish, face East.

Hold the ribbons with the end of the white ribbon covering the end of the red one (this represents the goddess being supported by the vitality of the god) and begin to plait them together and say:

Father and Mother Goddess, it is the time of your union.
Through your happy joining, so shall happiness spread
Through your abundance, so shall nature be abundant.

As you finish your plait, lay it in front of you.

While each individual is waiting, contemplate your flower, rededicating yourself through its perfection at this time to the service of the God and Goddess.

When everyone has finished, the leader or high priestess should gather the plaits together and bind them into one simple maypole symbol.

As this is done everyone should say:

Praise to you ancient God and Goddess.
You are our creators and from your union shall all beings rise and awaken.
Sacred art thou.

The flower petals can be strewn on the ground to signify abandonment.

Afterwards, the ribbon symbol might be hung in the sacred space or placed on the ground. Follow up the ritual with some sort of spring blessing or activity – a simple feast of breads, cereals and dairy foods perhaps.

Beltane Incense

1 part Rose
½ part Frankincense Resin
½ part Musk Root

Litha – 21 June (Summer Solstice)

Midsummer Night's Eve is of importance for many people because of the folk customs still associated with it. This is the longest day of the year – a day on which both light and life are plentiful.

This day is also known as Alban Heruin by the Druid. Known at this time as the Green Man with a face surrounded by foliage or the Lord of the Forests, the Sun God is at his strongest on this day. His day was celebrated by the burning of Sun Wheels, which were very large, to ensure fertility and prosperity in the coming year.

This ritual is also a celebration for the Goddess. She is now with child and nature reflects this with abundant growth. Now is a fine time for magical and purifying rites. In this ritual we commemorate those Sun Wheels and purification by fire.

Prior to attendance at this ritual, each individual should make a Sun Wheel in a similar way to the charm ball (see page 256). You can if you wish, use the charm ball you have already made.

Note: Make sure that if you are doing this ritual indoors, you have water on hand to douse any exuberant flames.

YOU WILL NEED
Red candle (to represent the Sun God)
Green candle (to represent the Goddess)
Sun Wheel for each individual
Cauldron or safe place in which to burn the wheels
Water
Midsummer incense (as below)

METHOD
Cast your circle.
Face South and say:

On this day the Sun is high, the light is bright and the Earth is warm.
As the Sun God blazes above, may the flames of our ritual blaze below.

Light the Goddess candle on the left of your sacred space and say:

Mother of Nature, Lady of the firmament,
Bless thy fruitful womb,
Which I honour.

Light the Sun God candle on the right of your sacred space and say:

God of fertility and fruitfulness,
Blessed Lord of the blazing sun,
Seed and nurturer of life,
May you be blessed.

Hold a Sun Wheel above your head and say:

May the Lord of the Sun burn away all that troubles, pains and distresses us.

The leader should light the Sun Wheel and when it is burning properly, drop it into the cauldron or prepared space and say:

By the powers of all that is,
Two who are one,
We banish all negativity from our lives.

Each individual should then consign their own Sun Wheel to the fire repeating the same words.

Note: If the group is a very large one, obviously more than one cauldron or burning space can be used.

When all are burnt, add water to the ashes then each individual may, if they wish, touch their Third Eye with the forefinger of their right hand which has been dipped in the ash and say:

Let my mind, my heart and my hands
Be dedicated to the service of the God and the Goddess.

Midsummer workings usually include those for prosperity, fertility and plentiful harvest. If you are working outdoors, make sure you have safely buried the ashes. Your feast at this time might be of cakes and mead.

Midsummer Incense

2 parts Sandalwood

1 part Mugwort

1 part Camomile

1 part Gardenia petals

Few drops of Rose Oil

Few drops of Lavender Oil

Few drops of Yarrow Oil

Mabon – 21 September

This is the second harvest Sabbat of the pagan year and is known by the Druids as Mea'n Fo'mhair. It is the time of the Crone – the God prepares for death and rebirth at this time of the Autumn equinox when the dark days of the year are looming. It is a time connected with mystery and the balance of light and dark. When working with a group, everyone can follow the actions of the leader in this simple ceremony. It can be performed in the open without an altar if preferred.

YOU WILL NEED

Willow staff to cast your circle

Red candles

A basket of autumn leaves

Fruits, berries, pine cones and oak sprigs

Brown altar cloth

Mabon incense (see below)

METHOD

Dress your altar if using one.

Cast your circle using your stave or enter your sacred space.

Light the candles and incense.

The leader or High Priestess lifts the basket of leaves in both hands and says:

The bitter fevered days move in, watching the trees and the leaves as they fall.
Our Lord of the Sun rides the wild wind horses westerly
As the ghostly night wraps its arms around the world.
Fruits flourish and the seeds fall into waiting earth.
I know this to be a time of equals, where nature's scales come into balance.
Through the deathly veil I know life finds a way.
Life's glory needs death's silence.
The dark winter shadows reveal the wheel a-turning.

Then the basket is passed around the circle and everyone takes a handful of leaves.
Let the leaves fall gently within the circle.
Place the offerings on the altar or in the circle.
Place the basket of leaves within the circle and say:

O cauldron protector, great Goddess of the decreasing moon,
Watcher of secret magic and long gone myths,
Show me the way to greater wisdom.
Show me the way O Goddess!
Show me the way to peace in all things.
I will bear thy knowledge well.

The fruits, berries and pine cones may be left in place as offerings to the Goddess
and nature spirits (if doing the ritual in the open).
Magical pastimes such as the collection of seeds to ensure next year's harvest can
be carried out at this point (do not forget to ask permission as you do so).
Have a simple feast and close the circle.

Mabon Incense

1 part Sandalwood
1 part Cypress
1 part Juniper
1 part Pine
½ part Oakmoss
¼ part Oak

Lughnasadh – 2 August

Lughnasadh is the first of the three harvest Sabbats and is also known as Lammas in Scotland where it is celebrated on 1 August. The word 'Lughnasadh' means 'the funeral games of Lugh'. Lugh was the Irish Sun God and he hosted the games in honour of Tailte, his foster-mother – hence the presence of the corn dolly. This day originally coincided with the first reapings of the harvest, giving the first seeds and fruit for storage in order to ensure future crops. At this time autumn begins; the Sun God is not yet dead, but allegorically loses some of his strength as the nights grow longer and the Sun rises farther towards the South.

For the feast afterwards, it is usual to have cider and bread. The colours for dressing your altar, if you use one, are red and orange.

YOU WILL NEED

Basket of grain heads

Basket of ripe fruit, berries and seeds

A corn dolly placed in a prominent position

Red altar cloth if used

Orange candles

Lugnasadh incense (see below)

METHOD

Cast the protective circle.

Light the incense and candles.

Pass the basket of grain around the group so that everyone has a handful.

Face East and say:

Now let us honour the Goddess in her fullness,

Her nurturing allows us to conserve her fruitfulness as the energy of the God wanes.

We love and honour her as the mother of all nature and share the power of her

beneficence.

Everyone should rub the grain heads together in their hands and allow the grains to fall on the ground.

(This is ritual grain threshing.)

Take a piece of fruit.
Taste it and appreciate its flavour then say:

We are one with the fruits of the harvest. Their energies are our energies.
Hail Goddess of the Moon, Hail worldly Mother, Hail Sun Lord.
Show us the path to goodness and light.
May all your harvests be bountiful.

Finish off the fruit, berries and seeds.
Spend some time meditating on the sense of community brought about in the sharing of the fruit.

Join in with a communal activity such as a walk in a forest or, when in an urban situation, through parks or alongside water.

Lughnasadh Incense

2 parts Frankincense Resin
1 part Heather
1 part Dried Apple Blossoms or peel
1 part Blackberry Leaves

PERSONAL DEVELOPMENT

The more proficient you become in using spells and rituals, the more naturally your development will unfold. We have already talked of the chakras and their meaning and now we move on to the development of the powers and qualities that working with the chakras brings.

THE SIDDHIS

Siddhis are totally natural abilities that can be explained in rational terms. They are simply perceptual states which are available to all human beings, given that the person is minded to develop those powers. They can be defined as a magical or spiritual power, although in fact there is nothing mysterious or magical about them. They are simply tools to be used for the purpose of the control of self, of others and of the forces of nature. They build up in response to the natural development which goes on as one gets to know oneself better.

Many people have difficulty in accepting the concept of siddhis, but before dismissing them out of hand, those who wish to challenge the claim to their existence must recognize that the nature of the siddhis does not fit easily into any accepted psychological category. They might be thought of as a very subtle development of the five senses and yet they are both more, and less, than that. They are more than that in that they give a heightened perception of ordinary everyday reality and less in that the abilities which can develop are sometimes completely misunderstood.

Most people present differing attitudes towards learning about, or spontaneously displaying, siddhis. Some people are born with powers that they exercise without being aware that their psychic gift is particularly unusual. For instance, they 'just know' when something is going to happen or are aware that their world works in a particular way if they take time to think about it. They may be quite used, for instance, to seeing shadowy spirit forms without much effort. In such cases it may come as a somewhat traumatic shock to the individual when they learn that their ability is not common. Children are often much more clued in than adults and are quite disorientated when they realize that they see things differently to others and are considered a 'misfit' by other people who do not possess the psychic ability. This often causes the child to suppress this ability which they can only then reactivate by a course of instruction.

According to occult theory, practising yoga and the use of other eastern disciplines is a rational and desirable way to go about achieving enlightenment. Actively developing the siddhis as an end in itself using these means is not however a good idea and, as we have repeated several times, the siddhis will develop naturally in due course using these disciplines. They then become qualities of your personality rather than tools that you use.

Hallucinogenic drugs such as LSD, mescaline and peyote stimulate the siddhis in an uncontrolled fashion, as indeed can any sort of unexpected trauma such as a blow to the head. The taking of hallucinogenic drugs and stimulants is a very dangerous practice and can lead to great psychological trauma, since it is the more negative side of the 'powers' which tend to be activated in this way. Such difficulties as voices in the head, uncontrollable urges and confusion of two realities can frequently occur, not to mention the additional strain which is put on the physical body.

Psychotic episodes and periods of schizophrenia after the protracted use of such drugs can cause extreme problems; the distortion of normal perceptions (what one expects to see) and those experienced as hallucinations can fall foul of modern psychological explanation. Taking this one stage further, because there is such a fine line between our accepted everyday physical reality and the more spiritual – perhaps magical – realm, the medical world has difficulty in accepting that the development of altered perception is something which can be natural and desirable. It will therefore tend to see any evidence of the development of psychic ability, even when carefully managed, as a sickness and will attempt to 'treat' the problem. It requires a fair degree of discipline – if not courage – to continue on the path of development in the face of such disbelief.

The yogis believe that there are three separate aspects to the development of the powers. They first arise from the 'warrior' aspect which is principally connected with the physical realm in which we live. Five qualities are developed and are as follows:

✦ Knowing the past, present and future.

✦ Being able to be beyond duality and not needing to suffer pleasure/pain, cold/heat, soft/hard. All are equal.

✦ Knowing the way the mind works and being able to work with dreams.

✦ Being able to control the effect of fire, wind, water, poisons, weapons and the sun.

✦ Wins battles and is invincible.

The second aspect only develops in response to concerted efforts to have the heart begin to purify and expand its reach beyond the emotional realm. It can be seen that many of these powers are what might be called magical:

✦ Physical concerns have no effect on the body. The mind does not get confused and emotional conflicts, old age and death have little effect on the body.

✦ The individual is able to know what has been said, no matter how far away the speaker is. This is what is sometimes known as 'far viewing'.

✦ The novice learns to 'see' events and outcomes at all levels of existence. Thus they can assess the overall effect of an action.

✦ The body is capable of travelling at the speed of thought to any place. This is astral projection.

✦ The individual is able to shapeshift and thus to assume any form. There must be good intent behind this.

✦ There is an ability to enter into another's body, whether they are dead or alive. This can be quite dangerous and should only be practised in the company of an adept.

✦ The initiate is able to die when he so desires and death has no meaning.

✦ There is an ability to see the 'sports of gods' and be able to participate in those games. For a warrior race this would have similarities to being able to enter Valhalla and consort with the gods.

✦ The individual develops the ability to attain whatever is desired. (This gift has to be treated with respect since often you can get more than you bargained for.)

✦ Obstacles, physical or otherwise, tend to melt into thin air and life is much easier to manage.

The third group of powers, while seemingly to do with control of the physical, are actually rather more spiritual gifts where the physical has little relevance. They are considered to be the highest siddhi powers:

✦ The reduction of one's form to one atom gives invisibility.
✦ The body weight can be made to be very heavy.
✦ The body can be made light enough to levitate.
✦ Each respective organ is sensed in its entirety.
✦ To perceive other realms and those things not normally visible.
✦ To control the forces of nature and arouse specific energies in others.
✦ To have complete control over the physical senses, thereby arousing the subtle aspects.
✦ To achieve joy and tranquillity simply by willing it to be so. All misery and desires are meaningless. This last quality is the one that is most sought after, most difficult to obtain but is the highest state of bliss.

In the Chakra Development exercise, you learnt how to bring a sphere of coloured light down to each chakra. As a further development of that, you may wish to concentrate on other qualities of the chakras as you hold the sphere of light steady at each point. Below you will find some of the qualities and possible problems associated with each chakra. Since this system is based on the Sanskrit, we have here given the Sanskrit name followed by its English equivalent.

Mooladhara ('Foundation' or Root Chakra) When the awareness point is in the foundation or root chakra, there is frequently great anger or passion and the individual will often be seen with clenched fists and tightened jaw. Violent or angry behaviour is often based on insecurity. Lack of sufficient sleep can be a problem since the individual probably needs up to 12 hours rest. The meditative colour is red.

Positive qualities which can be developed are that the mind is brought under control and doubts become manageable. Whatever one thinks will happen, does and there is freedom from disease. Past lives may be remembered and there is some access to information from universal sources. It is possible to achieve a degree of levitation, though this is often simply for effect.

Swadistana ('Dwelling Place of the Self' or Second Chakra) The desire for physical sensations and the creation of fantasy are obstacles in the development here as is restlessness, anxiety, confusion and delusion. One such delusion may be the Messiah complex, when the individual thinks himself to be a king, a saviour or a destroyer of evil – superhuman in some way – perhaps even alien. Such an individual usually requires 8 to 10 hours sleep. The meditative colour is orange. Charisma, psychic powers and control of the senses all develop when working with this chakra. Creative ability and a deep inner peace are also manifested and a reflective nature leads to freedom from jealousy, greed, lust and anger and to the perfection of relationships. There is often a high self-esteem.

Manipura ('The City of Gems' or Third Chakra) The negative aspect of the third chakra is the desire for personal power and recognition. When the point of awareness is in the third chakra one will often sleep 6 or 8 hours a night often on the back. The meditative colour is yellow.

Here there is an understanding of physiology; disease is overcome and one understands the reason for the use of medicines in the curing of disease. The power to create and destroy is understood, time is conquered and the Fire of Life is radiant. This is the plane of 'dharma' and selfless serving where egotism no longer exists. When healing or spell working, it is possible to enter the body of another though this is not always recommended.

Anahata ('Unstricken' Fourth or Heart Chakra) Obstacles in Anahata are experiences of purgatory, a kind of restless wandering and emotional disturbances. Sleep is from 4 to 6 hours a night, often on the left side. The meditative colour is green.

Several abilities are developed in working with the fourth chakra. First there has to be self-awareness, an appreciation of oneself as a valid human being. There is clairaudience and clairvoyance (clear hearing and seeing) which means that things not normally made visible are understood along with a knowledge of past, present and future. There is the ability to walk in the air and to travel at the speed of thought all over the world (astral travel). Finally there is the experience of seeing God in everything, of recognizing the divine spark, however it manifests. Here the individual is also aware of the Law of Cause and Effect (Karma) as it relates to him or her.

Vishuddhi ('Pure' or Throat Chakra) Obstacles on this level are experienced through the misuse of knowledge and a lack of wisdom. Knowing when to speak and when to remain silent is an art, but while this is developing many mistakes can be made and misunderstandings arise. The individual usually needs about 4 to 6 hours sleep and there is a tendency to move from side to side. The meditative colour is blue.

Calmness and serenity become evident as one gains mastery over the self. The individual becomes less conscious of the outer world and develops an understanding of dreams. The mind by now is well under control and reasoning takes precedence over emotion. On this chakra there is a state of non-judgement and an awareness of Cosmic Consciousness.

Ajnea ('Authority, Unlimited Power' or Brow Chakra) The biggest problem on this chakra is the recognition that all may be illusion. This can give difficulty in functioning meaningfully within the everyday world. Little sleep is needed – usually about 2 hours. The meditative colour is indigo.

The individual recognizes that he receives the benefits of all chakras while meditating on this one. There is freedom from all previous conditioning and whatever he desires comes to pass. He is capable of inducing visions of the past, present and future and through this comes to terms with the Karma of past lives. Obsessional behaviour becomes a thing of the past and the individual accepts a continuous state of samadhi – the oneness of all things.

Sahasrara ('Thousand Petalled, the Void' or Crown Chakra) In theory, there should be no problem with the development of this chakra for all siddhis are obtained. However, the individual must transcend the desire to use those siddhis or manifest his desires. The meditation colour is a deep violet.

This is the plane of happiness and all is completely 'one'. Union with the Divine is achieved. There is no differentiation between knowledge, the knower and the known. They are seen as having become one and the same thing and therefore liberated. The true meaning of Karma, the cause of law and effect, is recognized and enlightenment is the recognition of 'Tat Vat Sat' ('I am that'). Meditation is effortless.

For those of you with a practical turn of mind, here are some Romany beliefs on how to help the development of clairvoyance.

✦ Saffron is ruled by the sun and is dedicated to magic and love because of its yellow colour. Romanies say bathing the eyes with saffron not only increases clairvoyant vision, it instantly soothes painful eyes.

✦ To improve eyesight and clairvoyant vision, on a Sunday boil a little spring water with a pinch of saffron and use it to bathe the eyes.

✦ Another method of relieving sore eyes is to put gold rings in the ears. It may well be that this is why Romany people have their ears pierced at such a young age.

RITUALS FOR DEVELOPMENT

By the time you reach a fuller understanding of the chakras, rituals become unnecessary because the processes which are going on are mostly internal. However, many people find the use of ritual comforting as they learn more and more about themselves, so we include a few here to help in that process. Other rituals which may be helpful are the Change and Dark Moon rituals in the section on Lunar Magic and Communication with the Horned God. The first ritual here deliberately calls on one of the manifestations of the Earth Mother.

Divination Ritual

Themis is an ancient Greek goddess of justice; carrying a pair of scales she was a personification of the Earth Mother. By taking an oath in her name, the oath-taker risked losing their life if they lied to her.

A trusted adviser of Zeus and looked up to by all the Olympians, Themis protected the innocent and punished the guilty. In her original form she perceived all in the past, the present and the future and was the originator of the arts and magic.

This ritual is best performed during the waxing of or at the Full Moon. It is a way of taking your divination skills, such as prophecy and access to the collective unconscious, one stage further.

YOU WILL NEED

Jasmine or lotus incense (or use 'law incense' below)
Your particular divination tools (e.g. Tarot cards, Runes)
A chalice with red wine or juice
Two purple candles in holders

METHOD

Light your incense.
Light your candles, one on each side of the chalice.
Place your divination tools in between the candles and the chalice above them.

Hold your hands over your divination tools or pick them up and say:

Goddess of Justice, Goddess of Law,
Bless my working here today.
Goddess of Mysteries, Goddess of Power,
Show me the answer that I seek,
Through these tools, I bid you speak.

Take three sips of the juice.
Do whatever you have to do with your tools – shuffle the cards and lay them out or lay out the runes.
When you divination is done, raise your arms and say:

May the gods be thanked,
May they aid me with their guidance.

The candles do not have to burn out, but can be used for another divinatory spell.

Law Incense

This incense can be used to smooth the path in all matters involving the law or legal profession.

1 part Sandalwood
¼ part Cascara
¼ part Onion

Prophecy

The spell is best done during the Waxing or Full Moon and is good while training yourself to concentrate your mind to develop the art of clairvoyance.

YOU WILL NEED

Your cauldron or a scrying bowl half full of water
Two purple candles
Peppermint oil or suitable incense

METHOD

Place the cauldron/bowl on a table. Make sure you can see into it comfortably while seated.
Light the candles, making sure that their light does not shine into the water or your eyes
Ignite the incense or place the peppermint oil in your burner, concentrating on your chosen task.

Sit and focus your attention on the bottom of the cauldron/bowl with your hands placed lightly on either side.
Breathe gently onto the water and say:

Waters deep reveal to me,
That which I beseech of thee.
Open my eye with clarity
That I may truly see.

Allow your mind to become peaceful and remain relaxed while looking deep into the cauldron/bowl.

Be patient and wait a while. The answers to your question may come as images in the water, pictures in your mind or possibly as a strong awareness.

When you have finished, blow out the candles and dispose of the water, preferably directly onto the earth.

Should you not wish to say the verse, simply sit quietly for a few moments until your mind become still.

To Increase Spiritual Insight

In this technique you are combining knowledge from several disciplines. You are developing your powers of perception through the chakras but also using plant magic and candle magic as well.

If you have a serious problem in life, barley, which is sacred to Jupiter and to Demeter, attracts their help. Star anise is used to increase intuition. If you can find a whole pod in the shape of a perfect star, you can carry it to clarify your purpose and direction in life.

YOU WILL NEED
Barley

Star Anise

Purple Candle

METHOD
Sit quietly for a few minutes, outlining the problem to yourself and the Gods

To gain insight and vision concentrate on your Third Eye or Brow Chakra.

Inscribe some words about the situation onto the candle.

Surround the candle with a circle of uncooked barley.

Place a perfect star anise inside the circle of barley.

When the candle has completely burned out, place the star anise under your pillow to gain insight in your dreams.

You can also carry the star anise with you to lead you in the right direction.

As you become more proficient and the qualities of the Third Eye develop you will find that you not only develop clairvoyance but also the type of insights mentioned above.

To help you in your chosen task of self-development there are a number of incense which you can use while meditating. These are all shown on page 297 in the incense section entitled Psychic Powers, Divination and Prophetic Dreams.

This section has been an exploration of how to set up the environment for a ritual, the way to structure a ritual and how to use the 'tools of the trade'. This means being able to use ritual tools, those of both the mind and the spirit. We show how developing these tools leads to the use of self in a way that is different to that used by most people. You have, in fact, developed a magical self.

CONCLUSION

In today's climate, it is important to understand the past, the present and the future. In the past, those trained in the art of magic adhered rigidly to their rituals, ways of thought, techniques and what was known to work. Many people did not understand these ways of working and accusations flew backwards and forwards, resulting in persecution and disapproval. Even within each system of magic, belief led to a perception of rightness and wrongness which has lasted right up to our own time.

As we have learnt to adapt to the wider world in which we live, we have discovered many different ways of using the energies and powers previously called supernatural and magical. Today's rituals are an eclectic blend of those of the past, those of other cultures and those necessary to accommodate the technological world in which we live. If we are to move forward into the future we have to synthesize our own personal power with the greater energy available to us. This gives us a freedom that we have not had before as magical practitioners. We can appeal to the gods of other cultures, we can use the knowledge of 'lotions and potions' that others have accrued and, above all, we can allow ourselves to develop a personal magic that works for us.

This book has tended to concentrate mostly on group ritual because it is an immutable spiritual law that the power generated by a group is the power for change. Whether we wish to heal the individual, to create a better future or manifest a new way of being, it is undeniable that the joining together of individuals in love and harmony can achieve miracles. Ultimately, however, using natural magic well and wisely comes back to developing personal power and having the conviction to be able to move beyond the self and tap into the power of the Ultimate. Whether we do this through thaumaturgy (working miracles for ourselves) or theurgy (divine agency) does not matter.

There comes a time when ritual, and the flamboyance associated with it, is no longer necessary. Magic becomes the quiet application of power and knowledge. We wish you well in your search for power and knowledge and leave you with this blessing:

> *May your Gods support you in all that you should,*
> *May all that you do be done for good,*
> *May love, life and happiness be all that you would.*

SOURCES

The sources listed below are among the many which we consulted
and found particularly useful.

BOOKS
*Alexander's Hebrew Ritual, and doctrinal explanation of the whole
ceremonial Law, oral and traditional, of the Jewish community in England
and foreign parts*
　　　(Alexander Levy) Published by the author, London, 1819
The British Occult Subculture. Identity, gender and morality
　　　(Susan Greenwood) University of London, 1998
Buckland's Complete Book of Witchcraft
　　　(Raymond Buckland) Llewellyn Publications, St. Paul,
Minnesota, 1997
A Compleat History of Magick, Sorcery and Witchcraft
　　　(Richard Boulton)E Curll, London, 1715
The Crone: Woman of Age, Wisdom and Power
　　　(Barbara G. Walker) HarperSanFrancisco, New York, 1985
Drawing Down the Moon
　　　(Margot Adler) Beacon Press, Boston, 1986
An Encyclopedia of Occultism
　　　(Lewis Spence) Carol Publishing Group, New York, 1996
Encyclopedia of Religion
　　　(Mircea Eliade, Editor-in-Chief) Macmillan, New York, 1987
The European Witch-Craze of the Sixteenth and Seventeenth Centuries
　　　(H. R. Trevor-Roper) Peregrine Books, London, 1978
God is a Verb; Kabbalah and the Practice of Mystical Judaism
　　　(Rabbi David A. Cooper) Riverhead Books, 1998
The Golden Bough
　　　(Sir James George Frazer) MacMillan, London, 1922
*The Good Spell Book. Love Charms, Magical Cures and other Practical
Sorcery*
　　　(Gillian Kemp) Victor Gollancz, London, 2000
The Hermetica
　　　(Timothy Frekeand Peter Gandy) Judy Piatkus Publishers,
London, 1998
A History of Magic, Witchcraft and Occultism
　　　(William Bernard Crow) Aquarian Press, London, 1968

Incense. Its ritual significance, preparation and use
    (Leo Vinci) Aquarian Press, Wellingborough, 1980
The Jewish Ritual: or, the Religious Customs and Ceremonies of the Jews, used in their publick worship and private devotions... extracted from the Talmuds
    London, 1753
Lives of Twelve Bad Men. Original Studies of Eminent Scoundrels by Various Hands
    (Thomas Seccombe, Ed.) T. Fisher Unwin, London, 1894
The Magic Arts in Celtic Britain
    (Lewis Spence) Constable, London, 1945
Magical Religion and Modern Witchcraft
    (James R. Lewis, Ed.) University of New York Press, Albany N.Y., 1996
The Magical Universe. Everyday ritual and magic in pre-modern Europe
    (Stephen Wilson) Hambledon and London, London, 2000
Man and his Symbols
    (Carl G. Jung) Doubleday, Garden City, NY, 1964
Man and temple in ancient Jewish myth and ritual
    (Raphael Patia) Ktav Publishing House, New York, 1967
Matthew Hopkins: Witchfinder General
    (Richard Deacon) Frederick Muller Ltd, 1976
Moon Magick
    (D. J. Conway) Llewellyn Publications, 1998
Native Religions of North America
    (Ake Hultkrantz) Harpers and Row, New York, 1987
The new sacrifice of Christian Incense. Or the true entrie to the tree of life, and gratious gate of glorious Paradise
    (William D. D. Guild) Clement Knight, London, 1608
Real Magic: an introductory treatise as the basic principle of yellow magic
    (Philip Emmons Isaac Bonewits) Samuel Weiser, York Beach, 1989
The Rise of Magic in Early Medieval Europe
    (Valerie I. J. Flints) Clarendon Press, Oxford, 1991
Spells, Charms, Talismans and Amulets. A Complete Guide to Magical Enchantment
    (Pamela Ball) Arcturus Publishing, London, 2001
Voodoo; Its Origins and Practices
    (Henry Gilfond) F. Watts, London, 1976